The Complete Artist

The Complete Artist

Hazel Harrison & Alfred Daniels

Quantum
Books

A QUANTUM BOOK

This book is produced by
Quantum Publishing Ltd.
6 Blundell Street
London N7 9BH

ISBN 1-86160-531-5

QUMCPC

Printed in Singapore by
Star Standard Industries Pte Ltd.

CONTENTS

CHAPTER ONE

INTRODUCTION

The main body of Samuel Palmer's work was in oil. It was highly accomplished, but uninspired. His early watercolours, drawings and etchings, however, were works of true poetic imagination and owed much to the influence of William Blake, whom he met in 1824. Paintings such as the one shown here, The Magic Apple Tree, have their starting points in nature, but go far beyond it to create dream-like fantasy worlds, personal visions expressed in strange, emotive colours and almost Expressionist brush work. Unlike the 18th-century watercolourists, Palmer used semi-opaque paint. But his handling of it was so sure that the colours never became muddy or muted, as they often do with gouache paints in less skilful hands.

'I DON'T DO WATERCOLOUR; it's far too difficult' is a remark often heard from amateur painters, even those who regard themselves as reasonably proficient in other media, such as oils. It cannot be denied that some people find watercolours a little harder to use than oils. This very attractive medium is sometimes unpredictable, but this very unpredictability should be regarded as a virtue, not a drawback. What people really mean when they make this kind of remark is that watercolours cannot be altered over and over again as oils can; a colour or wash, once laid down on the paper, must stay there. To some extent this is true, and it is understandable that people should feel a certain nervousness when approaching a watercolour. But, in fact, many alterations can be made, and often are, as a painting progresses: a wash in a colour that has not come out quite right can be changed dramatically by applying another wash on top of it; areas can be sponged out or worked over; and if the worst comes to the worst the whole painting can be put under running water and washed away.

Watercolour has many virtues, its main attraction for artists being its freshness and translucence, making it ideal for a variety of subjects, especially landscapes and flower paintings. As its name implies, pure watercolour is mixed with water and is transparent, so that it must be applied from light to dark, unlike oil paint or acrylics which are opaque and can be built up from dark to light. Highlights consist of areas of the paper left white or very pale washes surrounded by darker ones. A certain amount of pre-planning is necessary at an early stage to work out where the highlights are to be, but some planning is always needed for any painting or drawing, whatever medium is being used.

No one ever quite knows how watercolour will behave, and many watercolour artists find this very unpredictability one of its greatest assets. The medium itself will often begin to 'take over' a painting, suggesting ways of creating interesting effects and lending a sparkle and spontaneity to the work. Experience is needed to make the most of the chance effects that occur in watercolour painting. A real feeling for the medium may not be achieved until several attempts have been abandoned, but there are many ways of using watercolour and with perseverance you will evolve your own style and method. The purely practical advantages of watercolour painting are that you need little expensive equipment, the painting can be done more or less anywhere provided there is enough light, and paints can be cleared up quickly, leaving no mess. Since the paper is relatively cheap, experiments and mistakes are not very expensive.

♦ THE MEDIUM ♦

Watercolour, like all paint, is made by mixing pigment with a binding agent, in this case gum arabic, which is soluble in water. There are two types of watercolour, 'pure' or 'classical' watercolour, which is transparent, and gouache, or 'body colour', which is the same pigment made opaque by adding white pigment to the binder. The

ABOVE *John Sell Cotman was the leading watercolourist of the 18th-century British School. In paintings like this one,* St Benet's Abbey, Norfolk, *he used paint in a bold, free and imaginative way to create marvellous effects of space, light and texture. Notice particularly the broad, overlapping brush strokes in the foreground and the swirling, directional ones in the sky.*

technique of gouache painting is similar to that of oil or acrylic, since light colour can be laid over dark, and is outside the scope of this book; but gouache is quite frequently used in conjunction with pure watercolour. Its use is a source of constant controversy among water-colourists: some claim that it destroys the character of the medium — its luminosity — and should never be used; others combine the two with considerable success. Nowadays there is a general trend towards mixing differ-ent media, and watercolour is often used with pastel, pen and ink, pencils or crayons (see Chapter 3). It can be a useful exercise, when a watercolour has 'gone wrong', to draw into it with inks or pastels to see the effects that can be achieved.

◆ THE HISTORY OF ◆
WATERCOLOUR PAINTING

It is commonly believed that watercolour was invented by the English landscape painters of the 18th century, but this is far from so. Watercolour has been in use in various

John Sell Cotman worked on a fairly small scale, but his landscapes and seascapes give an impressive feeling of space, strength and power, and are extraordinarily modern in approach. Many have an almost abstract quality, as in this painting, The Dismasted Brig, *where the rain-swept sky has been treated in bold, broad masses, and the swirling movement of the waves has been used to make a geometric pattern of different-sized triangles.*

RIGHT Albrecht Dürer, who painted this painting, which has come to be known as The Great Piece of Turf, *found watercolour a particularly sympathetic medium for detailed studies of nature. We cannot be sure of his precise method, but he probably began by* *using transparent washes to establish broad areas, such as the large leaves, and then built up intricate details with tiny strokes of opaque paint (or body colour).*

forms for many centuries. Indeed the ancient Egyptians used a form of it for painting on plaster to decorate their tombs; the great frescoes of Renaissance Italy were painted in a kind of watercolour; it was used by medieval manuscript illuminators, both in its 'pure' form and mixed with body colour; the great German artist, Albrecht Dürer (1471-1528), made use of it extensively, and so did many botanical illustrators of the 16th century and the Dutch flower painters of the 17th century.

It was, even so, in 18th-century England that watercolour painting was elevated to the status of a national art. A new interest in landscape painting for its own sake culminated in the work of John Constable (1776-1837), the forerunner of the Impressionists. Landscape had hitherto been purely topographical — a truthful and detailed record of a particular place — but in the hands of artists such as Paul Sandby (1725-1809), John Cozens (1752-97), Thomas Girtin (1775-1802), Francis Towne (1740-1816), John Sell Cotman (1782-1842) and Peter de Wint (1784-1849) it became much more than that. Watercolour was at last fully exploited and given the recognition that was its due.

Most of these artists worked in watercolour alone, regarding it as the perfect medium for creating the light, airy, atmospheric effects they sought; Constable used watercolour mainly for quick sketches of skies. The greatest watercolourist of all, J M W Turner (1775-1851), achieved his fame as an oil painter, but he produced watercolours of an amazing depth and richness. Quite uninhibited by any 'rules', he exploited accidental effects like thumbprints and haphazard blobs of paint, turning them into some of the most magical depictions of light and colour that have ever been seen in paint.

Throughout the 19th century the techniques of watercolour continued to be developed and the subject matter became more varied. The poet and artist, William Blake (1757-1827), evolved his own method of conveying his poetic vision in watercolour, as did his follower, Samuel Palmer (1805-81), who used swirls and blocks of opaque colour in his visionary and symbolic landscapes. With the end of the Napoleonic Wars in 1815, travel once again became easier, and the topographical tradition reached new heights in the work of artists like Samuel Prout (1783-1852), a superlative draughtsman who painted the buildings and scenery of western Europe in faithful detail. Travelling further afield, John Frederick Lewis (1805-76) made glowing studies of Middle Eastern scenes, and new techniques, such as the 'dragged' wash, were pioneered by Richard Parkes Bonington (1802-28) for both landscape and figure subjects, to be taken further by his friend, the French artist, Eugène Delacroix (1798-1863).

British artists of the 20th century have not ignored the possibilities of watercolour, its greatest exponents being Graham Sutherland (1903-80) and Paul Nash (1889-1946) and his brother John (1893-). It remains a popular medium with both professional artists and amateurs, and new ways are constantly being found of exploring its full potential.

CHAPTER TWO

MATERIALS AND EQUIPMENT

This paintbox might be regarded by some as messy, but this artist finds that he achieves a greater unity of colour by allowing traces of old colour to remain on the palette. He cleans the mixing trays only when the colours become muddied or when a different range of colours is required.

Payne's grey and cadmium yellow.

Prussian blue and cadmium yellow.

Cobalt and cadmium yellow.

Prussian blue and lemon yellow.

Viridian and lemon.

Black and cadmium yellow.

Cobalt blue and alizarin crimson.

Payne's grey and alizarin crimson.

Prussian blue and alizarin crimson.

Cobalt blue and Payne's grey.

Black and Prussian blue.

Black and alizarin crimson.

Cadmium yellow and cadmium red.

Alizarin crimson and cadmium yellow.

Lemon yellow and cadmium red.

Burnt umber and black.

Payne's grey and cadmium red.

Burnt umber and cobalt blue.

PERHAPS THE GREATEST single advantage of watercolour painting is that only a small amount of equipment is needed, equipment which is easy to store. Paints and brushes, although not cheap, last for a long time; indeed brushes should last virtually for ever if looked after properly. Hand-made paper is, of course, expensive, but beginners will find that many perfectly satisfactory machine-made papers are available from artist's suppliers.

♦ PAINTS AND COLOURS ♦

Ready-made watercolour paint is sold in various forms, the commonest being tubes, pans and half-pans. These all contain glycerine and are known as semi-moist colours, unlike the traditional dry cakes, which are still available in some artist's suppliers, but are not much used today. Dry cakes require considerable rubbing with water before the colour is released. It is a slow process, but the paints are therefore economical.

Gouache paints, or designer's colours as they are sometimes called, are normally sold in tubes. These paints, and the cheaper versions of them, poster colours and powder paints, have chalk added to the pigment to thicken it, and are thus opaque, unlike true watercolour. Water-colours themselves can be mixed with Chinese white to make them opaque or semi-opaque, so that they become a softer and more subtle form of gouache.

Success in watercolour painting depends so much on applying layers of transparent, but rich, colour that it is a mistake to buy any but the best-quality paints, known as 'artist's quality'. There are cheaper paints, sold for 'sketching', but since these contain a filler to extend the pigment, the colour is weaker and the paint tends to be chalky and unpredictable in use.

Whether to use pans, half-pans or tubes is a personal choice. Each type has its advantages and disadvantages. Tubes are excellent for those who work mainly indoors on a fairly large scale, as any quantity of paint can be squeezed out of them on to the palette. Any paint left on the palette after a painting is completed can be used again later, simply by moistening it with a wet brush. Pans and half-pans, which can be bought in sets in their own palette and are easy to carry, are the most popular choice for working out of doors on a small scale. Watercolours can also be bought in concentrated form in bottles, with droppers to transfer the paint to the palette. These are eminently suitable for broad washes which require a large quantity of paint, but they are less easy to mix than the other types.

The choice of colours is also personal, though there are some colours that everyone must have. Nowadays there is such a vast range of colours to choose from that a beginner is justified in feeling somewhat bewildered, but, in fact, only a few are really necessary. One point to bear in mind is that some colours are considerably less permanent than

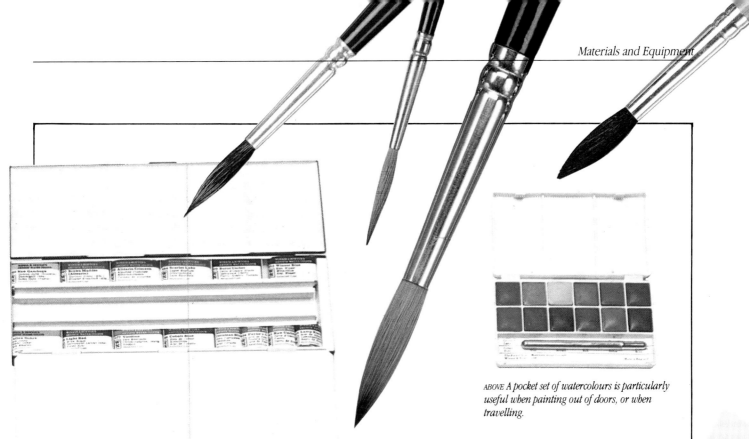

LEFT: These swatches show some of
the effects that can be achieved by
mixing in a limited colour range.

ABOVE Semi-moist pans must be carried in tins
and boxes, which can then be used as palettes.

BELOW MIDDLE Half pans are available individually
as well as in sets. The artist can replace the most
frequently used colours, and also build up a
palette to suit his own style.

ABOVE Bottled watercolours are concentrated, and
quicker to use than dry cakes or semi-moist pans
when a large area of wash is required.

RIGHT Watercolour in tube form is popular and
convenient. Do not squeeze too many colours onto
your palette at a time, or they will run together.

LEFT Gouache is available in tube
or pot form in an enormous
range of colours. From left to right:
lamp black, zinc white, burnt
sienna, raw umber, yellow ochre,
cadmium red (pale) cadmium
yellow (pale), Winsor emerald,
cobalt blue.

others, which may not be an important consideration for quick sketches and 'note-taking', but clearly is for any painting that is intended to be hung or exhibited. A wise course, therefore, is to rule out any colours classified as 'fugitive'. All the major paint manufacturers have systems of grading permanence. These are not always marked on the tubes or pans, but they appear on the manufacturers' colour charts; if in doubt, ask the shopkeeper or manager for advice. The tubes or pans will also bear a code indicating the relative price of each colour, some being more expensive than others according to the cost of the pigment used.

The golden rule when choosing a range of colours, or 'palette' as professionals call it, is to keep it as simple as possible. Few watercolourists use more than a dozen colours. For landscape painting, useful additions to the basic palette are sap green, Hooker's green, raw umber and cerulean blue, while monastral blue (called Winsor blue in the Winsor and Newton range) is sometimes recommended instead of Prussian blue. For flower painting the basic range might be enlarged by the addition of cobalt violet and lemon yellow.

◆ PAPER ◆

The traditional support — the term used for the surface on which any painting is done — is white or pale-coloured paper, which reflects back through the transparent paint to give the translucent quality so characteristic of watercolours. There are many types of watercolour paper. Each individual will probably need to try several before establishing which one suits his method of working, though sometimes a particular paper may be chosen to create a special effect.

The three main types of machine-made paper are hot-pressed (HP), cold-pressed (CP), which is also rather quaintly known as 'not' for 'not hot-pressed' and rough. Hot-pressed paper is very smooth and, although suitable

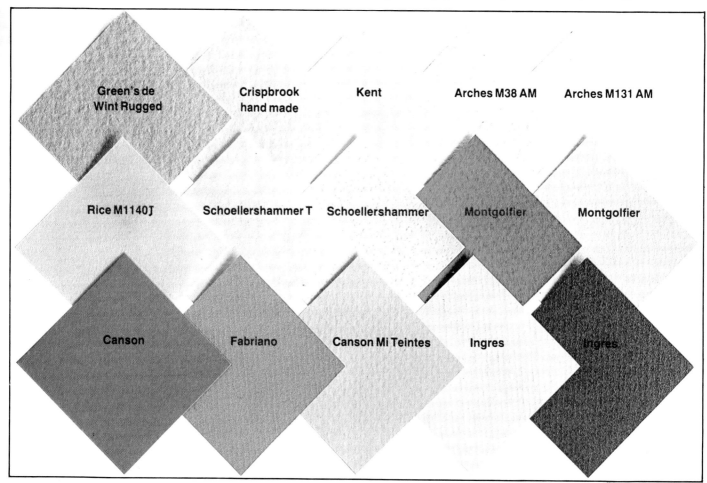

ABOVE The range of papers available is vast and can be bewildering even for the experienced artist. In order to find the paper which suits your particular style and immediate needs, buy only a few sheets at a time. The heavier papers are more expensive but can absorb large amounts of water; they do not, therefore, need stretching, which makes them useful for outdoor work. Toned papers provide a convenient middle ground for some subjects, from which to work darks and lights.

for drawing or pen-and-wash, is not a good choice for building up layers of washes in the standard watercolour technique as it becomes clogged very quickly. Cold-pressed paper, which is slightly textured, is the most popular and is suitable for both broad washes and fine detail. Rough paper, as its name implies, is much more heavily textured, and the paint will settle in the 'troughs' while sliding off the 'peaks', giving a speckled effect which can be effective for some subjects but is difficult to exploit successfully. Among the best-known makes of good water-colour papers are Saunders, Fabriano, Arches, Bockingford, Strathmore in the US, Ingres in the UK, and R.W.S. (Royal Watercolour Society), some of which also include hand-made papers.

Hand-made papers are made from pure linen rag and specially treated with size to provide the best possible surface for watercolour work. Such papers are sized on one side only and thus have a right and a wrong side, which can be checked by holding the paper up to the light so that the watermark becomes visible. Many of the better machine-made papers also have a watermark and hence a right and wrong side.

Some papers have surfaces which are tough enough to withstand a great deal of preliminary drawing and rubbing out without damage, but others do not. Bockingford paper, for instance, although excellent in many ways, is quickly damaged by erasing, and the paint will take on a patchy appearance wherever the surface has been spoiled. One of its advantages, however, is that paint can easily be removed by washing out where necessary; the paint, moreover, can be manipulated and moved around in a very free way. Arches paper and Saunders paper are both strong enough to stand up to erasing, but mistakes are difficult to remove from the former, which holds the paint very firmly. Saunders paper is a good choice for beginners: it is strong, stretches well and has a pleasant surface with enough grain to give a little, but not too much, texture.

♦ STRETCHING THE PAPER ♦

Watercolour papers vary widely in weight, or thickness, and the lighter ones need to be stretched or they will buckle as soon as wet paint is applied to them. The weight is usually expressed in pounds and refers to the weight of a ream (480 sheets), not to each individual sheet. The thinner papers, ranging from 70 to 140 pounds, must be stretched; any paper weighing 200 pounds or more can be used without this treatment. Watercolour boards can be bought. These have watercolour paper mounted on heavy board, so that the stretching has already been done. They are particularly useful for outdoor work, since no drawing board is needed.

Stretching paper is not difficult, but since the paper must be soaked, it takes some time to dry thoroughly and needs to be done at least two hours before you intend to start work. Cut the paper to the size required (if you do not want to use the whole sheet) and wet it well on both sides by laying it in a bath or tray of water. When it is well soaked, hold it up by the corners to drain off the excess

1. *Cut the paper to size and place it right-side up in a bath or tray of water. Leave it to soak for a few minutes.*

2. *Lift out the paper and drain off the excess water.*

3. *Lay the paper on a drawing board at least 1 in/2.5 cm larger than the paper all around. Make sure that the paper is still the right way up.*

4. *Smooth the paper quite flat and stick gumstrip around the edges, starting with opposite sides.*

5. *Finish by putting a drawing pin in each corner. Do not dry the paper in front of a fire, which will buckle it.*

water, then lay it right-side-up on a drawing board and stick down each edge with the gummed brown paper known as gumstrip (do not use masking tape or sellotape). Finally, place a drawing pin in each corner. The paper will dry taut and flat and should not buckle when paint is applied. Occasionally, however, stretching does go wrong and the paper buckles at one corner or tears away from the gumstrip; if that happens there is no other course but to repeat the process. Drying can be hastened with a hair-drier, but it is not a good practice to leave the board in front of a fire. Ideally the paper should dry naturally.

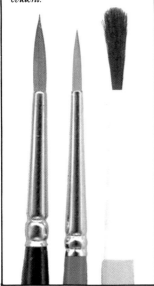

The differences between a quality sable brush (left), or synthetic sable (middle), and the kind of cheap brush sometimes provided in watercolour boxes (right), are self-evident.

♦ # BRUSHES ♦

Soft brushes are normally used for watercolour. The best ones are sable, made from the tips of the tail hairs of the small rodent found chiefly in Siberia. Sable brushes are extremely expensive, but if looked after properly they should last a lifetime. Watercolour brushes are also made from squirrel-hair (known as 'camel hair' for some reason) and ox-hair. These are good substitutes for sable, but have less spring. There is now a wide range of synthetic brushes, usually made of nylon or a mixture of nylon and sable, and although they do not hold the paint as well as sable and are thus less suitable for broad washes, they are excellent for finer details and are very much chaper.

Brushes come in a variety of shapes and only by experiment will an individual discover which shapes and sizes suit him. It is not necessary to have a great many brushes for watercolour work; for most purposes three or four will be adequate, and many artists use only two. A practical range would be one large chisel-end for laying washes and two or three rounds in different sizes. Some watercolourists use ordinary household brushes for washes, but care must be taken to prevent hairs from falling out as you work.

If you want your brushes to last, it is essential to look

BELOW Soft sable brushes are the best brushes, but they are very expensive and many synthetic and sable and synthetic mixtures are now available. A beginner should not need more than one flat brush and two or three rounds; specialized brushes such as blenders and fans are used for particular techniques.

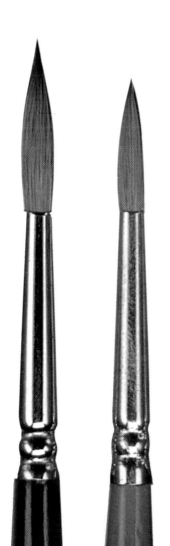

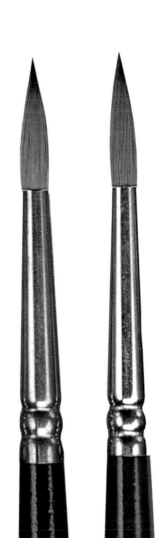

Japanese and Chinese brushes are versatile, and are very well suited to fine calligraphic work, but they require some practice and are not recommended for beginners.

LEFT *The complete range of sizes available of one make of brush.*

BELOW *A range of brush types used for particular techniques. From left to right: fine synthetic round, broad synthetic round, mixed fibres round, ox hair round, squirrel hair round, sable fan, sable bright, sable round, fine sable round.*

after them well. Wash them thoroughly in running water after use — if they are still stained use a little soap. Never leave brushes pointing downwards in a glass of water, as this will bend the hairs out of shape, possibly permanently. If they need to be stored for a length of time in a box or tin make sure that they are absolutely dry; otherwise mildew may form. Store them upright if possible.

A combined satchel and stool can make life easier when painting out of doors.

◆ EASELS ◆

Watercolours, unlike oils, are best done at close quarters, with the support held nearly horizontal, so that an easel is not really necessary for indoor work. However, an easel can be helpful. It allows you to tilt the work at different angles (many artists prefer to do preliminary drawings with the board held vertical) and to move it around to the best light, which is more difficult with a table. The most important aspects to consider — apart, of course, from price — are stability and the facility for holding the work firmly in a horizontal position. For outdoor work, the combined seat and easel, which folds and is carried by a handle, is particularly useful. For indoor work, the combination easel, which can be used both as a drawing table and a studio easel, is more convenient. Both are adjustable to any angle from vertical to horizontal. Good easels are not cheap, however, so that it is wise to do without one until you are sure of your requirements; many professional watercolourists work at an ordinary table with their board supported by a book or brick.

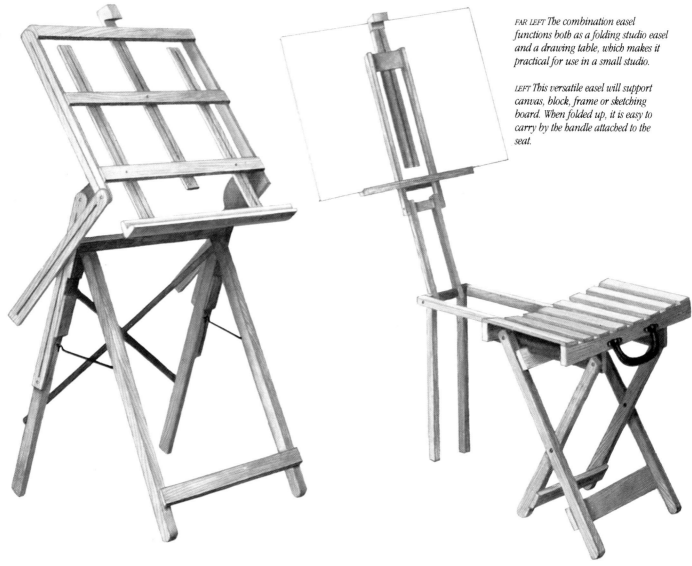

FAR LEFT The combination easel functions both as a folding studio easel and a drawing table, which makes it practical for use in a small studio.

LEFT This versatile easel will support canvas, block, frame or sketching board. When folded up, it is easy to carry by the handle attached to the seat.

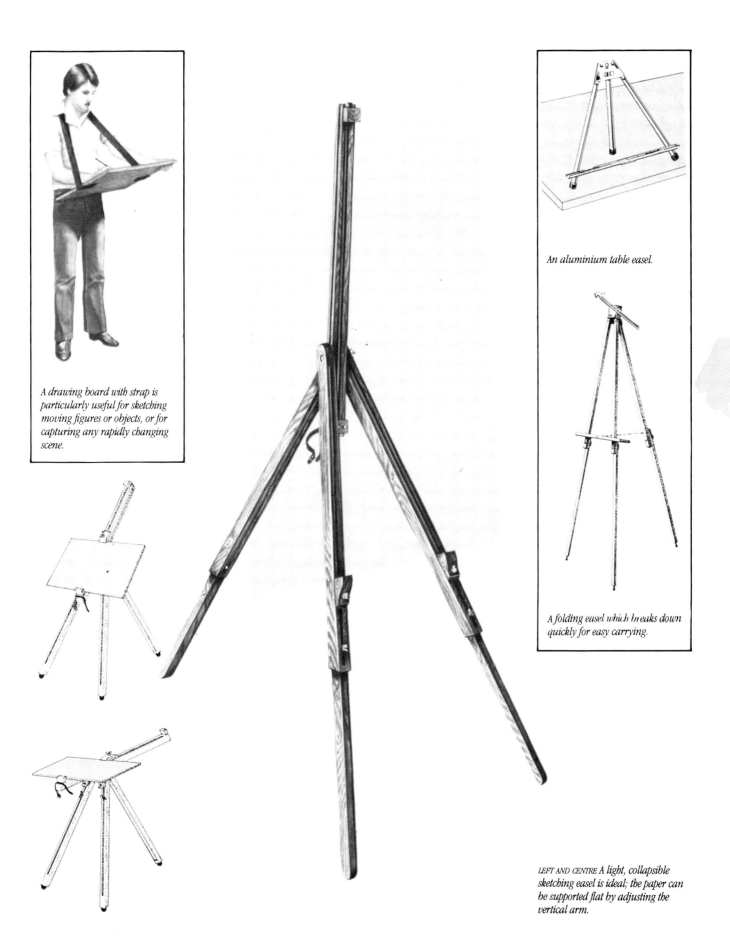

A drawing board with strap is particularly useful for sketching moving figures or objects, or for capturing any rapidly changing scene.

An aluminium table easel.

A folding easel which breaks down quickly for easy carrying.

LEFT AND CENTRE A light, collapsible sketching easel is ideal; the paper can be supported flat by adjusting the vertical arm.

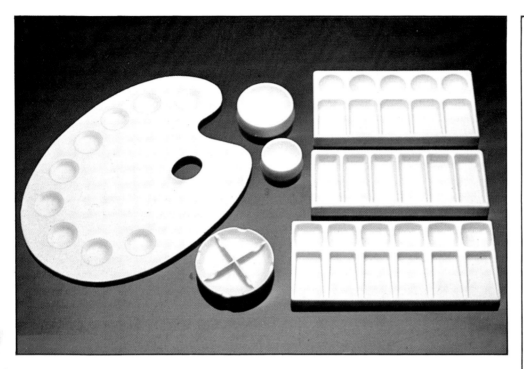

ABOVE *Any plate or dish can be used for mixing watercolour, but there are several specially made palettes on the market. The thumbhole variety is especially useful for outdoor work.*

These colours will provide a perfectly adequate range for most needs. Some artists work with fewer. From top to bottom: cobalt blue, Prussian blue, viridian, yellow ochre, cadmium yellow, lemon yellow, cadmium red, alizarin crimson, burnt umber, Payne's grey and ivory black.

♦ LIGHTING ♦

For indoor work it is vital to organize a good system of lighting. Working by a window with light coming over your left shoulder (or right shoulder if you are left-handed) can be quite satisfactory if the window faces north and gives an even and relatively unchanging light. It is less so if the window faces the sun, since the light may constantly change from brilliant to murky and may even throw distracting patches of light and shade across your work. An artificial light of the fluorescent 'daylight' type will enable you to work in a poorly lit room or corner and to continue working when the light has faded — winter days can seem very short for those dependent on daylight. Such light can be used either instead of natural light or to supplement it, and there is one type with a screw base that can be fitted to the edge of a table or an adjacent shelf.

♦ BOARDS, PALETTES AND OTHER EQUIPMENT ♦

You will need a drawing board, or possibly two boards of different sizes, to support the paper and stretch it where necessary. A piece of plywood or blockboard is perfectly adequate provided the surface is smooth and the wood soft enough to take drawing pins. For outdoor work a piece of hardboard can be used, with the paper clipped to it, though the paper must be heavy enough not to require stretching.

If you buy paints in paintbox form you will already have a palette; if not, you will need one with compartments for mixing paint. Watercolour palettes are made in plastic, metal or ceramic, in a variety of sizes, and some have a thumbhole so that they can be held in the non-painting

Small natural sponges are an invaluable aid to watercolour painting, both for applying paint and for correcting or modifying areas. Rags, kitchen paper and cotton buds should also form part of the basic equipment.

hand when working out of doors. Water containers are another necessity for outdoor work; there is nothing worse than arriving at your chosen spot to find that you have forgotten the water. Containers can be bought, plastic soft-drink bottles can be used to carry the water and any light (unbreakable) container such as a yogurt pot will suffice to put it in.

Various other items, though not strictly essential, can be useful and inexpensive aids for watercolour work. Small sponges can be used instead of brushes to apply washes, to sponge out areas and to create soft, smudgy cloud effects; kitchen roll, blotting paper and cotton wool can be used in much the same way. Toothbrushes are useful for spattering paint to create textured effects, to suggest sand or pebbles on a beach, for example. A scalpel, or a razor blade, is often used to scrape away small areas of paint in a highlight area. And both masking tape and masking fluid can serve to stop out areas while a wash is laid over the top, leaving a hard-edged area of white paper when removed. The specific uses of such aids and devices are more fully explained in the following chapter, and examples are given in the step-by-step demonstrations in the latter part of the book.

CHAPTER THREE

TECHNIQUE

*A detail from a painting of a French vineyard: the artist
decided that the converging lines of the field were too heavily
coloured. He loosens the colour with a soft brush and clean
water, before lifting it off with tissue.*

*P*URE WATERCOLOUR, being transparent, must be applied from light to dark. The paper itself is used to create the pure white or light tones which, with opaque paints, would be made by using white alone or mixed with coloured pigment.

Any area required to be white is simply 'reserved', or left unpainted, so that when it is surrounded with darker washes it will shine out with great brilliance. Pale tones are created in the same way, with a light-coloured wash put on first and then surrounded with darker tones. Light reflected off the paper, back through these thin skins of paint known as washes, gives a watercolour painting a spontaneity and sparkle which cannot be achieved with any other medium. Hence watercolour's popularity with artists both past and present.

The two most important facts about watercolour are, first, that it is always to some extent unpredictable, even in the hands of experts, and, second, that because dark is always worked over light, some planning is needed before beginning the painting. It is not always necessary to do a detailed and complicated drawing on the paper, only enough to work out the basic shapes and design; this really should be done however, or you will begin without really knowing which areas are to be left white or pale and how they will fit into the painting as a whole.

Thus the first step in any painting is to establish where the first wash is to be applied; and the first step in watercolour technique is to learn how to put on the wash.

◆ LAYING A FLAT WASH ◆

The wash is the basis of all watercolour painting, whether it is a broad, sweeping one, covering a large expanse, such as a sky or the background to a portrait, or a much smaller one laid on a particular area. Washes need not be totally flat. They can be gradated in both tone and colour, or broken up and varied. But the technique of laying a flat wash must be mastered, even if you subsequently find that you seldom use it.

The support should be tilted at a slight angle so that the brush strokes flow into one another, but do not run down the paper. For a broad wash a large chisel-end brush is normally used; for a smaller one, or a wash which is to be laid against a complicated edge, a smaller round brush may be more manageable. Laying a wash must be done quickly or hard edges will form between brush strokes. Therefore mix up more paint than you think you will need. Start by damping the paper with clear water (this is not actually essential, but helps the paint to go on evenly). Working in one direction, lay a horizontal line of colour at the top of the area, then another below it, working in the opposite direction, and continue working in alternate directions until the area is covered. Never go back over the wet paint because you feel it is uneven or not dark enough, as this will result in the paint's 'flooding' and leave blobs and patches. A final word of caution: if the doorbell or the

FLAT WASH.

A flat wash in a vivid colour is being laid on dampened paper with a broad, flat-ended brush. It is not strictly necessary to dampen the paper (many artists prefer the slightly 'dragged' look given by working on dry paper) but dampening facilitates an even covering. Tilt the board slightly so that the brush strokes flow into one another, and work backwards and forwards down the paper until the whole area is covered.

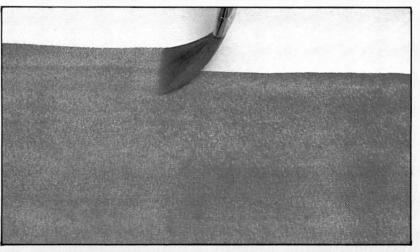

SPONGE WASH.

Often a wash needs to be slightly textured or varied in strength, for which purpose a sponge is useful.
1. *The wash is mixed with a brush and tested on a piece of spare paper.*

2. *Enough paint is mixed to cover the area and the sponge is dipped into it. For a lighter covering, some of the paint can be squeezed out.*

3. *A variegated effect is achieved by applying the paint quite thickly with the first stroke, much more thinly with the second.*

4. *The final wash can be worked into with the sponge while it is still wet in order to lighten some areas and produce a soft, shimmering effect.*

VARIEGATED WASH.

1. *The paper is dampened with a sponge and a thin wash of colour is applied, also with a sponge.*

2. *A second colour is then flooded on, using the tip of the sponge so that the two run together.*

3. *A brush is now used to touch in darker areas on the still-wet paint. Very subtle effects can be created by this wet-into-wet technique, but they are always to some extent unpredictable.*

telephone rings while you are in the middle of a wash, ignore it; otherwise you will return to a hard edge which is impossible, or at least very difficult to remove.

Leave the wash to dry before working on adjacent areas of the painting. Not until the wash is completely dry will you be able to establish either how even it is or what its true colour value is (watercolour dries much paler than it appears when wet). The ability to assess the precise tone of a wash comes only with experience, but it can be helpful to lay down one or two patches of flat colour on a spare piece of paper and allow them to dry as a preliminary test. Washes can be laid on top of the first one to strengthen the colour or darken the tone, though too many will turn the painting muddy. Purists claim that more than three layers spoils the quality.

Another method of laying a wash is to use a sponge. This is particularly useful when a slightly variegated or textured wash is required, as the sponge can either be filled with paint for a dense covering or used relatively dry for a paler effect. A sponge can also be used in conjunction with a brush. If, for instance, you rinse it in clean water and squeeze it out you can remove some of the paint laid by a brush while it is still wet, thus lightening selected areas — a good technique for skies or distant hills.

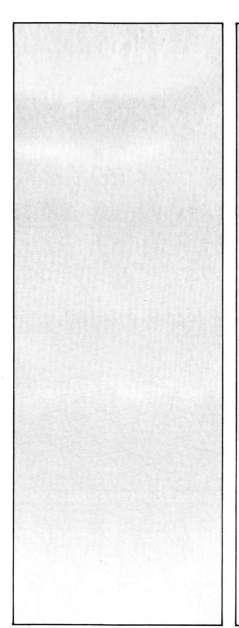

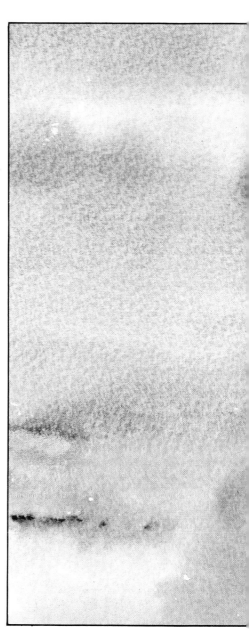

◆ COMPLEX EDGES ◆

Sometimes a wash must be laid against a complicated edge, for example, a group of roofs and chimneys with an intricate outline. The wash must then start from the edge rather than end at it, which may necessitate turning the board sideways or upside down. When dampening the paper before putting on the wash take care to dampen only up to this edge; otherwise the wash will flow into the areas to be reserved.

This kind of technical problem highlights the need for initial planning — the success of a painting may hinge on the precise way a certain area has been outlined by reserving. Another method for dealing with intricate shapes is to stop out the parts to be reserved with masking fluid.

◆ GRADATED AND VARIEGATED ◆ WASHES

Colours in nature are seldom totally flat or one solid hue. It is often desirable, therefore, to lay a gradated wash, which becomes darker or lighter at the top or bottom or changes from one colour to another. For a gradated wash, simply mix more water with the paint to make each successive strip lighter or more pigment to darken them.

For a variegated wash, mix up the two or more colours to be used, dampen the paper as usual, and then lay on the colours so that they blend into one another. The effect of such a wash cannot be worked out precisely in advance, even with practice — you should be prepared for a happy (or unhappy) accident. As with a flat wash, never make corrections while the paint is still wet; if you are dissatis-

DRY-BRUSH.

Dry-brush work is an excellent method of suggesting texture, such as that of grass or a corn field, but it becomes monotonous if used too much in one painting. Here a number of similar colours have been used over a pale underlying wash to give tonal variation.

FAR LEFT Prussian blue and alizarin crimson have been allowed to run into one another, just as they would with a wash of only one colour. Such effects are impossible to control accurately; the artist must be prepared for an element of 'happy accident'.

MIDDLE Laying one wash on top of another often gives textural variety as well as intensifying the colour. Notice that the bottom band, a pale wash of Payne's grey, is quite even, while the one at the top, a third application of the same wash, shows distinct brush marks.

ABOVE The possibilities of working wet into wet may be explored by producing this kind of doodle in a matter of minutes. The wet-into-wet technique is often used in the early stages of a painting, or for the background, more precise work being done at a later stage or in another area of the painting.

1. The artist uses detail paper to trace the area he wants to mask.

2. He then carefully cuts the mask with a scalpel.

4. More sap green, again mixed with gum water, is spattered on the area with an ordinary household brush.

5. The slightly irregular stippled effect is clear, even before the mask is peeled off.

fied when it is dry it can be sponged out and a further wash laid on top.

Some watercolourists use variegated washes in a particularly free way. Each individual arrives at his own technique by trial and error. Attractive efforts can sometimes be achieved by deliberately allowing the paint to flood in the middle of a wash, by introducing blobs of strong colour to a paler wash while the paint is damp, or by laying one wash over a dry one, thus producing a slight granulation of the paper. Such effects are unpredictable. For one thing, they vary widely according to the type of paper used. But one of the great joys of watercolour is the opportunity it provides for turning accidental effects to advantage.

♦ DRY-BRUSH AND TEXTURAL ♦ METHODS

Painting with a small amount of paint on a fine brush which is almost dry is a method most frequently used for the fine details of a painting, but dry-brush is also a technique in its own right and can be used very effectively for large areas, either over a wash which has already been laid down or straight on to white paper. For landscape work it can be used to suggest the texture of grass, trees, rocks, stone walls and the like. For portraits and still-lifes it can model forms more easily than washes of wet paint can.

Like all watercolour techniques dry-brush requires practice. If the paint is too wet it will go on as a solid wash; if too dry it will not go on at all. The brush normally used for large areas of dry-brush work is a large chisel-end, with the bristles slightly splayed to produce a series of fine lines, rather like hatching and cross-hatching in drawing. One colour and tone can be laid over another, and the brush strokes can be put on in different directions as the shape suggests.

The Victorian artist, William Holman Hunt (1827-1910) used this method extensively, together with stippling, in which small dots of colour are applied to the paper very close together, in rather the way that the

3. *The mask is applied and the tree is painted in sap green, mixed with a little gum water to give it extra body and brilliance.*

6. *The mask is removed, leaving a sharp, clean outline. The slightly irregular texture is very effective in suggesting foliage.*

French artist, Georges Seurat (1859-91), applied oil paint.

Scumbling is a method of applying fairly thick paint in a circular scrubbing motion so that the paint goes on to the paper from all directions and picks up the texture of the surface. It is effective when used for relatively small areas to provide contrast to flat washes, but if used too extensively in one painting it can become monotonous.

Another common method of suggesting texture is to spatter wet paint on to the paper with a toothbrush or bristle-brush. This technique, too, should be reserved for certain areas only, but it is an excellent way of dealing with a pebble beach, say, or a rough stone wall. The paint is usually spattered over an existing wash not directly on to white paper, and to make the result look natural care must be taken to use paint which is not much darker than the wash. Mask off surrounding areas if they are lighter in tone.

Masking tape can be used for a straight edge; for more complex shapes, a rough mask can be cut from cartridge paper.

USING MASKING FLUID.

Masking fluid provides a way of painting in 'negative', which can give very subtle and exciting effects.
1. *The areas to be masked are carefully drawn and the fluid is applied with a fine brush.*

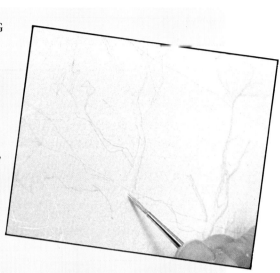

2. *The fluid is allowed to dry and a yellow-brown wash is laid over the top.*

3. *A blue wash for the sky is added and allowed to dry, after which the fluid is peeled off by gentle rubbing with a finger.*

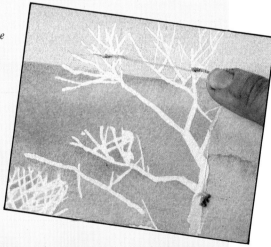

♦ MASKING OUT AND CREATING ♦ HIGHLIGHTS

Many watercolourists use masking fluid and masking tape for reserving areas of white paper. Masking fluid, which is specially made for the purpose, is a kind of liquid rubber sold in small bottles and applied with a brush. Purists disdain to use it, but their scorn is baseless. Very attractive and exciting effects, quite different from those produced by the classic method of laying washes around an area, can be gained by it. Stopping out with masking fluid is a method of painting in 'negative'; the precise and subtle shades made by the brush remain when the liquid is removed.

The paper must be quite dry before the fluid is applied, and the fluid itself must be allowed to dry before a wash is laid on top. Once the wash has dried, the fluid can be rubbed off with a finger or a soft eraser, leaving the white area, which can be modified and worked into if required. Masking fluid should never be left on the paper for longer than necessary, and care must be taken to wash the brushes immediately; otherwise fluid will harden in the hairs and ruin them. Masking fluid is not suitable for all papers, especially ones with a rough surface.

Masking tape is particularly useful for straight-edged areas, such as the light-catching side of a building or the edge of a window-sill. There is no reason why all painting should be done freehand; just as few people can draw a circle without recourse to compasses, few people can paint a really straight line without splashing paint over the edge. Masking tape enables you to use the paint freely without worrying about spoiling the area to be reserved.

Yet another way of keeping the paint away from the paper is to use wax in what is called the resist method, like that used in batik fabrics. This differs from the previous techniques in being permanent; once the wax is on the paper it cannot be removed except by laborious scraping with a razor blade. The paint, moreover, will lie on top of the wax to some extent (this varies according to the paper used), leaving a slightly textured surface. The effect can be very attractive, particularly for flowers or fabrics. An ordinary household candle can be used, or a white wax crayon for finer lines.

The best method of creating fine, delicate highlights when a painting is nearly complete is to scrape into the paint with a sharp point, of a scalpel, say, so that the white paper is revealed. Very fine lines can be drawn in this way to suggest a blade of grass or a flower stem catching the light in the foreground of a landscape. Such touches often give a painting that extra something it seems to need. They can also be achieved by applying Chinese white with a fine brush, but scraping back tends to give a cleaner line.

♦ MIXING MEDIA ♦

Many other media can be used in combination with watercolour; indeed, the mixing of media is now commonplace, whereas in the past it was regarded as

ABOVE *Watercolour has been used in conjunction with pastel to give liveliness and textural contrast to this painting. Both the building itself and and the dark tree on the left are in pure watercolour, while the foreground grass is pure pastel. The sky is a combination of the two. Pastel combines well with watercolour, and a painting such as this often benefits from a 'non-purist' approach.*

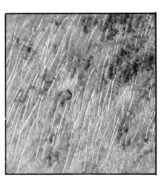

LEFT Sharp, clean lines and highlights can be made by scraping into dry paint with a scalpel or other sharp knife. Take care not to damage the paper by pressing too hard.

A wash which has 'gone wrong' ABOVE and flooded, has been worked into to create a sky effect not originally planned TOP. One of the attractions of watercolour is that new uses of the medium are often supported by 'mistakes'.

breaking the rules. Watercolour used with pen and ink has a long history; in the days before watercolour became recognized as a medium in its own right, it was used mainly to give touches of colour to drawings or to tint black and white engravings. Nowadays there are many other media — some old and some new — that can be used with watercolour to good effect.

One traditional way to change the nature of paint by thickening it is to mix it with a little gum arabic, which gives it both texture and lasting lustre. Soap can be used in much the same way, and it makes the paint easier to scrape back. Soap can also be used to make imprints of objects such as leaves or flowers. Coat the object with soap, apply paint to it and then press it on to the paper.

Watercolours can be drawn into with pens, pencils, crayons or pastels, and areas can be stressed or lightened with gouache or Chinese white. Watercolour pencils and crayons, a relatively new invention, are particularly suitable for this purpose. When dry they behave like crayons or hard pastels, but if dipped in water or used on wet paper they will dissolve, forming a wash. Using these, or ordinary pastels, on top of watercolour can turn a painting which has 'gone wrong' and become dull and lifeless into something quite new and different. It is always worth experimenting with such media on a painting that you are less than happy with; you may evolve a personal technique that you can use again. Wax oil pastels can create interesting textured areas when laid underneath a wash, as can treating the paper, or parts of it, with white spirit before painting, which has a similar effect. The possibilities are almost endless, and experimentation is sure to reward you with interesting discoveries.

PROBLEM-SOLVING

Although watercolours cannot be altered so drastically or so often as paintings in any of the opaque media, changes are possible. It is a mistake to abandon a picture because a first wash has not gone on quite right.

The first thing to remember is that a wash which looks too dark or too vivid on a sheet of otherwise white paper will dry much lighter and may look quite pale when surrounded by other colours. If the first wash looks wrong, let it dry. If you are still quite sure it is not what you intended, sponge it out with a clean sponge and clear water. This may leave a slight stain on the paper, depending on the paper used and the colour itself (some colours stain the paper, like a dye, while others do not) but when dry it will be too faint to spoil the new wash. When a wash has flooded, sponge it out immediately without waiting for it to dry; flooding cannot be entirely remedied, though it can sometimes create an effect not originally planned.

One of the commonest faults is accidentally to take a wash over the edge of an area to be reserved. There are three ways of dealing with this, depending on the size of the area and the type of edge desired. If the wash is pale and the area to be reserved is a broad and imprecise shape, such as a stone in the foreground of a landscape, you can simply sponge out the excess paint with a small sponge or cotton wool damped in clean water. A soft edge will be left. For a more intricate shape, or one requiring a sharp, clear edge, you may have to scrape the paint away (after it is dry) with a razor blade or scalpel, the former for broad areas, the latter for small ones. Hold the blade flat on the paper so that the corners do not dig in and scrape gently. The same method can be used to lighten an area or to create texture by removing a top layer of paint. The third rescue technique — to apply Chinese white with a fine brush — should be used only when the painting is otherwise complete; if the white is allowed to mix with other colours it will muddy them and spoil the translucency.

The small blots and smudges that often occur when you take a loaded brush over a painting or rest your hand on a still-damp area can also be razored out when dry. If a splash of paint or dirty water falls on the painting, quickly soak up the excess with a twist of tissue or a cotton bud, let it dry and then razor it out gently. If you are intending to apply more paint to the area, rub it down lightly with a soft eraser to smooth the surface, which will have been slightly roughened.

Even professionals, of course, sometimes find that a painting has gone so wrong that small corrections will not suffice or has become so clogged with paint that further work is impossible. If this happens you can, of course, throw it away. But you can also wash out the whole painting, or large parts of it, by putting the paper under running water and sponging the surface. Leave it on its board if you have stretched it. A slight stain may be left, but this can be an advantage as the faint shadow will serve as a drawing for the next attempt. A whole sky or foreground can be removed in this way, while leaving intact those areas with which you are satisfied.

USING GUM WATER.

Gum water, which is gum arabic diluted in water, adds richness to watercolours and keeps the colours bright. It can also be used, as here, as a sort of resist method to create highlights.

1. The tree and hedge are painted in with pure watercolour.
2. A further wash of green is applied, this time mixed with gum water.
3. The area of the central tree is spattered with water, flicked on with a household brush.
4. The central tree is blotted with a rag, so that wherever the water has touched, small areas of paint are lifted off, the gum being soluble in water.
5. The lighter patches of colour give an extra sparkle to the tree, while the addition of the gum water imparts richness to the dark green on either side.

1

2

3

4

5

CHAPTER FOUR

BASIC RULES FOR ARTISTS

Working outdoors. Some artists find that they work best with the subject in front of them. Others will only work from sketches or photographs, or even (more rarely), from memory.

*E*VERY PAINTER, working in whatever medium, needs to understand the basic rules of his craft, even if sometimes only to break them. The underlying principles of such things as composition, perspective, drawing itself, apply to all kinds of painting. The novice watercolourist, who needs to plan his paintings especially carefully, should have a firm grasp of them from the beginning.

♦ COMPOSING AND SELECTING ♦

Whether you are painting outdoors or indoors, whether your chosen subject is a landscape, a group of buildings, a portrait or a single flower in a vase, you need to have a clear idea of what the main elements are and of how you will place them on the paper before you begin to paint. Painting a landscape out of doors requires you to decide where the view is to begin and end, where to place the horizon, whether to emphasize or alter features in the foreground, and so on. For a portrait, still-life or flower painting you must decide how much to show, the proportion of the figure or flower in relation to the background, the general colour scheme and the balance of lights and darks. Composition and selection thus go hand in hand: an artist first selects which aspects of the subject are important and then composes the picture by placing them in a certain way.

There are well-tested mathematical rules for 'good composition'. The ancient Greeks, for instance, devised the system known as the Golden Section (or Golden Mean), in which the area of the painting is divided by a line in such a way that the smaller part is to the larger what the larger is to the whole. This ensures that the picture plane is divided in a balanced and symmetrical way, and countless artists have made use of the principle. The triangle is another basis for composition (many paintings are based on the framework of a single triangle) as is a series of intersecting geometric shapes such as squares, rectangles and circles.

It is unlikely that someone sitting down to an outdoor watercolour sketch will need a full knowledge of such principles, but there are some simple and practical ones that should be borne in mind. Basically, a good composi-

ABOVE *Figure paintings are more difficult to compose than landscapes because the choices are so much wider. A figure can be disposed in an almost infinite number of ways, while a landscape often needs only minor re-arranging. Here the artist has placed his subject in the centre of the picture, with the diagonal of the leg balancing the angle of the head: He has allowed one leg and the legs of the chair to 'bust' the frame at the bottom, thus bringing the figure forward on to the picture plane and avoiding a cramped and awkward appearance.*

Painters of the Renaissance usually planned the composition of a painting on a geometric grid structure. This example, by Piero della Francesca, is based on a triangle, a common compositional device which is still much used, as are circles and rectangles. The drawing on the right shows how other triangles can be discerned within the main one formed by the figures.

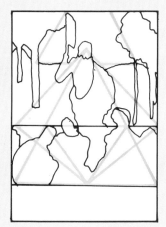

LEFT Converging lines in landscapes are often used to lead the viewer's eye to the focal point, in this case the buildings. Unusually, the artist has divided the picture into two nearly equal parts, the land and the sky; but monotony has been avoided by allowing the buildings and trees to break into the skyline and by dividing the foreground by the broken line of white road in the middle distance.

tion is one in which there are no jarring elements; all the parts of the picture balance one another in a pleasing way, and the viewer's eye is led into the picture rather than out of it. Whatever the subject, it is almost never advisable to divide the painting into two equal halves, such as sea and land, or table-top and background in a still-life. The result is at once monotonous and disjointed. The viewer's eye should not be led to one part of the painting to the exclusion of others, but there should usually be a 'focal point'. For example, a group of buildings in a landscape can be used simply as a counterpoint to other elements, such as trees and hills, or they may be what interests you most about the scene, with the trees, hills and foreground used as a 'backdrop'. The buildings need not be large, nor placed directly in the centre of the picture (this is not normally advisable); what matters is that the eye should be consistently led to them as the focal point. Compositional devices often used to lead the eye in this way are the curving lines of a path, stream, ploughed field or fence, along which the viewer's eye must travel. Such lines should never lead out of the picture unless for a deliberately sought effect.

The focal point of a portrait is almost always the face, the eyes in particular for a front or three-quarter view, and care must be taken not to detract from it by placing too much emphasis on other elements, such as the background, or the hands. Hands and clothing are often treated in a sketchy way so that they do not assume too much importance. A figure or face should be placed in a well-considered and deliberate way against the background to create a feeling of harmony and balance. There should not be too much space at the top. Nor, usually, should the subject be placed squarely in the middle of the picture, though a central position can sometimes be effective.

Backgrounds are part of a portrait painting, as are skies in landscapes, even when they are quite plain and muted in colour. If a picture is placed against a stark white background, the white areas will have their own shapes and thus make their contribution to the balance of the painting. Such flat areas are known as 'negative space'. A more decorative background, such as a boldly patterned wallpaper or still-life of a vase of flowers on a table, can be used to complement the main subject, just as the colours in the sky or the direction of clouds do in a landscape.

Many artists use viewing frames to help them work out a satisfactory composition, and some also use polaroid cameras for indoor work, taking several shots of a portrait or still-life until they find a satisfactory arrangement. A viewing frame is simply a piece of cardboard with an oblong hole cut in it (a good size of aperture is $4\frac{1}{2} \times 6$ in /11×15 cm), which is held up at about arm's length to

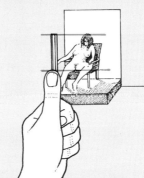

When drawing a figure from life measurements and angles need constant checking. By holding up a pencil and moving your thumb up and down on it you can check proportions; angling the pencil to follow the line of the body or limb shows you the precise slope, which can be double-checked by relating it to a vertical, such as a chair leg.

work out the best placing of the subject. It is particularly useful for on-the-spot landscape work, as it is very difficult to assess large landscape subjects without some form of framing device. Making small, quick sketches, often referred to as thumbnail sketches, is another good way to work out a composition. A rough scribble, even a few lines, will often provide a clear idea of how the main shapes should be placed within the picture area.

◆ DRAWING ◆

Drawing is the basis of all painting. Indeed, painting is simply drawing with a brush and colour. Although much of the more detailed drawing in a watercolour is done at the final stages with a fine brush, it is nearly always necessary to make some form of pencil drawing on the paper before beginning to paint. Without this, you will have no idea where to place the first wash or which areas to reserve as paler ones. Obviously there are exceptions to this general rule. A very quick study in which colour is the most important aspect or a broad and impressionistic landscape with little detail may not need a drawing. But, even so, a few lines can provide a helpful guide.

Few people draw with the ease and assurance that produce the confident and flowing lines of really fine drawings. However, a drawing which is to be used only as the guideline for a painting need not be of high quality. What matters is getting the proportions and shapes right. Everybody tends to draw what he knows, or thinks he knows, rather than what he actually sees. The first step in drawing is to take a good long look at the subject and try to get rid of any preconceptions about it. By holding a pencil up at arm's length and closing one eye it is possible to check whether a line which appears vertical or horizontal really is so; and the size of one object in relation to another can be measured in the same way. Once one part of a scene, or figure, has been described accurately all the others can be related to it. But if you begin with a false 'statement', misunderstanding the angle at which a roof top slopes away from you, for example, and then try to relate the other shapes and lines to it, the drawing will go progressively awry. It pays to take time over a preliminary drawing, especially if the subject is complex; otherwise you will become increasingly frustrated when you start to paint.

Never try to draw any subject from too close a viewpoint, which distorts the view. And make sure that you do not have to move your head to see different parts of the subject. Your line of vision should be central. Try to make sure that you are reasonably comfortable (not always possible when working out of doors) and hold the drawing board in such a way that it does not obscure any part of the subject. Check sizes and measurements continually by holding up your pencil and moving your thumb up and down on it, closing one eye to measure distances. Avoid making the drawing too fussy. Too many pencil marks may muddy the paint. An HB or B pencil is the best to use, as softer ones may smudge the paper. The drawing can be erased at any stage during the painting as long as the paper

TRANSFERRING THE IMAGE.

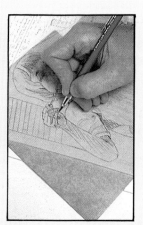

In portraiture precise drawing is very important. It is often wise to make a preliminary drawing and then transfer it to the painting surface, thus avoiding too much erasing on the surface itself. Here the artist has worked from a photograph, enlarged to the required size by means of a grid. The drawing line transferred to the support by using a form of carbon paper called iron-oxide paper, which provides a clear outline. The finished painting can be seen on page 102.

LEFT At first sight this appears to be a rapidly executed, spontaneous sketch, as indeed it is; but its composition has been sufficiently worked out to present a pleasing unity as well as a strong feeling of life and movement. The lights and darks are well balanced, the colours are harmonious, and the eye is led into the picture by the gently curving path with its pattern of shadows. This kind of planning is often instinctive; some people have a natural feel for a good composition, while others have to rely on theory and hard work.

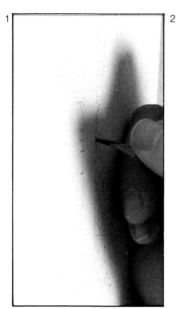

LEFT This study of a motel required a careful outline drawing to enable the artist to place his first wash accurately.

TOP RIGHT AND ABOVE Since only an outline was needed, the drawing was done directly on the support with a sharp 2B pencil. The first wash was then laid around the shapes of the building and trees.

is quite dry. On most papers pencil marks can be erased without affecting the paint on top, though the surface of a few, rather smooth, papers may be spoiled by too much erasing.

◆ PERSPECTIVE ◆

Perspective is sometimes believed to be the concern only of those who paint buildings. In fact, the laws of perspective govern everything, simply because drawing and painting transfer three-dimensional shapes on to a two-dimensional surface.

In theory, a perfectly adequate drawing with a fairly accurate rendering of perspective could be produced by simply drawing what is seen. Some knowledge of the basic principles of perspective is nevertheless helpful, if only

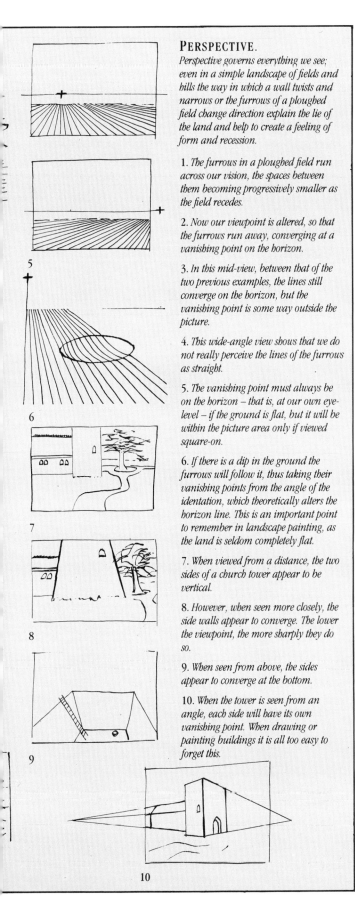

PERSPECTIVE.

Perspective governs everything we see; even in a simple landscape of fields and hills the way in which a wall twists and narrows or the furrows of a ploughed field change direction explain the lie of the land and help to create a feeling of form and recession.

1. The furrows in a ploughed field run across our vision, the spaces between them becoming progressively smaller as the field recedes.

2. Now our viewpoint is altered, so that the furrows run away, converging at a vanishing point on the horizon.

3. In this mid-view, between that of the two previous examples, the lines still converge on the horizon, but the vanishing point is some way outside the picture.

4. This wide-angle view shows that we do not really perceive the lines of the furrows as straight.

5. The vanishing point must always be on the horizon – that is, at our own eye-level – if the ground is flat, but it will be within the picture area only if viewed square-on.

6. If there is a dip in the ground the furrows will follow it, thus taking their vanishing points from the angle of the identation, which theoretically alters the horizon line. This is an important point to remember in landscape painting, as the land is seldom completely flat.

7. When viewed from a distance, the two sides of a church tower appear to be vertical.

8. However, when seen more closely, the side walls appear to converge. The lower the viewpoint, the more sharply they do so.

9. When seen from above, the sides appear to converge at the bottom.

10. When the tower is seen from an angle, each side will have its own vanishing point. When drawing or painting buildings it is all too easy to forget this.

because it will enable you to know when something has gone wrong. The 'golden rule', which most people learn at school, is that receding parallel lines meet at a vanishing point. That vanishing point, which is on the horizon, may be inside the picture area or outside it. The horizon itself is your own eye-level, so that if you are lying down or crouching it will be low, with a large expanse of sky, whereas if you are looking down on a scene, from a top-floor window, say, it will be very high, perhaps with no sky visible at all, and a receding parallel line of rooftops below you will slope upwards. The real difficulty in drawing complex perspective subjects, such as urban scenes, is that buildings have several different planes, each with its own vanishing point, and sometimes one building or group of buildings is set at angles to another, giving yet another set of points, many of which will be outside the picture plane. These must be guessed at to some extent, but the pencil-and-thumb measuring system described earlier is helpful, or a small plastic ruler can be held up to assess the angles of parallel lines.

Artists frequently distort perspective intentionally, or use it in an inventive way by choosing an artificially high or low viewpoint. Others ignore it altogether, to create paintings with a strong pattern, rather as children do. There is no reason why the rules should not be broken if doing so makes a better painting. But to break rules successfully it is necessary first to understand them.

◆ TONE AND COLOUR ◆

Colour theory can be enormously complicated. It is a fascinating study in itself, about which whole books have been written. But there are really only a few facts about colour which the average painter needs to know. Colour has two main components, tone and hue, the former being its lightness or darkness and the latter its intensity, or vividness. If you were to take both a black-and-white photograph and a colour one of a landscape composed almost entirely of greens, the black-and-white one would show the tones quite clearly as a series of dark greys and light greys shading to white and black. It is important to balance tones, or lights and darks, in a painting, but they can be rather hard to assess, particularly outdoors in a changing light. You may wonder whether the sky is lighter or darker than the sea or land, or whether the leaves of a tree are lighter or darker than the hills behind. Tones are much easier to judge if you half-close your eyes, thus eliminating distracting details.

In the colour photograph of the landscape some of the greens will appear more vivid than others, to have a brighter hue. You may notice that the brightest colours are in the foreground, where the contrasts in tone are also the strongest, those in the background tending to merge into one another and become barely distinguishable in places. An understanding of this phenomenon, called aerial perspective, is vitally important, especially for the land-scape painter. As a landscape recedes into the middle and then the far distance, objects appear much less distinct and become paler and bluer because the light is filtered

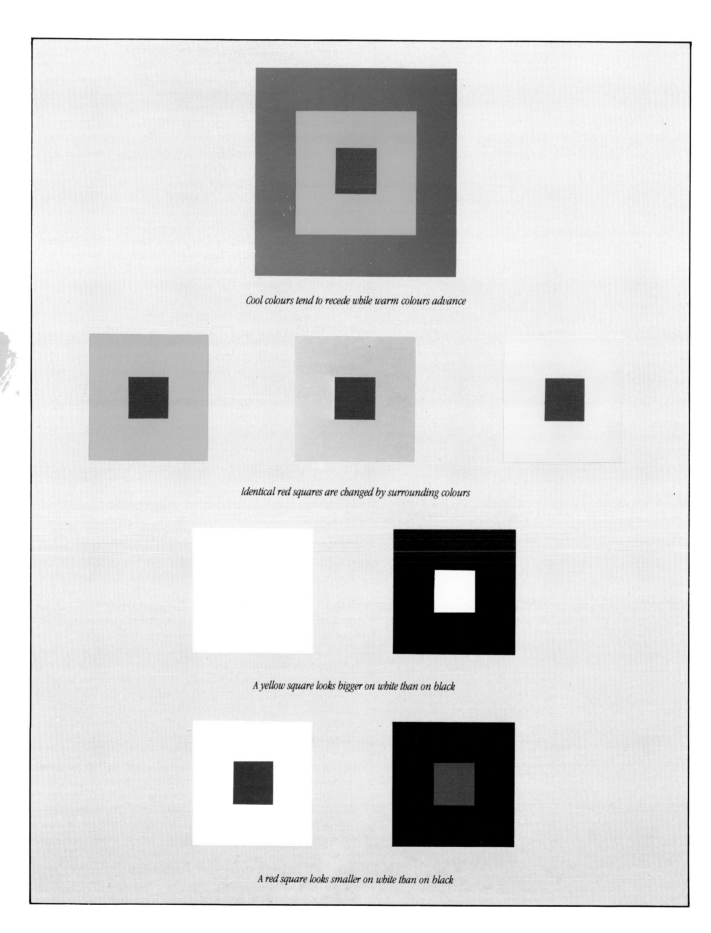

Cool colours tend to recede while warm colours advance

Identical red squares are changed by surrounding colours

A yellow square looks bigger on white than on black

A red square looks smaller on white than on black

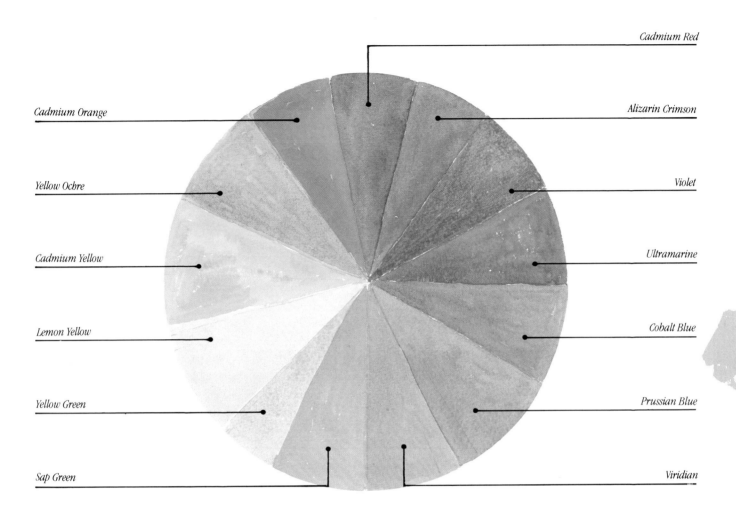

Cadmium Red

Alizarin Crimson

Cadmium Orange

Violet

Yellow Ochre

Ultramarine

Cadmium Yellow

Cobalt Blue

Lemon Yellow

Prussian Blue

Yellow Green

Viridian

Sap Green

LEFT The single most important fact to realize about colour is that each colour exists only in relation to those surrounding it. Not only does the relative 'temperature' of a colour, that is, its warmness or coolness change, but the apparent size of an area of colour also changes according to its surroundings. These are examples of optical illusions produced by such juxtapositions.

through dust and moisture in the atmosphere. It is possible to suggest distance and recession in a painting by using this kind of perspective alone, and such effects are easier to achieve in watercolour than in oil: a pale, flat wash can be put on and then the tiny differences in tones suggested by just a dab or two of barely tinted water.

Colours in the foreground tend to be 'warmer' than those in the background as well as brighter in hue. All colours can be broadly classified as either 'warm' or 'cool'. Reds, yellows and oranges, for instance, are warm, and tend to push themselves forward, or 'advance'; blues, and colours with blue in them, such as blue-grey and blue-green, will recede. However, colours can be perceived as colours only in relation to one another, and some blues are warmer than others while some reds are cooler. You can see this by placing ultramarine blue, which is relatively warm, next to the cold Prussian blue, or alizarin crimson, which is quite cool, next to cadmium red or orange, both of which are very warm.

Another way of using colour effectively is to make use of complementary colours, those that are opposite one another on the colour wheel. Red and green are complementaries, as are blue and yellow. A large expanse of green grass or blue sea can often be heightened by a small patch of bright red or yellow respectively. Landscape

ABOVE The colour wheel, which is really just a spectrum bent into a circle, is a useful device for working out combinations of colours. Notice how the colours on the red and yellow side appear warm, while those on the green and blue side are much cooler.

ABOVE *In this painting all the colours are cool, just a range of blues and greys with a touch of warmer greenish brown on the left side of the building. Foregrounds are often brought forward and emphasized by using warmer colours in the front of the picture; but here the foreground has been made to 'advance' by the use of much darker tones, aided by the very clear definition of the spiky foliage on the left.*

RIGHT *Warm colours have been used throughout this painting, those in the foreground being repeated in smaller quantities in the background. The artist's concern was with the pattern created by the various elements rather than with a strict three-dimensional representation, though the background recedes just enough to allow us to 'read' the picture as an urban landscape.*

and seascape painters often use a figure or the sail of a boat as a means of introducing a complementary colour.

Perhaps the single most important fact about colour is that there is no colour at all without light. The quality, strength and direction of the light changes colours constantly, a problem when working out of doors, as a landscape which might have seemed to be composed of tones of greenish grey in the morning could by evening have become golden ochre, even red, in places. The best ways to overcome the difficulty are to work quickly, possibly making several sketches under different lights, or to decide on a colour scheme and stick to it, ignoring subsequent changes. The problem is less acute when working indoors, though if natural light is being used for a portrait or still-life the colours will undoubtedly change, as will the way the shadows fall.

♦ USING REFERENCE MATERIAL ♦

Paintings do not, of course, have to be done from life: many fine landscapes are painted in the studio, and excellent portraits are done from photographs or drawings or a combination of both. Few good paintings, however, are done from memory. Even professional artists, who are trained to observe and assess and are constantly on the lookout for visual stimulus, make use of reference material for their paintings. These may be sketches or photographs, sometimes even picture postcards. You may think that you remember a scene very well, but you will be surprised how the details escape you as soon as you sit down to paint it. It is therefore wise to amass as much reference material as possible, even if it seems to be much more than you need.

Carrying a sketchbook is recommended — if nothing else it encourages the analytical observation of things, which is quite different from just looking and admiring. The trouble with sketches is that it takes experience to know which particular aspect or detail of a scene you will want to refer to later. Also, unless you draw with assurance, you may find that you have failed to capture the essence of what you wished to record — rather like taking notes and finding you cannot read your own shorthand or handwriting.

The camera is useful as a notetaker, but it should not be regarded as any more than this. Never try to copy a photograph slavishly. If you are out walking and see a promising subject, take several photographs, and when you begin the painting try to use them constructively, as a starting point, together with your own recollections of the scene, departing from both if you feel it would improve the painting. Portrait painters often have a preliminary live sitting and then photographs for later stages, or for the clothes and background.

The great advantage of photographs is that they can capture fleeting moments and impressions, such as the light falling in a certain way on a stretch of water, the eerie purple and gold light before a storm, children playing, or a cat asleep in a patch of sunlight. The disadvantage is that they do not actually tell the truth: the camera distorts perspective, flattens colour and fudges detail. When you want a clear visual description of some small, but vital, part of a subject, you find only a vague blur. A sketch, even a less than brilliant one, would probably have been more useful, because you would have been forced to look hard at the subject and thus have gained more understanding of it.

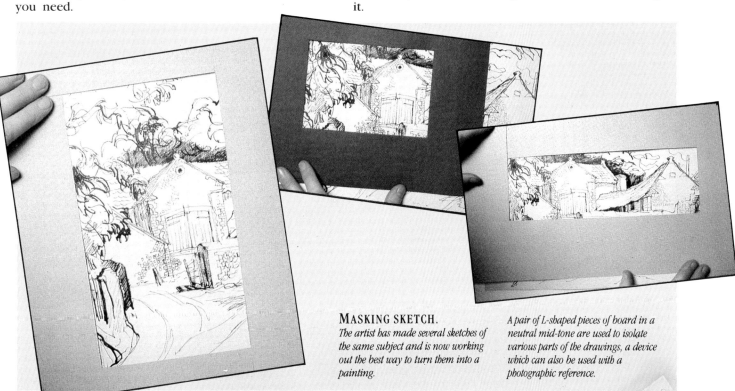

MASKING SKETCH.
The artist has made several sketches of the same subject and is now working out the best way to turn them into a painting.

A pair of L-shaped pieces of board in a neutral mid-tone are used to isolate various parts of the drawings, a device which can also be used with a photographic reference.

CHAPTER FIVE

LANDSCAPE AND SEASCAPE

*Earth colours and a vibrant green form the basic palette for
this watercolour of a twisting harbour wall. The tones of the
background were harmonized and blended by laying more
paint into damp washes.*

WATERCOLOUR HAS ALWAYS BEEN closely associated with landscape and seascape painting, and even with today's proliferation of new media for the artist there is still none more able to render the transient and atmospheric qualities of countryside, sea and sky.

♦ THE ENGLISH WATERCOLOUR ♦ TRADITION

In England, the country which more than any other can claim to have founded the great tradition of landscape painting in watercolour, landscape was not really considered a suitable subject in its own right until the late 18th century. The formal, classical landscapes of the French artists, Claude Lorraine (1600-82) and Nicolas Poussin (1594-1665), were much admired by artists and discerning collectors, as were the realistic landscapes of artists of the Dutch school such as Jacob van Ruisdael (1629-82), but the general public in the main wanted portraits and historical subjects. The great English portrait painter, Thomas Gainsborough (1727-88), had a deep love of his native landscape and regarded it as his true subject, but in order to earn a living he painted many more portraits than landscapes.

The two artists who elevated landscape and seascape to the status of fine art were Constable and Turner. Their influence on painting, not only in Great Britain but all over the world, was immeasurable. By the early 19th century landscape had arrived, and at the same time watercolour, a medium hitherto used for quick sketches and for colouring maps and prints, had become the chief medium for many landscape artists. Constable used it as his predeces-

ABOVE *Peter de Wint, an English painter of Dutch extraction, was drawn to flat, panoramic landscapes. His great sweeping views seem to extend beyond the confines of the paintings themselves. Observe the sure and confident handling of the trees and water in* Walton-on-Thames, *and the tiny areas of unpainted paper which give extra sparkle to the picture.*

LEFT *Thomas Girtin was a pioneer of watercolour painting much admired by his contemporary, Turner. He worked with only five colours – black, monastral blue, yellow ochre, burnt sienna and light red – to create subtle evocations of atmosphere.* The White House, Chelsea *shows both his fine sense of composition and his mastery of tone and colour. In the darker areas, washes have been laid one over another with great skill. The focal point, the house, is slightly off-centre and has been left as white paper, showing through with such brilliance that it appears almost as if floodlit.*

sors had, as a rapid means of recording impressions, but Turner used it in a new and daring way and exploited its potential fully to express his feelings about light and colour.

At much the same time John Sell Cotman, the co-founder of the school of painting known as the Norwich School after its other founder, John Crome (1768-1821), who lived in that town, was producing some of the finest watercolour landscapes ever seen before or since. These paintings by the artists of the English watercolour school have never been surpassed; they became an inspiration to artists everywhere, and remain so today.

♦ PRACTICAL HINTS FOR ♦ OUTDOOR PAINTING

Once landscape had become an 'official' subject for painters, working out of doors directly from nature became increasingly common, the more so after the French Impressionists set the example. It is not now so popular. Photographers queueing up to record a beauty spot are a more usual sight than artists doing so. It is, however, an excellent discipline, which forces you to look hard at a subject and make rapid decisions about how to

ABOVE *Francis Towne's work was not appreciated in the 19th century, but he has since been recognized as one of the great names of British watercolour painting. He felt a particular fascination for grand mountain landscapes, finding much of his inspiration in the wild scenery of the Alps, North Wales and England's Lake District. This painting,* Grasmere by the Road, *is typical of his technique, in which pen outline is used to isolate areas of contrasting colour.*

ABOVE RIGHT *A watercolour of stones at Avebury. The cool tones express the clarity of daylight and the calm grandeur of this ancient monument.*

treat it and lends immediacy and spontaneity to the work itself.

Watercolour is a light and portable medium, ideally suited to outdoor work, but on-the-spot painting, whatever the medium, always presents problems. Chief among them is the weather. You may have to contend with blazing heat which dries the paint as soon as it is laid down, freezing winds which numb your hands, sudden showers which blotch your best efforts or wash them away altogether, and changing light which confuses you and makes you doubt your initial drawing and composition. If the weather looks unpredictable, take extra clothes (a pair of old gloves with the fingers cut off the painting hand are a help in winter), a plastic bag or carrier large enough to hold your board in case of rain, and anything else you can think of for your comfort, such as a thermos of tea or coffee and a radio. If the sun is bright try to sit in a shaded place; otherwise the light will bounce back at you off the white paper, which makes it difficult or sometimes impossible to see what you are doing. If you are embarrassed by the comments of passers-by, a 'walkman' serves as an efficient insulation device. Some people also find it an aid to concentration, though others do not. Always take sufficient water and receptacles to put it in, and restrict your palette to as few colours as possible.

Choose a subject that genuinely interests you rather than one you feel you 'ought' to paint, even if it is only a back garden or local park. If you are familiar with a particular area you will probably already have a subject, or several subjects, in mind. On holiday in an unfamiliar place, try to assess a subject in advance by carrying out a preliminary reconaissance rather than dashing straight out with your paints. Finally, try to work as quickly as you can without rushing, so that the first important stages of the painting are complete before the light changes. If necessary make a start on one day and complete the work on another. Seascapes are especially difficult, since the colour of the sea can change drastically — from dark indigo to bright blue-green, for example — in a matter of minutes. It is often advisable to make several quick colour sketches and then work indoors from them.

Although Turner's watercolours are less well known than his oils, they rank among his finest works. He was clearly extremely taken with watercolour and used it brilliantly and experimentally to express his preoccupation with light and atmosphere, often making use of the semi-accidental effects that occur in watercolour painting. In Venice from the Giudecca he has created distance by using thin layers of paint and cool blues in the background; the darker and warmer details in the foreground are suggested lightly enough to retain the feeling of hazy, shimmering light.

♦ SUMMER PAINTING ♦

This landscape is a fine evocation of the drama of the ever-changing countryside, here seen under the kind of summer squall of rain which causes the sky and hills to merge into one another. Watercolour is an ideal medium for capturing such atmospheric effects, but although the painting looks spontaneous (as the artist intended) it is actually very carefully planned.

The technique could not be more dissimilar to that used in the following example. Here an unusually large selection of colours has been used, and they have been deliberately allowed to mix on the paper to create soft, blurring effects. The natural translucence of watercolour has been exploited to the full to allow the bright colours, such as the greens of the foreground and the patch of sunlight on the hills, to shine out with brilliance and clarity.

Since the time of Turner the effects of light have been among the prime concerns of landscape painters, particularly those living in the temperate zones, where the landscape is subject to sudden changes. It is not easy, however, to capture light and atmosphere with brushes and paints, and a painting like this one relies for its success on a deliberate use of certain techniques as well as on fast working — freshness and spontaneity is quickly destroyed if the brushwork becomes too laboured. Here the brush strokes themselves form an integral part of the painting, having been used to suggest the uneven shroud of rain, with brighter and darker colours laid on in places with great accuracy and assurance. There are no totally flat washes anywhere in the painting. Even in the distant hills different tones and colours are visible, but a feeling of space and recession has been rendered by the use of very bright colours and greater tonal contrasts in the foreground.

MATERIALS USED

- ♦ SUPPORT: pre-stretched watercolour paper with a Not surface, measuring 9½ × 13 in/24 × 33 cm.
- ♦ COLOURS: Hooker's green, oxide of chromium, Indian yellow, Naples yellow, raw sienna, raw umber, cobalt blue, ultramarine and permanent rose, plus a little Chinese white.
- ♦ BRUSHES: a selection of soft brushes and a small household brush.

1. The paper was stretched before use and the board was laid flat, not propped at a slight angle as it would be for laying flat washes. In this way the paint was allowed to mix on the paper without running down it uncontrollably.

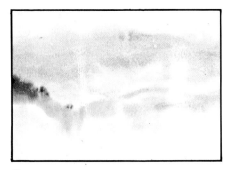

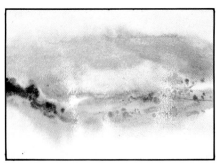

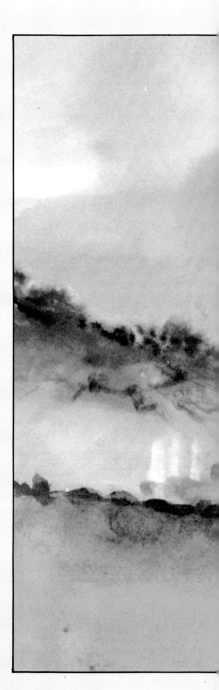

2. As the first colours began to dry slightly a warmer pink tone was introduced to the sky and touches of blue added to the middle distance. In this technique, called working wet into wet, the paint is never allowed to dry entirely; but if new paint is added when the first layer is too wet it will flood rather than merge softly into the other colours.

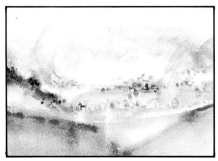

3. A broad bristle-brush was used to block in the colours for the foreground, the greens being chosen to balance the yellow-green patch of sunlight on the hills. Oil-painting brushes and household brushes can often be used in watercolour painting to create particular effects.

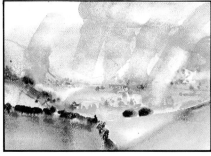

4. Next, bold brush strokes were introduced into the sky to indicate the rain clouds, and the sky was given a yellow hue and then overlaid with grey-blue. At the same time the foreground colours were strengthened and further definition was added.

5. Finished painting: to give a softer, more blurred, effect to the rain a little white was added to the paint in the final stages. Adding white to watercolour gives an effect quite unlike the harsher one provided by gouache paints, but it should not be used until the painting is near completion; otherwise it may muddy the other colours.

Raw Umber   *Cobalt Blue*

Summer Painting

marine   *Permanent Rose*   *Hooker's Green*   *Oxide of Chromium*   *Indian Yellow*   *Naples Yellow*   *Raw Sienna*

1. This photograph gives an idea of how much paint is needed for a wash over a large area. Until you are used to laying washes it is wise to mix more than you think you will need. This wash, for the sky, is diluted cobalt blue.

♦ DISTANT HILLS ♦

This painting relies for its effect on the use of linear shapes arranged in such a way as to create an atmosphere of gentle harmony. The colour range is very limited, almost monochromatic, and the minimum of detail, even in the foreground, gives the elegantly uncluttered and stylized look characteristic of many Chinese paintings.

One of the artist's main concerns was to indicate the spaciousness and recession of the landscape. He used two methods to do this. The first was aerial perspective, the term used for the way that the features of a landscape become less distinct as they recede, with the colours becoming paler and cooler. Tonal contrasts are greater in the foreground, where the colours are strong and warm. The second method was to allow the tree on the right to go out of the frame at the top, thus clearly indicating that the group of trees is on the picture plane (the front of the painting).

The painting provides an excellent example of the 'classical' approach to watercolour, in which the paint is laid on in a series of thin washes, allowing the brilliance of the white paper to reflect back through them. Unusually, an HP (hot-pressed) paper was used instead of the more popular Not, or cold-pressed, but this artist finds that the smoother paper suits his style, and he mixes a little gum arabic with the water to give extra body and adherence. Each wash, once laid down, has been left without any further paint being laid on top, and the painting was worked from the top downward, with the foreground trees painted over the washes for the sky and hills. It was done in the studio from a sketch and the drawing on the support was restricted to a few lines drawn with an HB pencil.

2. The wash for the sky, put on with a No.10 squirrel brush, was deliberately laid slightly unevenly to suggest a pale blue sky with a light cloud cover.

3. As soon as the wash for the sky was dry, the same squirrel brush was used to put on a darker shade, with Payne's grey added to the cobalt blue, to the area of the far hills.

4. The second wash had to be darker than that for the sky but not too dark, as the artist knew that he would have to increase the tonal contrasts in the middle distance to suggest its relative nearness to the picture plane.

5 and 6. As each wash has to be allowed to dry before putting on the next, in this particular technique, a hairdrier is sometimes used to hasten the process. The third and fourth washes, darker shades of the second, were laid on next, leaving the whole of the foreground and middle distance still untouched.

7. The tone of the darker area of the middle distance had to be very carefully calculated to make it appear to be in front of the far hills. This wash has been put on slightly thicker in places to suggest the shapes of the trees.

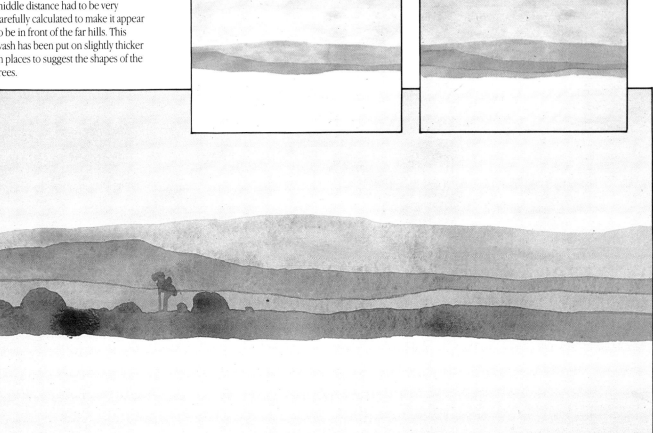

8 . The trees in the foreground were worked on next, the darker paint being taken over the background and sky washes. This overlapping device is most successful when the colours are similar; overlapping two quite different colours, for instance red-brown tree trunks over a bright green middle distance, would give a third colour, which could provide a jarring element if not planned.

9 and 10. At this stage both the background and foreground were complete, but the area between the two was still unpainted. Because warm colours tend to advance and cool ones recede, the artist laid a warm greenish wash over this area to make it come forward toward the picture plane.

MATERIALS USED

- ◆ SUPPORT: pre-stretched watercolour paper with an HP surface, measuring 14 × 21½ in/35 × 53 cm.
- ◆ COLOURS: cobalt blue, Payne's grey, raw umber and sap green.
- ◆ BRUSHES: a No. 10 squirrel and a No. 4 sable.
- ◆ ADDITIONAL EQUIPMENT: a selection of ceramic palettes for mixing the paint; a little gum arabic for mixing with the water.

Distant Hills

1. Having made a careful outline drawing of the main shapes, the artist blocked out the brightest areas of the rocks with masking fluid. This method highlights the importance of an accurate drawing, since the artist has to know from the outset exactly where to place the masking fluid.

♦ OLD HARRY AND HIS WIFE ♦

A large variety of different techniques has been used to create the deceptively simple effect of this painting. The subject is bold and dramatic, and its drama has been emphasized by the juxtaposition of large, solid shapes. The tonal contrasts between the rocks and the sea are distinct enough for the rocks to stand out as light against dark, but not so great as to spoil the delicate balance. Greater contrasts might have looked overstated.

Seascapes can be tricky subjects. It is difficult to decide whether to treat the sea as a flat area or to try to show the movement of the water by 'filling in' every wave and ripple. Also, when painting outdoors, you will see the colours constantly changing, which can give rise to uncertainty about the best approach. Here the sea has been treated fairly flat, with just enough unevenness and broken texture to suggest water; the sky hints at clouds, nothing more. The artist did not have to contend with changing colours and lights, since the painting was done in the studio. He used a photograph as his main reference for the shapes and was thus free to decide on a colour scheme without external distraction. The light falling on the rock, which the photograph features very vividly, has been given a minor role in the painting, as the artist was more concerned with the texture of the rock, which is echoed in the rippling reflection below.

Masking fluid provided the ideal way of dealing with the rock. The brightly lit areas were covered with the fluid, so that the shadow areas could be built up without the paints encroaching on the highlights. In places the dry-brush technique was used, together with that of spattering the paint. Both techniques are excellent for suggesting texture, though they should always be used sparingly.

2. Masking fluid gives a different effect from that obtained by painting around areas to be reserved. The marks of the brush are visible when the fluid is removed, thus making it a method of painting in 'negative'. When the masking fluid was dry, a broken wash was laid over the sky area and then a darker one for the line of distant cliffs.

3. The sea was laid in with a soft brush and a dilute wash of Payne's grey. This wash was deliberately kept loose and fluid, and the paint was moved around to create different tones.

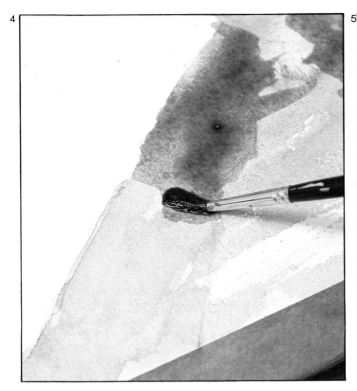

4. Here the artist is using a darker tone of Payne's grey, mixed with ultramarine, a warm blue, to darken the sea in places.

5. At this stage the entire surface has been covered and the masking fluid, yellowish in colour, is still on. A pale wash of lemon yellow was laid on the reflection area and greyish washes put over the darker parts of the rocks.

6. Using diluted black paint, the artist works the darkest shadows between the rocks and at the bottom of the central rock.

7. Once the dark tones have been put on, the masking fluid is removed by rubbing gently with the finger. Masking fluid is not suitable for use on rough paper, as it sinks into the hollows and cannot be removed.

8. The grassy tops of the cliffs are now painted sap green with a fine brush. Note how the artist darkens the colour at the edge to produce a crisp line of shadow.

9. Here the artist is preparing the brush for dry-brush work by spreading the bristles below the ferrule so that they will give a series of fine lines. The minimum of paint is put on the brush for this technique.

10. Another technique used for this painting was to cover an area already painted with gummed water, leave it to dry, and then gently work into it with a brush dipped in clear water to give small areas of lighter tone.

11. Here the artist is using a broad bristle-brush to spatter paint on to the surface. Surrounding areas were masked off first. This is an effective texture-creating technique, but care must be taken to mix a colour which is only slightly darker than that underneath; otherwise you will create a spotted, rather than an unobtrusively textured, effect.

12. As a final touch, the line of wavelets at the bottom of the rocks is added with opaque white paint, which is allowed to mix a little with the blue to give the broken effect of foamy water.

MATERIALS USED

♦ SUPPORT: pre-stretched watercolour paper with a Not surface, measuring 21 × 30 in/54 × 75 cm.
♦ COLOURS: black, Payne's grey, ultramarine, cobalt blue, sap green, lemon yellow, yellow ochre and raw umber, plus a little white gouache.
♦ BRUSHES AND OTHER EQUIPMENT: a selection of large and small soft brushes, a broad bristle-brush, gum arabic, masking fluid and masking tape.

Old Harry and His Wife

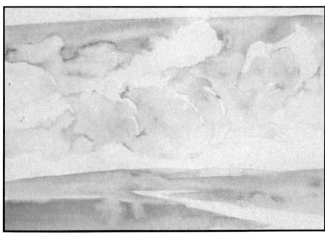

1. The artist started with some pencil lines to indicate the position of the horizon and the diagonal line of the river. He then began to lay wet washes on the sky and distant hills, using the brush as a drawing implement to describe the shapes of the clouds.

2. The artist continued to build up wet washes, keeping the middle ground fairly light at this stage, and repeating the warm pink tones on the undersides of the clouds.

3. The hills on the left have now been deepened in tone, so that they separate themselves from the more distant hills behind. At the same time further modelling has been added to the clouds by building up the mid-tones with Payne's grey, warm blue-grey and pink.

♦ CLOUDS ♦

In a landscape painting, sky and land should always be seen together and in relation to one another, since the particular light cast by the sky — varying according to the amount of cloud cover and the position of the sun — has a direct influence on the colours and tones of the land below. Also, the shapes and colours of clouds can be used as an important part of a composition, perhaps to act as a counterfoil to some feature of the foreground or to echo a shape or colour in the middle distance.

Watercolour lends itself very well to sky painting, since by working wet into wet effects can often be produced which resemble those seen in skies. Care must be taken, however, not to allow too many hard edges to form or the soft, rounded appearance of the clouds will be lost. Here the artist has kept the paint quite loose and fluid, using the brush to draw the cloud shapes and laying one wash over another to build up the forms. He has worked all over the painting at the same time, repeating some of the warm pinky-browns of the foreground and middle distance in the clouds themselves, so that the painting has a feeling of unity, with no artificial division between sky and land. The horizon has been placed quite low, as the sky is the main focus of interest.

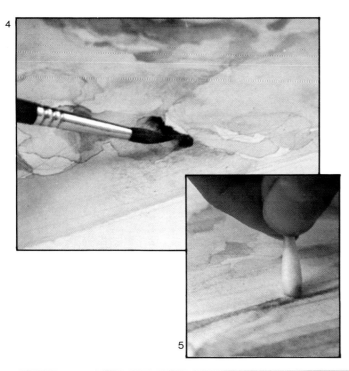

4

5

4. Here the artist is seen working wet into wet, adding small touches of Payne's grey to parts of the clouds. Notice how the fine lines which have formed in places where the paint has flooded have been cleverly exploited to give a crisp look to the clouds.

5. Sponges and cotton buds are particularly useful for a painting like this, as they can be used to soften edges, as here, or to draw paler shapes into an existing wash.

6. The final touches, which have brought the whole painting together, were to add some definition to the foreground and to increase the intensity of the blue above the clouds, so that the darker tones of land and sky are pleasingly balanced.

MATERIALS USED

♦ SUPPORT: pre-stretched watercolour paper, measuring 10 × 14 in/25 × 35 cm.
♦ COLOURS: ultramarine, cobalt blue, olive green, burnt sienna, cadmium yellow, alizarin crimson, Payne's grey.
♦ BRUSHES AND OTHER EQUIPMENT: Nos. 12, 8 and 4 soft brushes, cotton buds.

6

Clouds

CHAPTER SIX

BUILDINGS

Bonington's paintings, in both oil and watercolour, were much admired in his lifetime. He died of consumption at the age of 26 without having fully exploited his gift. As a colourist he was superb, and he was a pioneer in the use of watercolour, but it is said of him that he never fully understood perspective. In this painting, Castelbarco Tomb, the subject is sufficiently simple to disguise any possible weakness, and it comes across as a bold and dramatic statement of form and colour.

ALTHOUGH PAINTINGS which take a building or a group of buildings as their subject are usually regarded as a branch of landscape painting, it is more practical to regard architectural painting and drawing as a separate subject. It presents its own problems, not the least of them being the intricacies of perspective. Obviously not all paintings of buildings need be as accurate and precise as an architect's drawings — this is seldom desirable — but a painting of a house, church or ruin is similar to a portrait. It is that particular building you want to paint, because you are attracted to its shape, colour or general atmosphere. It is therefore important to get the proportions and perspective right, just as you would the features of a face.

THE TOPOGRAPHICAL TRADITION

Before the time of the great watercolour landscape painters of the later 18th and early 19th centuries, watercolour had been used mainly for quick sketches and topographical drawings, that is, precise visual records of landscapes or buildings. Many such drawings and paintings were intended as the basis for engravings or etchings, and were not really painterly in approach, colour being used in flat washes to supplement a linear drawing, often in pen and ink. In the 19th century interest in buildings was stimulated by the comparative ease of travel to foreign parts. Crumbling medieval ruins, Roman remains and picturesque streets in old towns became favourite subjects for artists. By then, too, the use of watercolour had become much more daring and inventive, and artists were concerned with conveying the feeling and atmosphere of buildings, not simply recording their outward appearance and superficial details as an architect or draughtsman

would. Paintings such as Bonington's *Castelbarco Tomb* and Turner's *Tintern Abbey* are faithful and accurate records of the buildings, but they are also full of life and vigour, thus combining the topographical tradition with that of poetic landscape.

♦ PRACTICAL HINTS ♦

Some knowledge of perspective is needed to make a building look solid and convincing, but the most important factor is close and careful observation, which leads to a good foundation drawing. Try to work directly from the subject itself wherever possible: photographs, which distort the perspective, are not the ideal source of reference for architectural subjects. A photograph taken with a standard instant camera, which usually has a wide-angle lens (35–45mm focal length) will cause a tall building to look much shorter and wider; and any details in shadow, such as the top of a wall under the eaves of a roof, will probably be indistinguishable.

Watercolourists of the past sometimes paid a draughtsman to make a preliminary drawing for them. They would simply put on the colour! Most of us, however, have to do our own donkey-work, and with a complicated subject it can take time. Fortunately, the drawing can be done on one day (and can take as long as necessary, since changing light does not matter very much at this stage) and the actual painting on another, or even indoors. A photograph might then be used as a reference for the colour only.

A small ruler is a useful addition to your usual drawing kit as it can be used to check angles, verticals and horizontals by holding it up at arm's length and to draw guidelines on the paper. There is no reason why all drawing should be done freehand; the rather mechanical-looking lines

LEFT Turner was a master of every kind of painting he turned his hand to, and he could portray the intricate details of a building with the same skill and sensitivity that he brought to atmospheric landscapes. This detail from his Study of Tintern Abbey *shows a combination of the topographical draughtman's precision and the painter's eye for mood, tone and colour.*

Seaside Pavilion, *by Moira Clinch, is a good example of an intricately detailed architectural study which nevertheless retains the freshness and sparkle of more spontaneous sketches. Light and shade are cleverly handled, the clear, fresh, pale colours of the regular squares of paving stones providing a pleasing contrast to the deeper blues of the sky and parts of the building. On the pavilion itself every minute detail of the position itself has been recorded with faithful accuracy, yet the painting nowhere looks overworked or tired.*

given by ruling will be obscured once the paint is laid on. Proportions can be measured by the pencil-and-thumb method, and all such measurements should be constantly checked and re-assessed as the work progresses.

Once the painting itself is begun, you can work in a much freer manner, altering small details to improve the composition. But architecture generally calls for a more methodical approach than landscape. Lines usually need to be crisp and clear. So allow each wash to dry before putting on the next, turning the board sideways or upside

down, if need be, to fill in each area.

When the first washes have been laid on, texture, such as that of brickwork or stone, can be suggested by any of the various methods described in Chapter 3 and small, precise details can be added carefully with a fine brush. Final touches are often added with a pencil or pen and ink to give a crisp definition to the painting, but they must be handled carefully. A heavy, black line can destroy the delicacy of a painting.

1. When painting on the spot, making a preliminary sketch is a good way to sort out your ideas before committing yourself to paint. It is essential to be sure of the most important elements of a landscape. Resist the temptation to put everything in just because it is there.

2. The artist's first step was to lay a neutral wash on the foreground area. This was a mixture of raw umber, Prussian blue and permanent yellow. He then laid a second wash over it, using the same mixture, to create slight tonal differences and texture.

♦ VINEYARD IN ITALY ♦

This painting is more a landscape than an architectural study. The buildings are just one of the features in a land-scape, not the whole subject. They are treated quite sketchily and their appeal lies in the way that the planes of the walls catch the light and the colours of the roofs balance the greens of the foliage. However, although not drawn in any great detail, the buildings are a large part of what the painting is about, and hence its focal point, and they have been treated with sufficient attention to per-spective and proportion to ensure that they look solid and convincing.

The painting was done on the spot, but the artist worked out his composition first by making a charcoal sketch, which clarified the subject for him and enabled him to see how best to treat it. He placed the group of houses slightly higher than they are in the sketch, so that almost no sky was visible, and altered the foreground so that the sweeping lines of the vineyard were made much stronger, leading the eye into the picture and up to the houses. This is a good example of the way an artist can ignore, emphasize or alter any elements of the scene in front of him to make an interesting and lively composition. The busyness of the background, with the different shapes and colours of walls, roofs and foliage, is accentuated by the strong, regular and linear pattern of the foreground, so that the whole painting has a sparkling air of movement. The use of complementary colours is also exemplary: the red of the roofs and the green of the foliage engage in a lively interplay.

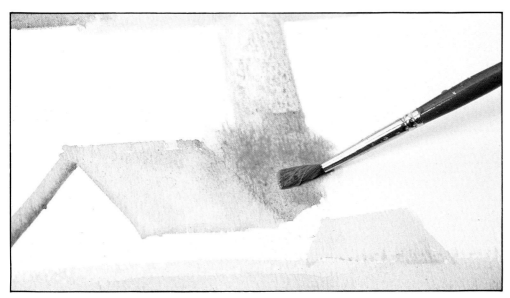

3. Having laid broad but precisely placed washes on the rooftops and shadowed sides of the buildings, the artist puts on an area of loosely applied bright green, thus juxtaposing complementary colours and establishing a key for the rest of the painting.

LAYING A WASH TO AN UNEVEN EDGE.

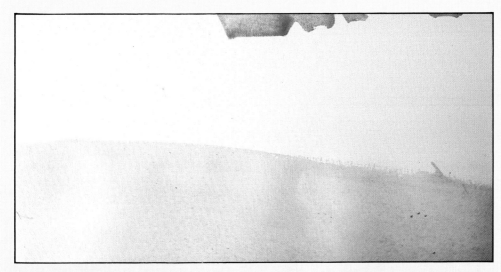

4 and 5. Here the artist had to lay a wash against a complicated edge, the rooftops on the right-hand side of the picture. He first wet the paper only in the area to be covered, then worked paint into it, and finally dabbed it with blotting paper to absorb some of the excess paint, lighten the tone and provide an even texture.

6. Here the artist is defining the shadows on the unlit sides of the buildings, allowing the paint to mix on the paper in order to produce a soft effect.

7. He uses a combination of Prussian blue and Payne's grey to achieve relatively strong tonal contrasts.

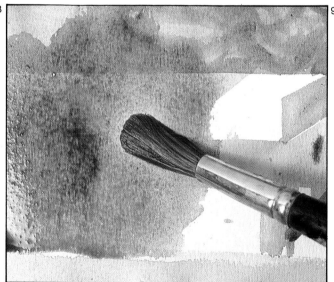

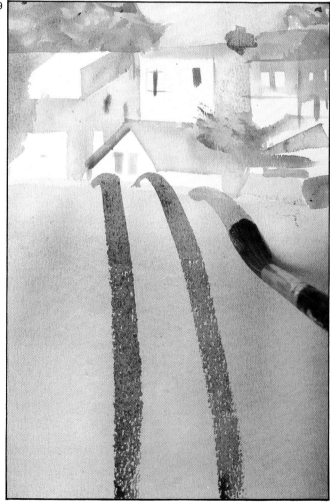

8. The paint was kept quite fluid throughout the painting, and the texture of the paper is an important element in the final effect. Here a large, soft brush is used to apply dark green over the light red of the roofs and the blue of the sky, so that the colours blend into one another in a pleasing way.

9. The lines of the vines are laid on with bold brush strokes and darkened in places to hint at shadow, without describing it in detail. Strong tonal contrasts help to bring the foreground forward toward the picture plane.

10

10. The rows of vines are reinforced with a mixture of terre verte and Payne's grey. Shadows are not usually merely darker shades of the same colour, but have their own colours.

MATERIALS USED

- ♦ SUPPORT: pre-stretched watercolour paper with a Not surface, measuring 12 × 16 in/30 × 40 cm.
- ♦ COLOURS: raw umber, burnt umber, Payne's grey, terre verte, Hooker's green, yellow ochre, permanent yellow, Prussian blue and cadmium red.
- ♦ BRUSHES: Nos. 4 and 11 sable.

Vineyard in Italy

◆ CHURCH IN FRANCE ◆

Buildings present special problems to the artist, especially the watercolourist, and they demand a fairly precise and planned method of approach. In a painting such as this, where the church is the *raison d'être* of the picture rather than being just one feature in a landscape, the perspective must be convincing, the lines sharp and clear, and some suggestion made of the texture and quality of the masonry.

This artist has worked in a very deliberate way, starting with a careful outline drawing made with a sharp pencil and ruler to map out the main areas, so that he is sure where to place his first wash. He then put on a series of flat washes, the first one being laid over the sky area and the second, very pale, over the building itself. Next he began to consider the best way of suggesting the stonework, and decided on masking fluid, applied in slightly uneven brush strokes. When this was dry he washed over the top with brownish grey paint and then removed the fluid, leaving lines of paint between and around the original brush strokes. Further texture was applied at a later stage by the spattering method, and crisp lines were given to details, such as the face and hands of the clock, by drawing with a sharp pencil. The whole painting has a pleasing crispness, produced by the very sharply defined areas of light and dark; no attempt has been made to blend the paint in the shadow areas, and very distinct tonal contrasts have been used — in the small round tree in front of the church, for example. The artist has also avoided the temptation to put in too much detail, which might have reduced the impact and made the picture look fussy and untidy. The tiled roof consists simply of a flat wash; although there is just enough variation in the sky to avoid a mechanical look, no attempt has been made to paint actual clouds.

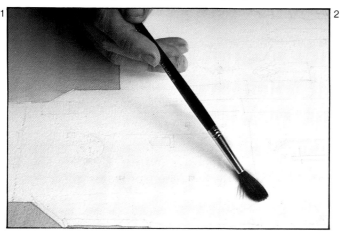

1 and 2. In a subject like this a careful outline drawing is essential. Once the drawing was complete the artist laid an almost flat wash over the sky and then a paler one over the building. These established his basic mid-tones, enabling him to gauge the tonal strength of the steeple.

3. The steeple was painted and allowed to dry, after which masking fluid was put on to areas of the masonry, not as a flat wash but as individual brush strokes. Fairly dark brownish paint was washed over this when dry so that it sank into the areas between the brush strokes.

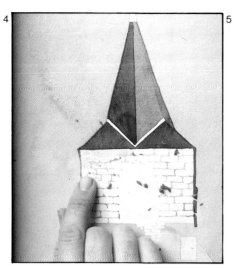

4. Here the masking fluid is being rubbed off with a finger, leaving the irregular lines of dark paint to suggest the edges of the stones. This is a more effective method than painting in the lines, and gives a much more natural look because the technique is a very slightly 'random' one.

5. Here the spattering technique is being used to give further texture to the walls. It is sometimes necessary to mask off surrounding areas so that they do not get splashed, but this artist makes use of the method quite often, and is confident of his ability to control the paint.

6. At this stage only the foreground, with the dark trees and bright grass, remain unpainted. The artist worked the painting piece by piece, as he found that having no overlapping layers of paint gave a crisper definition, but it is not a method recommended for beginners because it is difficult to judge tones and colours in isolation.

7. Here the hands and face of the clock are being carefully drawn in with a very sharp pencil over the original pale wash.

8. Further texture is given to the stonework by rubbing a candle over the paint. Candles or wax crayon can also be used as a resist method, like masking fluid, in which case they are applied before a final paint layer.

9. The mid-tones of the grass have now been laid in, providing a foil to the red-brown of the tiled roof.

10. The artist now works carefully on the shadow side of the tree, using a fine brush and very dense dark green paint.

11. The final touches were to darken the left hand tree and paint in the straight, dark shadow in the foreground. Two small trees were also added in the shadow area at the bottom of the church.

MATERIALS USED

- ♦ SUPPORT: pre-stretched 200 lb Bockingford paper
- ♦ BRUSHES: Nos. 2, 7 and 9 sables and a 1-in/2.5 cm bristle brush for spattering.
- ♦ COLOURS: cobalt blue, sap green, yellow ochre, raw umber, brown madder alizarin, Payne's grey and ivory black
- ♦ ADDITIONAL EQUIPMENT: masking fluid, a candle and gum water.

11

Church in France

CHAPTER SEVEN

NATURE

*Dürer's accurate and precise drawings and watercolours of
plants and animals are possibly the best examples of
natural-history painting in the entire history of art. The
Young Hare was probably begun with broad washes of
transparent paint to establish the main form. The fine details
were then built up with tiny brush strokes of opaque paint;
every hair and whisker has been precisely described, but the
hare is still quite evidently a living, breathing creature.*

*F*ROM THE 16TH CENTURY onwards watercolour became a favoured medium for botanical illustration, which, with the great upsurge of interest in describing and cataloguing plants and flowers, was very much in demand. Just as it did for architecture, the medium proved ideal for the detailed and delicate work demanded by such subjects.

◆ NATURAL-HISTORY PAINTING ◆

In the early years of the 16th century Dürer pioneered the use of watercolour with body colour for botanical subjects, and such works as *The Great Piece of Turf* and *Young Hare*, faithful renderings of nature, laid the basis for a tradition of botanical and natural-history painting which has continued down to the present day.

In the 18th and 19th centuries the majority of natural-history painters and illustrators made their initial watercolours as bases for engravings. Some, notably the famous French flower painter, Pierre-Joseph Redouté (1759-1840), mastered the art of engraving themselves, the techniques of which in turn influenced styles of painting. In America natural-history painting in watercolour reached new heights with the marvellous bird paintings of John James Audubon (1785-1851), paintings which became familiar to a wide public through the hand-coloured engravings done from them. These works, although they are in the illustrative tradition of accurate observation, are now regarded as art rather than illustration (there is really no dividing line between the two) and change hands at staggering prices.

Watercolour is still much used for precise botanical and natural-history illustration, but it has also come into its own as a medium for depicting nature, particularly flowers, in a more painterly way, either in its natural environment or in the studio as still-life.

The painting of water-lilies overleaf shows how superbly the medium can be used to give a feeling of life and immediacy: the water-lilies could almost be opening before your eyes.

◆ PRACTICAL HINTS ◆

Flowers and plants always make attractive subjects and present no particular problems other than the usual one of getting the drawing right. However, many people frequently buy a bunch of flowers and paint them at home, but do not think of going out to paint them in their natural environment. There is nothing at all wrong with the still-life approach. Countless superb paintings have been done of plants and flowers indoors. But painting or drawing on the spot is an excellent way of observing nature, and the plants or flowers do tend to look more at home in their natural setting.

Ring-tailed Lemur, *by Sally Michel, has something of the quality of Dürer's work. She works in watercolour and* pastel, *and always from life, though she takes the occasional polaroid for reference.*

Sally Michel

This study of waterlilies, by Marc Winer, was painted on the spot, with much use of the wet-into-wet technique. The artist allowed some colours to run into one another in a semi-random way, sometimes creating hard edges, sometimes more gentle transitions, an effective way to suggest the soft wetness of the leaves and flowers floating in water.

Animals and birds present much graver problems to the would-be wild-life painter. They simply will not sit still. For most professional wild-life artists, birds or animals are a life-long passion, and they have often made a long study of their chosen subject from books and museums before beginning to sketch and observe from nature. A family pet, however, can often be prevailed upon to stay in one place for long enough to be sketched — especially if it has just had a good meal — and photographs can sometimes be used in combination with sketches as the basis for a painting. Anyone who decides to make animals or birds his subject should try to observe them as often and as closely as possible, both in movement and in repose. You may think you know exactly what your dog or cat looks like, but if you try to.daw it from memory you will soon realize the limits of your knowledge.

◆ TROPICAL FISH ◆

It can be difficult to find natural-history subjects that remain still for long enough to be observed and studied by the artist, but fish in a tank almost beg to be looked at and admired, and although they are always on the move, at least they do not move very far. Many wild-life artists make a particular branch of the animal world their own, often because of a life-long interest. This artist has studied fish very closely, and has made a great many drawings of them over the years.

The painting was done from a series of drawings and from past observations of the structure and colours of the fish. It makes use of both the wet-into-wet technique, in which new colour is applied to a wash before it is dry, and the wet-into-dry technique, in which wet washes are laid over dry ones so that they overlap in places. The hard and soft edges formed in this way create the illusion of rippling water, a very important element in the painting. The background washes had to be applied extremely carefully and accurately so that they did not spoil the crisp edges of the fishes' bodies and fins. A careful drawing was made before any paint was put on.

Although people often think of watercolours as pale and delicate, the colours can be made as vivid as you like, simply by being less diluted. In places the artist has used the paint almost pure to create bright and glowing effects. She has also used complementary colours to good effect: the bright oranges of the fish are accentuated by the complementary greenish-browns in the background.

1. This sketch is just one of many that the artist has made in the past and uses as reference for her paintings.

2. Having made a careful drawing on her stretched paper with a sharp pencil, the artist began by painting in the shapes of the fish with a mixture of cadmium orange and cadmium yellow pale. The colours and tones were varied to show the lights and darks of the bodies as well as the individual differences between the fish. Some of the broader details were drawn into the bodies before the first wash was dry, giving a soft effect.

3. The background colour was a mixture of black and lemon yellow, which gives a warmer colour than blue and yellow. When laying the wash the artist took special care to work precisely and accurately between and around the fins and bodies in order to preserve the clean, crisp lines that are such a vital feature of the painting.

4. When the broad area of the background has been laid in with deliberately uneven washes to suggest ripples, the painting was allowed to dry. Further layers of colour were then added, so that the water became darker around the fish and lighter at the top, where the proportion of yellow to black was increased.

5. Here the artist is painting the leaves with a fine brush in a very strong lemon yellow, barely diluted. This covers the original pale wash and is slightly modified by it.

6. A very fine sable brush was used to paint the delicate details of the scales, and touches of white were added in places. When doing detailed work in the centre of a painting, make sure the area below is quite dry or you may ruin the painting by smudging it.

Tropical Fish

7. Final touches deepened and enriched the colours of the fins and tails and gave definition to the foreground, hitherto left as an area of water. Opaque paint (Chinese white) was mixed with the watercolour to produce greys and ochres, which were then used to pick out the pebbles. Opaque paint should be used sparingly and only in the final stages, but it is extremely useful for touches such as these.

MATERIALS USED

♦ SUPPORT: pre-stretched watercolour paper with a Not surface, measuring 14 × 20 in/35 × 50 cm.
♦ COLOURS: cadmium red, cadmium orange, cadmium yellow pale, lemon yellow, yellow ochre, sap green, Payne's grey and black, plus a little Chinese white.
♦ BRUSHES: Nos. 7, 5, 3 and 00 sable.

◆ PHEASANT ◆

This painting is both a bird study and still-life, since it was painted indoors and the subject is a stuffed pheasant borrowed from an antique shop. Artists whose particular interest is wildlife can study and observe nature at second hand as well as directly from life. Natural-history books and museums both offer opportunities for gaining a thorough knowledge about structure and detail.

Because there could be no attempt to make the stuffed bird appear anything other than what it was, the painting presented a different challenge from that of representing a live bird. With a live bird the prime consideration might have been to suggest movement, while the natural back-ground of trees or rocks might have formed part of the composition. Here the artist chose to treat the subject in a very formal way, setting it up as a rather stark still-life, but his enthusiasm for the bird itself comes across very strongly in the glowing colour and the delicately painted detail.

His technique was quite free and fluid, and he worked quickly, building up the form in the early stages from loose washes and working wet into wet in places. The background shows an interesting use of watercolour: with only one colour a wide variety of tonal contrasts has been achieved. This gives the painting extra drama and excitement as well as providing a balance to the texture of the pheasant itself.

1. A very hard (F) pencil was used to make a careful outline drawing to establish the forms of the bird as well as its relationship to the background and table-top. Composition is extremely important for this subject, which relies for its impact on the way the main shape is placed. Once he had planned the composition, allowing the tail to go out of the frame so that it appears longer, the artist first laid a pale wash on the body and tail.

2. Once the first wash, a mixture of raw umber and cadmium orange, was dry, a darker one using using the same colours was laid on top, after which blue and red were applied to the head and neck.

3. The same red, alizarin crimson, was put on the breast area, and the artist then began to work on the head feathers with a fine brush. He used a mixture of black, viridian and ultramarine for this, leaving parts of the original blue showing through.

4. Some artists work all over a painting at the same time, but in this painting the bird was completed before the artist turned his attention to the background. Here the feathers are being painted, with the paint kept quite loose and fluid to prevent a cramped, overworked look.

5. This detail shows the richness and variety of both the colours and the brushwork. In the red area a darker tone has been allowed to overlap the one below, creating a series of edges which give the impression of feathers. Note how small lines of white have been left in the original wash to stand for the wing feathers.

6. The painting of the bird is now complete, and the successive washes built up one over the other have created exactly the rich impression that the artist wanted. When putting washes over other washes in this way it is essential to know when to stop; if the surface of the paper becomes too clogged with paint the painting will begin to look tired. Judging the strength of colour needed for each wash takes some practice, since watercolour looks so much darker when it is wet.

7. Now the artist begins to work on the background, using a fairly strong mixture of Payne's grey and taking it very carefully around the bird's body. It is often necessary to turn the board sideways or upside down for this kind of work.

MATERIALS USED

♦ SUPPORT: pre-stretched Bockingford watercolour paper, measuring 22 × 30 in/55 × 75 cm.
♦ COLOURS: chrome orange, alizarin crimson, burn sienna, raw umber, ultramarine, viridian, Payne's grey and black.
♦ BRUSHES: Nos. 12 and 2 sable and a No. 7 synthetic round.

8. By varying the tones of the background wash the artist has made the bird stand out in a very three-dimensional way. The dark head is prevented from merging into the similar tone behind it by the thin line of white which has been left between the two. The white area of the table-top has been carefully placed so that it is not quite central and thus provides a balance to the long, almost horizontal, line of the tail.

Pheasant

◆ GERANIUM ◆

This painting demonstrates very well how in the right hands watercolour can be an ideal medium for capturing the rich colours and strong, yet intricate, forms of flowers and foliage. The starting-point was a single bloom in a garden trough, but the artist has transformed the rather ordinary subject seen in the photograph into a highly dramatic painting with a strong element of abstract pattern. He has reduced the background to an area of dark neutral colour, which allows the shapes of the leaves to stand out in bold contrast, but he has given it interest by varying the tonal contrasts while using only one colour. He has done this by allowing the paint and water to mix unevenly, and even form blobs in places, and by scrubbing the paint with a stiff household brush.

Although no preliminary drawing was done, the artist had a very clear idea of the composition before he began to paint; the positioning of the flowers against the background is a vital element in the effect of the painting. The leaves have been slightly cropped by the frame on both sides, thereby bringing the flowers and leaves towards the picture plane. The almost horizontal band of lighter colour in the foreground, suggesting the garden trough, adds to this effect, firmly 'mooring' the plant in the front of the picture. It is interesting to compare the finished painting with the penultimate stage, in which the flower appears to float in space.

1. The colours were built up gradually from very light to very dark, and the first step was to apply dilute washes of green and red to the leaves and flower head.

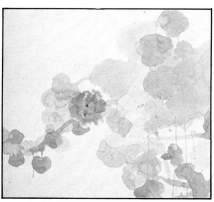

2. The leaves were then darkened in places and touches of cerulean blue added to the flower head with a No. 2 sable brush.

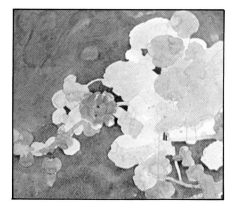

3. Once the main shapes of the leaves and flower had been established, the artist began to paint the background, using a mixture of Payne's grey and cerulean blue and judging the tones very carefully. Assessing the strength of a dark wash takes practice, as watercolour appears much lighter when it is dry.

4. Next the artist began to darken the tones on some of the leaves, mixing the Payne's grey used for the background with cadmium green. Using only a small selection of colours helps to give unity to a painting.

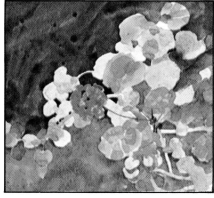

5. Payne's grey was again used, this time pure, to paint the fine, delicate lines formed by the stems and veins of the leaves. A No. 2 sable brush gave the fine brushmarks needed for this detailed work.

EXPLOITING THE WASH.

The general leaf shapes were produced with a very wet green wash. The paint was then drawn out, while still wet, into thin strands to create the leaf stems.

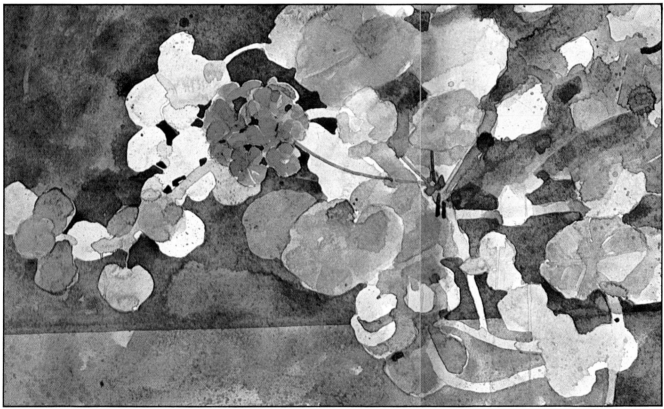

Geranium

6 The red of the flower head had to be as vivid as possible, and the depth of colour was achieved by laying deep washes of vermilion over paler ones in which a little blue had been added. Note how the artist has varied the intensity of the colours and left small lines of a lighter tone showing through to suggest the shapes of the petals.

MATERIALS USED

♦ SUPPORT: pre-stretched watercolour paper with a Not surface, measuring 18 × 23 in/45 × 57 cm.
♦ COLOURS: vermilion, yellow ochre, cadmium green, Payne's grey, cerulean blue and black.
♦ BRUSHES: Nos. 10, 6 and 2 sables and a small household brush for the background.

◆ FIELD OF DAISIES ◆

There is no better medium than watercolour for rendering the bright colours and delicate detail of flowers, but a painting like this one presents a technical problem which is not easy to overcome by traditional methods. Since watercolour must always be worked dark over light, white or pale shades are created by painting around them. Here the white shapes are smaller and more intricate than they are in most paintings, and if the artist had attempted to lay washes around them the painting would have run the risk of becoming niggly and tired-looking. He has solved this problem by using masking fluid for the heads of the flowers, laying washes of varying intensities on top and then removing the fluid to reveal the white paper.

Some artists find masking fluid a rather mechanical device, and in the past it was more often used for illustration and other graphic work, but in fact it can be used quite freely, as it was in this painting, and can either be applied with a brush or used for spattering effects. It is difficult to draw really fine lines with it, however, as it is thick and viscous. The artist has therefore used oil pastel to draw the stems of the flowers. This works as a resist medium in the same way as masking fluid; the oil repels the water, creating clear lines and interesting textures.

One of the most difficult decisions faced by painters attempting plant or flower studies outdoors is what to put in and leave out. Obviously, if you try to include every flower head and blade of grass, as well as large parts of background and sky, the painting will become a confused jumble.

A comparison of this painting with the reference photograph shows how the artist has simplified the subject, reducing the number of flowers to make a telling arrangement and allowing the background to become simply a dark, receding area suggestive of grass. No preliminary drawing was done, as the artist wanted to create a feeling of spontaneity, but less experienced painters would probably find an advance thumbnail sketch or two helpful in establishing the composition.

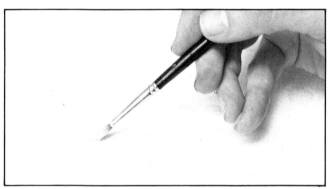

1. Without making a drawing on the support, the artist began by picking out the flower heads with masking fluid. Since this takes some time to dry, it should always be done in the very early stages.

2. Here the artist is using oil pastel to draw the stems, keeping the strokes as free as possible. When the watercolour washes are applied, the paint will slide off the pastel, leaving a clear line.

3. Before any paint was put on, the artist established the overall pattern with masking fluid and with lines and dots of oil pastel.

4. Next the whole picture area was covered with a wash of sap green and yellow, deliberately applied unevenly and loosely. The brush strokes, made with a No. 6 sable brush, were used to suggest the movement of wind-blown grass and leaves.

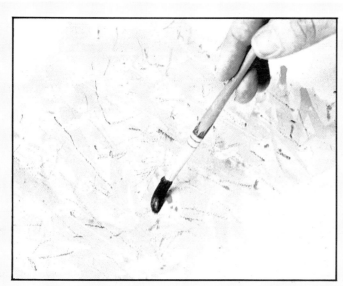

TEXTURING.
The green wash is enlivened by the strong brush strokes. This is purely a textural effect: note that the colour is exactly the same as the first.

5. Once the first wash was laid, the artist began to strengthen the colour in places with a dark mixture of chrome green and black. A slight sheen was given to the paint by mixing it with gum water.

6

REMOVING MASKING FLUID

Before removing masking fluid (by gently rubbing with the finger, as the artist does here), ensure that the paint is quite dry and that no further alterations or additions are needed.

6. The deepest shadows in the foreground have now been painted and the background has been darkened. The darker green areas were carefully drawn with a fine brush, as more accurate definition was needed at this stage.

7. The final touch was to paint in the flower centres with cadmium yellow.

MATERIALS USED

♦ Support: Arches watercolour paper with a Not surface, measuring 12 × 18 in/ 30 × 45 cm.
♦ Colours: watercolours in sap green, chrome green, cadmium yellow and black; oil pastels in olive green and yellow.
♦ Brushes and other equipment: Nos. 6 and 4 sable brushes, a small household brush for spattering, gum water and masking fluid.

7

Field of Daisies

CHAPTER EIGHT

PORTRAIT AND FIGURE

*John Frederick Lewis' paintings were often of Middle-Eastern
subjects. Like many 19th-century painters he travelled
widely in search of inspiration. He was attracted by the rich
colours and textures of the East and in* The Harem *he
rendered their bright, jewel-like quality in a painstaking
technique typical of the watercolours of the period.*

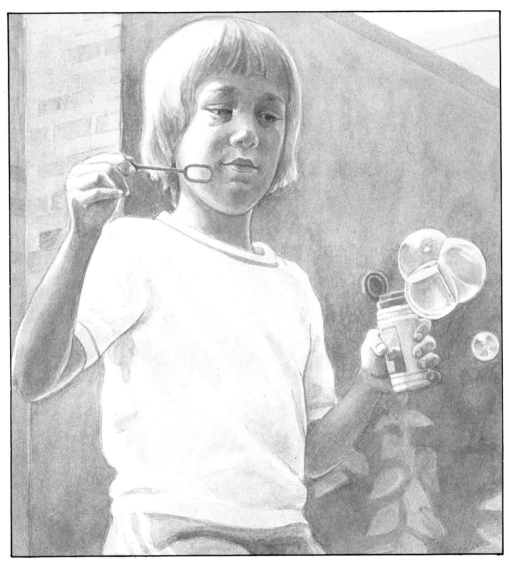

AS MORE AND MORE ARTISTS SUCCUMB to the charms of watercolour, it is becoming an accepted medium for portraits and figure paintings, hitherto regarded as the province of oils. Its softness and translucence make it ideal for capturing the living qualities of skin and hair, but it needs particularly careful handling in this branch of painting if the surface is not to become muddy and dull. Accurate drawing is also vital, especially for portrait work. Try to draw from life wherever possible and avoid the temptation to put the paint on before the drawing is right.

♦ PAST AND PRESENT ♦
APPROACHES

Although artists have always used watercolour or pen-and-wash to make quick studies of faces and figures, there is really no tradition of portraiture in watercolour, and until this century paintings of the figure have also usually been in oil. The reasons for this have nothing to do with any inherent unsuitability of the medium itself. In the past

RIGHT Edward Burra worked in watercolour because his severe arthritis made it difficult for him to handle oils. His use of the medium was truly amazing: he achieved a depth and richness of colour seldom seen in watercolour, and each detail was minutely described without ever appearing over-worked. In paintings such as Harlem *(1934) Burra's concern was with the general atmosphere and lifestyle of the people he encountered, and his juxtaposition of dark and light colours and harsh and soft textures is highly descriptive.*

portraits were the artist's bread and butter — they were seldom done for pure pleasure as they are today — and the sitter who paid to have his image or that of his family hung on his wall wanted a large and imposing painting as well as one that would stand up to the ravages of time. Watercolours, although we have better ways of preserving them now, as well as more permanent pigments, are prone to fade, and the paper can become mildewed and blotched. Figure paintings were also traditionally fairly large, and most artists found that they called for a slower and more deliberate approach than that normally used for watercolours. Nowadays we have a different attitude to such subjects. A rather sketchy and impressionistic treatment of a figure, either clothed or unclothed, is not only acceptable but often desirable, and can suggest light and movement more easily than a more heavily worked painting.

Figure paintings in watercolour became more usual during the 19th century, partly as a result of the far-reaching influence of William Blake's symbolic and allegorical paintings. The Pre-Raphaelites and Edward Burne-Jones (1833-98) pioneered new techniques, such as rubbing in dry colour and scratching out. Burne-Jones' watercolours are barely recognizable as such; they have rather the appearance of medieval manuscripts. Another 19th-century artist, influenced by the Pre-Raphaelites though, like Burne-Jones, not actually a member of the Brotherhood, was John Frederick Lewis (1805-76), whose paintings of Middle Eastern scenes such as *The Harem*, (see page 100), glow with a jewel-like brilliance. A comparison of *The Harem* with *Girl in Armchair* reveals startling differences in technique. It is difficult to believe that the same medium has been used. Painters such as Lewis used watercolour almost like oil, with the minimum use of washes and much fine-brush work, but his paintings never look tired, as an over-worked watercolour easily can. Today there is a tendency to favour the classical, broad-wash technique, but many others are also used, such as dry-brush and stippling, and some artists combine several techniques in one painting.

♦ PRACTICAL HINTS ♦

Photographs provide a very useful source of reference for portraiture and figure work, particularly if the subject is a figure in motion. *Blowing Bubbles* is an example of a painting done almost entirely from a photograph. It is advisable, even so, to work from life wherever possible, and since a watercolour study is not likely to take as long as an oil, it should not be difficult to persuade people to sit.

Good drawing is essential for human subjects, since a misplaced eye or an ill-drawn hand or foot can completely destroy the harmony of a painting. Never start painting until you are sure that the drawing is correct; and as you draw, check proportions and measurements constantly. When you are drawing a figure, it often helps to look at the space behind the head or between limbs. If a person is standing with one hand resting on a hip, for instance, the triangle formed between the arm and the body will be a particular shape. Foreshortened limbs, an arm resting on a

chair for example, are difficult to get right, but they can usually be checked by using some part of the background as a reference point. You can see at which particular point the arm would be intersected by a vertical line formed by the wall behind, or how the hand lines up with the legs of the chair.

Before you even begin to draw, compose the picture carefully and give thought to both the background and the lighting. The light will define the figure by casting shadows in a certain way, and lighting can also be used to create atmosphere. A figure seen against a window will appear almost in silhouette, the colours deep and merging into one another; a front light will give a hard, flat look, while a strong side light, or one from above, will give drama to the subject by producing strong tonal contrasts.

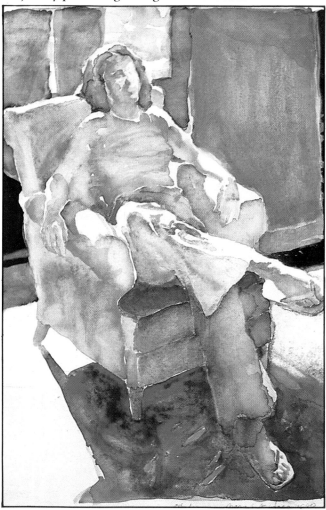

This painting presents a striking contrast to the previous example, both in its technique and in the atmosphere it conveys. The artist was interested in light and colour rather than in achieving a likeness of a particular person, and the paint was kept fluid and free, with the minimum of detail, thus enhancing the relaxed mood of the light-flooded figure in the armchair.

♦ AGAINST A STRIPED BLANKET ♦

This is an unusually large painting for a watercolour. The head is almost life-size. The colours are gentle and muted with the minimum of tonal contrast. This type of colour scheme, in which there are no dark tones or colours, is known as 'high-key'. Some artists always work in a high key, others always in a low one (using dark or vivid colours with strong contrasts); yet others are happy to work in both, the choice depending on their approach to the subject.

This portrait was done from life. The artist made sure that the model was really comfortable before work began, and makes the positions of her hands and feet so that she could resume exactly the same position after breaks. In a painting as subtle as this the drawing had to be very accurate and the tonal contrasts and variations extremely tightly controlled. The artist needed to observe the subject closely without being distracted by movement or complaints about discomfort.

The first stage was to draw a very careful outline, establishing the composition so that each wash could be placed quickly and accurately. The pale colours, as well as the sheer size of the painting, ruled out the possibility of major alterations once the painting had begun. Drawing is particularly important in a portrait, since if the proportions of the features are wrong, or the eyes or mouth placed crookedly, the painting will not only fail as a likeness, but will also lose structural credibility. The drawing need not be elaborate — too many pencil marks can confuse rather than clarify — but it must be clear and accurate enough to provide a guide for the painting; so if you are working from life, make sure that both you and your model have enough time to spare.

1. The photograph shows how different the actual colours were from those the artist has chosen. Even the strongly patterned blanket, which has been given a prominent role in the painting, is much paler and more muted.

2. The drawing was made with a mechanical lead-holder, sometimes called a clutch pencil, into which different leads can be inserted for different purposes. Any unnecessary lines were carefully removed with a soft putty eraser in order not to damage the surface of the paper. Bockingford paper, the one used here, is easily spoiled by excessive erasing.

3. The area around the eyes and brows is one of the most difficult to draw accurately, and the artist pays special attention to the structure and the way the eyes fit into the sockets. Pencil lines can either be rubbed out when the painting is partially done, but quite dry, or left as part of the image.

4. When the pencil drawing was complete the artist began to draw with the brush, painting in the shadow below the top eyelid. The eyes are the focal point of most portraits and need very careful treatment.

5. The next step was to get rid of some of the white paper by applying a pale wash to the background. A No. 2 sable brush was used to work on separate areas right across the painting.

6. The stripes of the blanket were intensified before any further work was done on the face, as this was a very important part of the painting and acted as a key for the colours and tones of the face and hair.

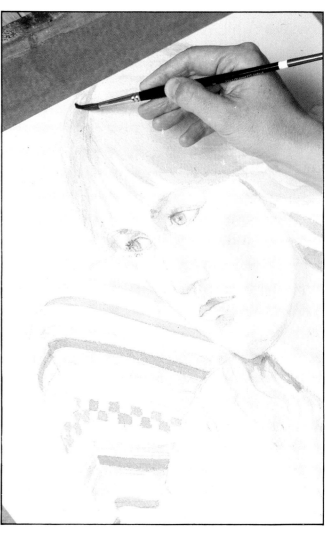

7. Here the artist paints the darkest part of the hair, using a No. 2 sable brush and a mixture of violet, Payne's grey and Indian red. The hair had hitherto been mainly yellow ochre with touches of Indian red.

8. By this stage the paper had been entirely covered, but the painting was somewhat weak and insubstantial, the flesh tones too pale and cool. The artist therefore intensified all the tones, adding warmth to the flesh and giving a more solid feel to the face. The final touches were to paint in the pattern of the blanket and add definition to the hair, so that it formed a pleasing pattern without being fussy.

MATERIALS USED

♦ SUPPORT: pre-stretched Bockingford paper, measuring 18 × 16 in/45 × 40 cm.
♦ COLOURS: Indian red, yellow ochre, violet, Payne's grey, cobalt blue, ultramarine, alizarin crimson, cadmium red and sap green.
♦ BRUSHES AND OTHER EQUIPMENT: Nos. 6 and 2 sable brushes, a mechanical lead-holder and a putty rubber.

Against a Striped Blanket

◆ PORTRAIT OF PAUL ◆

This sensitive study is much more graphic in approach than the previous portrait. The artist is more interested in line than in colour, and has used a technique which is a combination of drawing and painting, enabling her to express the character of the sitter in a way she found suited his thin, somewhat aquiline, features.

She used a quill pen made from a goose feather, a drawing tool much favoured by such artists as Rembrandt, but the medium was dilute watercolour instead of the more traditional ink. A quill pen produces a less mechanical line than a metal nib, because strokes of different thicknesses can be made by turning the quill. By this means, and by varying the strength and colours of the paint itself, the artist has produced a series of contrasting lines — some thick and soft, some short and stabbing, and some fine and taut. She used a Chinese brush in combination with the quill, both to lay washes across the whole image and to soften the line in places by dipping it in a little clean water. Using watercolour gives an artist more freedom to modify or alter lines.

1. A simple pose, seen directly from the front, was chosen for the painting, because it gave the artist the opportunity to explore fully the lines and contours of the features. No preliminary pencil drawing was made, since the painting was in itself a drawing, which could be corrected as the work progressed.

1

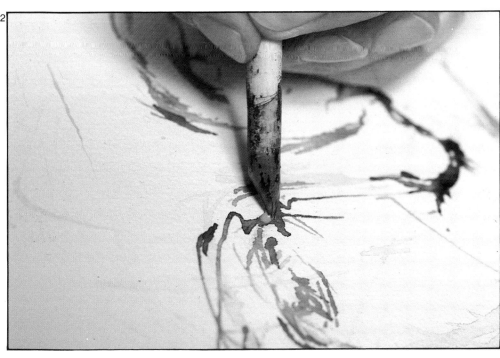

2. This photograph shows how the artist varied the strength of the watercolour when drawing with the quill. She used three different mixtures: raw sienna and cobalt blue; Prussian blue and cadmium red; and yellow ochre and cadmium yellow.

3. Here the artist has found that she is not satisfied with the line of the cheekbone; so she lightens it with a brush dipped in water before re-drawing it.

4. A Chinese brush was used to apply small areas of colour all over the image. No attempt was made to render the colours precisely; they were applied in a spontaneous manner to create an overall effect.

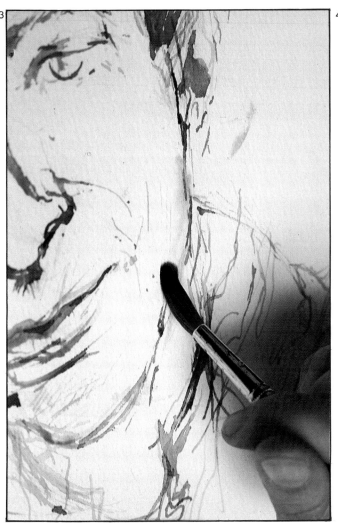

5

6

5. The artist has made little use of the traditional watercolour technique of flat washes. Instead, she has allowed the brushmarks to become part of the painting. The background was applied with two different brushes, a No. 9 sable round and a Chinese brush.

6. Once the lines had been firmly established and the artist was satisfied with the drawing, she laid a loose wash over the face and neck to build up the form and add warmth to the flesh.

rtrait of Paul

CHINESE BRUSHES.

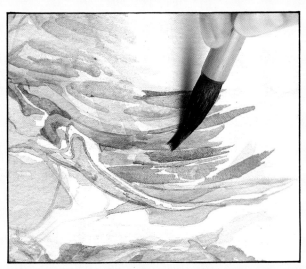

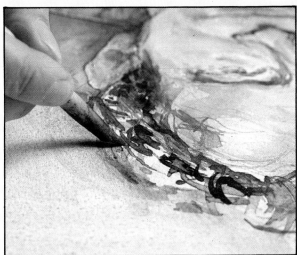

Although colour is not the most important aspect of the painting, it has been used boldly and sensitively. Here the artist is using a Chinese brush to apply small patches of bright colour to the clothing and darker tones to the hair.

MATERIALS USED

♦ SUPPORT: Langton watercolour paper with a Not surface, measuring 12 × 10 in/ 30 × 25 cm.
♦ COLOURS: raw sienna, cobalt blue, Prussian blue, cadmium red, cadmium yellow and yellow ochre.
♦ BRUSHES AND OTHER EQUIPMENT: A No. 9 sable round, a Chinese brush and a goose-feather quill pen.

1. The artist has deliberately chosen the pose to fit in with a pre-conceived composition, and he was sufficiently sure of the placing of the main shapes not to need a preliminary pencil drawing. Instead, the main lines and shapes were mapped out with much-diluted watercolour.

2. The tree just visible through the slats of the blind was painted in very freely over the orange-brown lines of the blind. The darker lines thus show through the green wash, giving the shimmering effect of light striking the soft, uneven form of the tree.

3. The next step was to lay a dark grey-blue wash at the top of the window area, leaving white below so that the light was chanelled through the bottom part of the window. The body was then established with a strong cadmium orange, balanced by the crimson of the skirt and the blue of the bed.

4. The artist continued to work all over the painting, modelling the outstretched leg and adding definition to the face and neck. A strong tint of raw sienna was used for the darker flesh tints in order to echo the orange-brown of the blind and window frame.

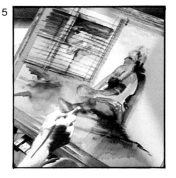
5

5. Although pure watercolour was used for most of the painting, some white gouache was added for the smaller highlights, such as those on the leg and face.

6. As a final touch, a deep pink flesh-tint was put on the body, and the area of the bed was strengthened by using a wash of blue gouache with white added. Too much use of gouache with watercolour can destroy its quality, but here it has been used skilfully.

MATERIALS USED

- ◆ SUPPORT: pre-stretched Arches watercolour paper with a fine grain, measuring 18 × 28 in/46 × 71 cm.
- ◆ COLOURS: lemon yellow, cadmium yellow, cadmium orange, cadmium red, alizarin crimson, raw sienna, sap green, cobalt blue and Payne's grey, plus cobalt blue and white gouache.
- ◆ BRUSHES: a selection of sables and a small bristle brush.

---

irl by a Window With a Blind

◆ GIRL BY A WINDOW WITH ◆ BLIND

In this painting the figure is seen in the context of an interior, and the effects of light interested the artist most. Watercolour has been used very loosely in thin washes, with a large amount of paper left uncovered, and the impression of a large, spacious room lit by diffused light has been created with minimal attention to detail. Although the paint has been used mainly pure, the artist also used gouache in the final stages for certain areas such as the blue bed and the smaller highlights on the face and body. Gouache can destroy the quality of a watercolour by giving a matt, dead surface, but here it has been used very skilfully without detriment to the painting.

The composition, with its careful arrangement of lights and darks, is well balanced. The crisp, diagonal lines of the blind contrast with the softer contours of the model, who is placed in silhouette against the white wall. It is the relationship between the figure and the window that gives the painting its interest, and the two are unified by the expanse of bright blue formed by the bed, which is in turn echoed by the cushion and shadow behind the model.

P. J. Redouté 1834.

CHAPTER NINE

STILL-LIFE

STILL-LIFE as its name implies, simply means a composition of objects which are not moving and which are incapable of doing so, usually arranged on a table; the French rather depressingly call it 'dead life' *(nature morte)*.

The subjects can be whatever you like, but traditionally the objects in a still-life group are in some way associated with each other — a vase of flowers with fruit, a selection of vegetables with cooking vessels or implements, and sometimes dead fish, game or fowl with a goblet of wine, perhaps, or a bunch of parsley. (Culinary still-lifes are less popular nowadays, possibly because they run the risk of looking like the cover of a cookery book.) Good paintings can be made from quite homely subjects. Vincent Van Gogh (1853-90) made a wonderful and moving still-life from nothing but a pile of books on a table.

Most artists have painted still-lifes at one time or another, and several, notably Jan Vermeer (1632-75), included them in their figure paintings. In the 17th century a group of Dutch artists became obsessed with still-life to the exclusion of all other subjects, and vied with one another to produce ever more lavish portrayals of table-tops gleaming with edible produce, rare porcelain and golden goblets. In many of these, tiny insects are visible among the foliage, blood drips from the mouths of freshly killed hares or rabbits, and bunches of grapes shine with tiny droplets of moisture, every object painted with breathtaking skill.

Because the subject of a still-life painting can be entirely controlled by the artist, as can its arrangement and lighting, still-lifes present an unusual opportunity for exploring ideas and experimenting with colour and composition. The greatest master of the still-life, Paul Cézanne (1839-1906), found that the form allowed him to concentrate on such fundamental problems as form and space and the paradox of transferring the three-dimensional world to a two-dimensional surface.

The ability to control the subject of a still-life means that you can take as much time as you like to work out the composition and complete the preliminary drawing, and you can practise painting techniques at leisure, trying out new ones as you feel inspired. Oddly, watercolour was seldom used in the past for still-lifes other than flower paintings, but it is now becoming extremely popular.

◆ SETTING UP A STILL LIFE ◆

There are no specific problems in painting a still-life or flower piece once it has been set up. The real challenge is arranging it, and this may take some time — plonking an assortment of objects down on a table will not give you a good painting. The wisest rule to follow at first is to keep the composition simple. The more objects you have the more difficult it is to arrange them in a harmonious way. It is also best to have a theme of some kind: if the various objects are too different in kind they will look uneasy together.

Start with something you like, a bowl of fruit on a patterned tablecloth, perhaps, or a pot plant, and keep arranging and re-arranging until you are satisfied that you have achieved a good balance of shapes and colours. Drapery is often used to balance and complement the main subject, and it is useful to have a selection of fabrics or tablecloths on hand for this purpose. Many artists make small sketches or diagrams to work out whether a vertical line is needed in the background, or a table-top shown as a diagonal in the foreground. Finally, when you are fairly sure that the arrangement will do, look at it through a viewing frame to assess how well it will fill the space

LEFT Cezanne used still-life to explore the relationships of forms and their interaction on various spatial planes. He usually worked in oils, but Still Life with Chair, Bottles and Apple, *shows his understanding of watercolour. ABOVE William Henry Hunt produced charming portraits as well as genre subjects, using his paint rather dry to depict colours and textures with great accuracy.* Plums *is an unusual approach to still life, as it has an outdoor setting but it was almost certainly done in the studio from preliminary sketches.*

allotted to it. Move the frame around so that you can assess several possibilities. Often you may find that allowing one of the objects to run out of the picture actually helps the composition.

Lighting is also very important. It defines the forms, heightens the colours and casts shadows which can become a vital component in the composition. If you are working by natural light other than a north light, it will, of course, change as the day wears on. This may not matter very much so long as you decide where the shadows are to be at the outset and do not keep trying to change them; but often it is more satisfactory to use artificial light. This solution sometimes brings its own problem, however, since if you are painting flowers or fruit they will wilt more quickly. You may simply have to decide which is the lesser evil.

♦ CYCLAMEN ♦

Flower arrangements are among the most popular of all still-life subjects. Indeed, they are often regarded as a separate branch of painting. In purely practical terms, however, they are a type of still-life, posing the same problems as well as sharing the major advantage of being a captive subject.

With any group of objects set up as a painting subject the main problem is arrangement, and hence the composition of the painting itself. Flowers in a vase, for example, do not always make a shape that fills a rectangle very well; so it is sometimes necessary to add other elements, such as a plate, some fruit or background drapery. Here the composition is simple but very effective: the table-top, with its checked cloth, provides foreground interest to balance the pattern formed by the flowers themselves against the plain background. It also adds to the impression of solidity and its intersecting diagonal lines provide a pleasing contrast with the curved shapes. Interestingly, the tablecloth was added as an afterthought, when the artist had already painted the flower and pot; without it the character of the painting would have been quite different. When arranging a still-life or flower piece it is helpful to make a few advance sketches, as alterations cannot always be made as easily as they were here.

1. A careful outline drawing was made of the flowers and pot, and then the flowers were painted in with a mixture of cadmium red and purple lake. Particular attention was paid to the arrangement of the spaces created by the flowers against the background.

2. The mid-to-light tones of the leaves in the centre were laid on quite freely, sharper definition being reserved for those at the sides, to form a clear, sharp outline. The colours — emerald green, sap green, Payne's grey and a touch of raw sienna — were put on wet and allowed to mix on the paper.

3. The leaves and flowers were darkened in places and a first wash was then laid on the pot. Here, too, the colours were applied wet and moved around on the paper until the artist was satisfied with the way they had blended together.

FREEDOM AND LIGHT

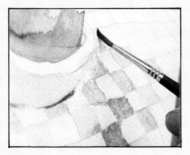

4. A very pale wash was put on the underside of the dish, leaving the rim white to stand out against the checks. The blue used was chosen to echo the blue on the pot, and the shadow was added later.

5. Here the artist is using the tip of a sable brush to paint the blue checks. Although they were painted carefully, and varied in size and colour to suggest recession, the artist has not attempted to produce perfectly straight or regular lines, which would have looked mechanical and monotonous.

6. The wet-into-wet technique was used for painting the pot, giving it a lively appearance suggestive of light and texture. Widely varying colours were applied with plenty of water and blended into one another. If the paint is too wet, or blends in the wrong way, it can be dabbed off with a sponge or tissue.

MATERIALS USED

♦ SUPPORT: pre-stretched
 watercolour paper with a Not
 surface, measuring
 12 × 16 in/30 × 40 cm.
♦ COLOURS: cadmium red,
 alizarin crimson, raw sienna,
 purple lake, emerald green,
 sap green, lemon yellow,
 ultramarine, cobalt blue and
 Payne's grey.
♦ BRUSHES: Nos. 7 and 3 sable.

Cyclamen

♦ STILL LIFE WITH FRUIT ♦

The artist has used a number of different techniques to give a lively look to this bright fruit and vegetable group. His approach was unusual too, since he began by painting in the basic colours of the fruit, leaving the background and the table unpainted until a relatively late stage. This artist frequently paints piece by piece in this way, instead of adopting the more usual method of working all over the painting at the same time. It can be very successful, as it is here, but it does rely on the ability to judge tones and colours very accurately and upon having a clear idea of how the painting is to look finally.

A watercolour containing small, intricate shapes like these requires some planning, as too much overpainting and overlapping of colours can result in a muddy, tired-looking painting in which the brilliance of the colours is lost or diminished. In this case, the artist has solved the problem by using the watercolour mixed with white gouache, which gives it extra covering power without dulling the colours.

Once the colours of the fruit had been established, the warm ochre of the table top was laid on. The paint was applied around the shapes of the fruit, but quite boldly and loosely without too much concern about occasional overlapping. Texture was given to the wood by spattering opaque paint from a stiff brush and then by dragging the same brush, used rather dry, along the surface to suggest wood grain. The fruit was worked up and given more colour and form, and then the near-black background was painted in, giving an even richer glow to the fruit and providing a diagonal which balances the composition and brings all the elements in the painting together.

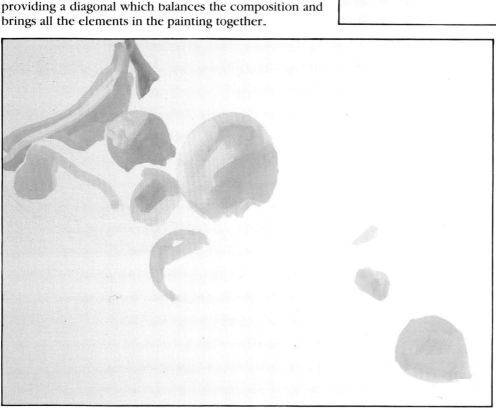

1. The artist begins by painting the lemons, using watercolour mixes with just a little white gouache.

2. By painting all the yellow areas first the artist has to a large extent established the composition. The pattern formed by the yellow shapes, interspersed with darker or more vivid forms and colours, is an important element in the painting.

3. Here the artist is working wet into wet to build up the forms and colours. Because he is using semi-opaque paint, he is able to lay a lighter yellow on top of the deep orange.

4. Now all the colours of the fruit have been laid on, although not in their final form. This enables the artist to gauge the colour and tone he needs for the table top.

ADDING TEXTURE

5. Having laid on the basic colour for the table top, taking it around the edges of the fruit, the artist now uses the spatter method to give a slight textural interest.

6. The grain of the wood is suggested by dragging a stiff, broad brush over the surface, using a darker colour in a slightly dry mixture.

7. This detail shows how well the solidity of the fruit has been depicted, being built up with quite broad and bold areas of colour. The dark shadows beneath them anchor them to the horizontal plane of the table.

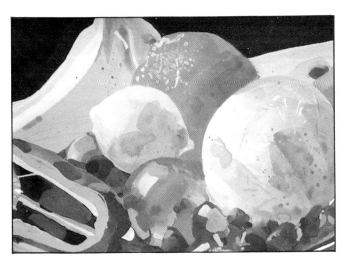

8. The addition of the black background gives a further sparkle to the clear, bright colours of the fruit. The textured highlights on the top of the orange were made by dribbling wet, opaque white paint from the brush on top of the darker colour.

9. The finished painting shows how important the greatly angled diagonal formed by the back edge of the table is to the composition. It balances the opposing diagonal formed by the group of fruit itself, a triangle with the bowl as the apex.

MATERIALS USED
♦ SUPPORT: plain white mounting board
♦ BRUSHES: Nos. 2, 7 and 9 sables and a 1-in/2.5 cm bristle brush
♦ COLOURS: lemon yellow, cadmium yellow, cadmium red, alizarin crimson, sap green, cobalt blue, raw umber and ivory black.

Still Life with Fruit

CHAPTER ONE

WHY OILS?

I<small>N</small> recent decades there has been an amazing proliferation of new materials for artists and designers, so much so that a visit to one of the larger artists' suppliers can leave an uninitiated person feeling confused and bewildered. There are pencils, pens, crayons and pastels in every colour of the rainbow; there are acrylic paints, both in tubes and in pots; there are watercolours in tubes, pans and boxes; there are gouaches and poster paints; there are even special paints for fabrics and ceramics. Indeed, special materials are now available for almost any surface that could conceivably be painted or decorated. And, often tucked away unobtrusively in one corner, there are oil paints.

Why, then, are oil paints still so popular with professional artists and 'Sunday painters' alike? There are two main reasons for this, the first being that oil paint is the most versatile of all the painting media, and can be used in any number of ways to suit all styles, subjects and sizes of work. The second is that it is the easiest medium for a beginner to use. Which is not to say, of course, that a novice will automatically be able to create a masterpiece at first try – that is most unlikely. But because oil paint can be manipulated, scraped off and overpainted, built up and then scraped down once again, it enables you to learn by trial and error, uninhibited by the thought of having 'to start all over again', or waste expensive materials. This is not true of any other medium: acrylic, for example, cannot be moved at all once it has been laid down, and watercolour – a lovely medium but a tricky once – quickly loses all its qualities of freshness and translucence if overworked. Of course, an overworked oil painting will not be a perfect picture, but it may at least be a creditable one, if only because of the knowledge gained in painting it.

OIL PAINT IN THE PAST

Oil paint, though regarded as a 'traditional' painting medium, is actually quite young in terms of art history. In Europe, before the invention of oil paint in the 15th century, artists painted with tempera, which is colour pigment bound with egg yolk. This was a difficult medium to use as it dried very fast, and thus called for a deliberate and meticulous approach.

The Flemish painter Jan van Eyck (*c.*1390-1441) was the first to experiment with raw pigments bound with an oil mixture, when he found that one of his tempera paintings had split while drying in the sun. Not only did the oil paints dry without cracking, but, as van Eyck discovered, they could be applied in thin, transparent layers which gave the colours a depth and luminosity hitherto unknown.

The early painters in oil, like van Eyck, used the paint thinly, with delicate brushstrokes that are almost invisible to the eye. But the full potential of oil paint was not really exploited until it was taken up by the Italian painters of the 15th and 16th centuries,

LEFT *Self Portrait* by
Rembrandt van Rijn (1606-
69). Rembrandt shocked
many of his contemporaries
by his bold use of paint,
which produced thick,
textured surfaces. The
popular Dutch paintings of
the time were characterized
by a very smooth finish, with
no visible brushstrokes,
while in Rembrandt's later
work brushstrokes and the
paint itself are used to
suggest texture, the paint
being used almost as a
modelling medium in places.

LEFT *Old Woman with a
Rosary* by Paul Cézanne
(1839-1906). By Cézanne's
time, the techniques of oil
painting had been largely
freed from the earlier
restrictions and prejudices.
The brushstrokes are an
integral part of this dramatic
composition, as are the areas
of broken colour, while the
face itself has been treated in
a bold, broad manner as a
series of planes.

RIGHT *Man in a Turban* by
Jan van Eyck (active 1422-
41). In his oil paintings, van
Eyck used much the same
methods as previously used
for tempera work, building
up thin layers of paint, one
over another, the technique
known as glazing. However,
oil paint used in this way
gives a depth and luminosity
of effect which cannot be
achieved with tempera.

notably Giorgione (1475-1510) and Titian (*c.*1487-1576).

In Titian's hands, and later in those of the great Dutch painter Rembrandt (1606-69), oil paint was at last used with a feeling for its own inherent qualities. Both artists combined delicately painted areas of glazing (thin paint applied in layers over one another) with thick brushstrokes in which the actual marks of the brush became a feature rather than something to be disguised. Rembrandt's later paintings must have seemed quite shocking to a public accustomed to the smooth, satin finish of other contemporary Dutch paintings – a common complaint was that they looked unfinished.

The English landscape painter John Constable (1776-1837), and the French Impressionists later in the 19th century, took the freedom of painting to even greater lengths by using oil as a quick sketching medium, often working out of doors. In Constable's day the camera had yet to be invented, and artists had of necessity to make a great many sketches as references for their finished works. Constable's wonderful sky and landscape studies, made rapidly, often on scraps of paper and cardboard, were never intended as finished works of art; but to our eyes they are much more pleasing, and infinitely more exciting, than his large polished studio paintings, because they have the quality of immediacy that landscape painting seems to demand.

The Impressionists, who drew inspiration from Constable, applied their paint in thick dabs and strokes of broken colour to depict what was their main preoccupation – the ever-changing effects of light on the landscape. Vincent van Gogh (1853-90), who was not an Impressionist but is sometimes grouped with them because he was working at much the same time, used both the colour and the texture of the paint to express his emotions and to define forms, treating the paint almost as a modelling medium. We are so familiar with van Gogh's paintings through countless reproductions that it is hard to appreciate how strange, indeed even offensive, those great, thick, swirling brushstrokes must have looked to his contemporaries (van Gogh sold only one painting during his entire lifetime).

OIL PAINT TODAY

The very diversity of painting techniques in the past has had the effect of freeing us from any preconceptions about the medium. It is what you want it to be; there is no 'right' or 'wrong' way of doing an oil painting. Today's painters use oil paint in so many different ways that it is often hard to believe that the same medium has been used. Interestingly, the art of tempera painting is now undergoing a revival, and some artists working in oil use a similar technique, applying thin layers of transparent glazes to produce a luminous, light-filled quality. Other artists apply paint thickly with a knife, building it up on the surface of the canvas so that it resembles a relief sculpture.

New painting mediums – oils, varnishes and extenders – are constantly being developed in recognition of these different needs; for example, you can choose one type of medium if you want to build up delicate glazes, another if you want to achieve a thick, textured surface using the impasto technique.

Oil paints can be mixed with other types of paint and even other media; for instance, they can be used in conjunction with oil pastels for quick and dramatic effects; they can be drawn into with pencils; and some artists even mix paint with sand to create areas of texture. A later chapter treats such special techniques in more detail, but the foregoing should give you some idea of the creative potential of this exciting and adaptable medium.

OPPOSITE TOP LEFT *Autumn at Argenteuil* by Claude Monet (1840-1926). The French Impressionists were very much influenced by Constable's landscape paintings, and Monet in particular took the preoccupation with the effects of light almost to the point of an obsession. He frequently worked out of doors, and would paint several versions of the same scene in different lights, building up the paint in thick impastos to achieve the ever-changing effects suggestive of motion which he sought.

FAR LEFT *Olive Trees* by Vincent van Gogh (1853-90). The Impressionists' use of paint was free and daring by the academic standards of the day, but van Gogh's was the most innovative by far, and even those accustomed to the newer styles found his paintings perplexing and even shocking. No one had hitherto dared to represent the sky or foliage as a series of thickly-painted swirls, as in this painting, or the ground as broken lines of bright, unblended colour.

LEFT *Chain Pier, Brighton* by John Constable (1776-1837). Constable was among the first artists to use oil paint as a sketching medium, and his small studies, often on pieces of paper or primed cardboard, are infinitely fresher and more spontaneous than his large studio canvases. This tiny sketch, no more than 25 cm (10 in) high, makes a complete statement about light and colour, as well as recording all the important details of the scene.

CHAPTER TWO
MATERIALS
AND
EQUIPMENT

ABOVE A suggested 'starter palette'. From right to left: white (above), yellow ochre, cadmium yellow, cadmium red, alizarin crimson, cobalt violet, ultramarine, Prussian blue and viridian.

The palette chosen depends very much on the subject to be painted: for instance, violet might not be needed at all, cobalt blue might be used instead of the other two blues, an additional green, such as chrome oxide, added, and a different yellow chosen.

The photograph shows the colours mixed with varying amounts of white.

MATERIALS for oil painting can be costly; so it is advisable to work out your 'starter kit' carefully. Begin by buying the minimum and adding extra colours, brushes and so on when you have progressed to the stage of understanding your particular requirements. For example, someone who intends to specialize in flower painting will need a different range of colours from someone whose chosen theme is seascapes, while a person working on a miniature scale will use brushes quite unlike those needed for large-scale paintings.

CHOOSING PAINTS

Oil paints are divided into two main categories: artists' and students' colours. The latter are cheaper because they contain less pure pigment and more fillers and extenders, but in general they are a false economy for that very reason; they cannot provide the same intensity of colour as the more expensive range. However, students' colours are fine for practising with, and it is possible to combine the two types using the students' colours for browns and other colours where intensity is not a prime requirement and artists' for the pure colours such as red, yellow and blue. A large-size tube of white works out most economical, since white is used more than most other colours.

Paints in the artists' range are not all the same price – a trap for the unwary. They are classified in series, usually from 1 to 7 (different manufacturers have different methods of classification), series 7 being extremely expensive. The price differences reflect the expense and/or scarcity of the pigment used. Nowadays, because there are so many excellent chemical pigments, it is seldom necessary to use the very expensive colours, such as vermilion, except in very special cases.

It is often said that all colours can be mixed from the three primaries, red, yellow and blue. To some extent this is true, but they will certainly not provide a subtle or exciting range, and in any case there are a great many different versions of red, yellow and blue. The illustration shows a suggested 'starter palette', which should provide an adequate mix of colours for most purposes. In general you will need, as well as white, a warm and a cool version of each of the primaries, plus a brown and a green and perhaps a violet or purple. Strictly speaking, greens are not essential as they can be mixed from blue and yellow, but it takes time and experience to arrive at the right hue, and there really is not much point in spending more time in mixing than you need. Vividian is a good choice, since it mixes well with any colour. Other useful additions to your palette are rose madder in the red group; a lemon yellow such as Winsor or cadmium lemon in the yellow group; cerulean blue and Antwerp or cobalt blue in the blue group; and sap green and chrome green in the greens. Good browns and greys are burnt sienna, burnt umber and Payne's grey. Flake white dries quickly and is resistant to cracking, but it contains poisonous lead; for this reason some artists prefer to use titanium white, which is non-toxic. The use of black is often frowned upon, and many artists never use it as it can have a deadening effect, but it can be mixed with yellow to produce a rich olive green, and many landscape artists use it for this purpose.

PAINTING MEDIUMS

Oil paint can be used just as it comes from the tube, or it can be a combination of oil and a thinner (what artists call a *medium*). If you try to apply undiluted paint accurately in a small area, you will see why such mediums are necessary; without them the paint is not easily malleable.

The most popular medium is the traditional blend of linseed oil and turpentine or white spirit, usually in a ratio of 60% oil and 40% thinner. Linseed oil dries to a glossy finish which is resistant to cracking – but be sure to buy either purified or cold-pressed linseed oil, which dry without yellowing. Boiled linseed oil – the sort found in DIY shops – contains impurities which cause rapid yellowing.

Linseed oil is slow to dry, which may not suit your way of working and can produce a rather churned-up paint surface. There are several faster-drying mediums available, such as drying linseed oil, drying poppy oil, stand oil (which also makes the paint flow well and disguises brushstrokes) and an alkyd-based medium sold under the name of *Liquin*.

Turpentine is the most commonly used artist's thinner, though in fact white spirit is just as good and is less likely to cause the headaches and allergic reactions which artists sometimes complain of when using turpentine. White spirit also has less odour, and stores without deteriorating.

Special ready-mixed painting mediums are sold for specific purposes. Linseed oil, for instance, is not suitable for glazing (see p. 27) as it will dribble down the surface of the canvas, but Liquin is excellent for this purpose. Another alkyd medium, *Oleopasto,* has been developed specially for impasto work (see p. 27). It is designed to extend the paint and add body to it so that it can be applied in thick layers, with the brush or knife marks clearly visible.

BRUSHES AND KNIVES

Paint brushes for oil painting come in a wide range of shapes, sizes and materials. Good-quality brushes cost more, but are worth the initial outlay as they last longer and hold their shape better. For oils, unlike for watercolours, you need more than just one or two brushes, otherwise you will be forever cleaning them between applying one colour and the next. The ideal is to have one brush for each colour, but a selection of six should be enough to start off with.

The illustration shows the main shapes and types of brush:

Flats have long bristles with square ends. They hold a lot of paint and can be used flat, for broad areas, or on edge for fine lines.

Brights have shorter bristles than flats and produce strongly textured strokes. They are ideal for applying thick paint for impasto effects.

Rounds have long bristles, tapered at the ends. Like flats, they produce a wide variety of strokes, but they give a softer effect which is excellent for backgrounds, skies and portraits.

Filberts are fuller in shape than flats, with slightly rounded ends that make soft, tapered strokes.

Of the four types of brush, rounds and flats are the most useful to begin with. Brights and filberts can be added later, should you require them.

Each type of brush comes in a range of up to 12 sizes; so choose the size that best suits the style and scale of your paintings.

Hog's-hair bristles and sable hair are the traditional materials for oil-painting brushes; hog's hair is fairly stiff and holds the paint well, while sable gives a much smoother and less obvious brushstroke. Sables are very expensive indeed, but there are now several synthetic versions of the softer type of brush, and also mixtures of sable and synthetic. In the case of the soft brushes, you may need several or none at all, according to the way in which you work; some artists use nothing but soft nylon brushes and others nothing but hog's hair. The projects on pages 42 to 123 will give you an idea of the differing requirements of different styles.

Palette knives, made of flexible steel, are used for cleaning the palette and mixing paint, while painting knives are designed specifically for painting. The latter are unlikely to be needed by a beginner unless you have a particular desire to experiment with this kind of painting, but an ordinary straight-bladed palette knife should form part of your 'starter kit'.

PALETTES

Palettes come in a variety of shapes, sizes and materials, designed to suit your individual requirements. Thumbhole palettes are designed for easel painting. They have a thumbhole and indentation for the fingers, and the palette is supported on the forearm. Before buying a palette, try out different sizes and shapes to see which feels the most comfortable.

New wooden palettes should be treated by rubbing with linseed oil to prevent them absorbing the oil in the paint. You can even improvize your own palette, from any non-absorbent surface, making it any size and colour you like. An old white dinner plate might do, or a sheet of glass with white or neutral-coloured paper underneath it. Disposable palettes made of oil-proof paper are a boon for outdoor work, and remove the necessity for cleaning.

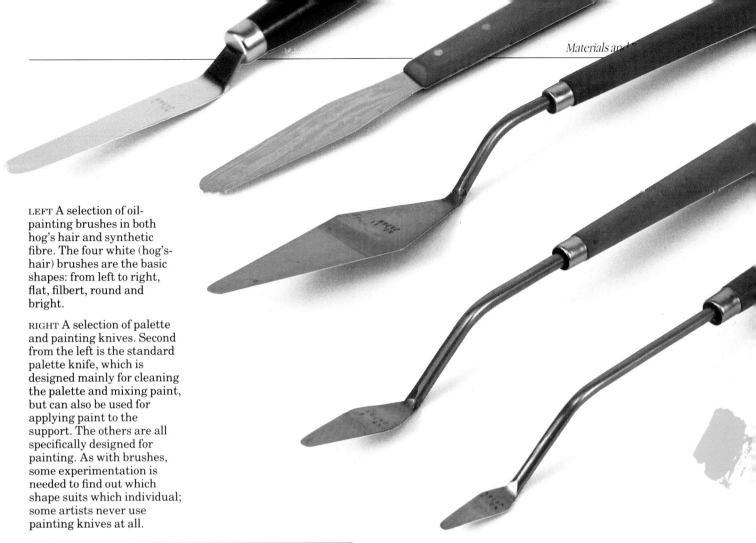

LEFT A selection of oil-painting brushes in both hog's hair and synthetic fibre. The four white (hog's-hair) brushes are the basic shapes: from left to right, flat, filbert, round and bright.

RIGHT A selection of palette and painting knives. Second from the left is the standard palette knife, which is designed mainly for cleaning the palette and mixing paint, but can also be used for applying paint to the support. The others are all specifically designed for painting. As with brushes, some experimentation is needed to find out which shape suits which individual; some artists never use painting knives at all.

PAINTBOXES

Theoretically, any old cardboard box will do to keep paints, brushes and media in, but if you are intending to carry paints around with you it is worth investing in a proper box with separate compartments for paints and brushes. Most of these are wooden, with a carrying handle, and are sold with their own palette which fits into the lid.

Alternatively you can improvize you own paintbox from a toolbox or fishing tackle box, which are less expensive and lighter to carry.

OIL PAINTING ACCESSORIES

Other essential items include dippers for your painting medium, which can be attached to the palette; jam jars or tin cans to hold white spirit for cleaning brushes; and of course a large supply of rags or kitchen paper (oil paint is very messy and needs to be cleaned up frequently).

Another useful painting aid is a mahl stick, which steadies your hand when you are painting small details or fine lines. The traditional mahl stick has a bamboo handle with a chamois cushion at one end. The stick is held across the canvas with the cushioned end resting lightly on a dry area of the painting, and you rest your painting arm on the stick to steady yourself as you paint. Mahl sticks are sold at artists' suppliers, but a piece of dowelling or garden cane with a bundle of rags tied to one end is quite adequate, and can be

rested on the side of the canvas or board if the paint surface is wet. Page 65 shows a mahl stick being used.

For anyone who intends to do a lot of outdoor work, a pair of canvas separators is very useful. These are designed to keep two wet canvases apart without damaging the paint, and have a handle for carrying. It is necessary to have two canvases of the same size with you, even if you intend to use only one.

VARNISHES

Ideally, paintings should be varnished to protect them from dust and to restore the colours, which tend to become toned down as the paint dries. Many people associate varnish with that dark-brown, sticky look that was such a feature of Victorian paintings, but several clear synthetic varnishes are now available, both matt and gloss. Most varnishes, however, cannot be applied for at least six months, even a year if the paint is very thick, as it takes this long for it to dry out thoroughly. The exceptions are the temporary varnishes, such as retouching varnish, which can be applied when the paint is 'skin dry', that is, in about two weeks to a month. It can also be used to brush over an area that may have become dull and matt during the painting, as sometimes happens, and can be removed if necessary by rubbing gently with distilled turpentine.

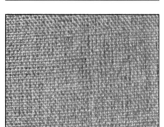
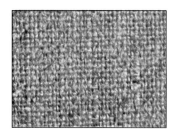

SUPPORTS

This is the term given to whatever surface is used to paint on, whether stretched canvas, hardboard or cardboard, paper – even a wall. The most commonly used support for oil painting is canvas, usually made of linen or cotton, and stretched to make it taut, but many other surfaces can be used, and each one has its own individual characteristics. Canvas provides a sympathetic surface and holds the paint well, while primed hardboard, favoured by some artists, is unyielding and holds the paint much less well, so that it tends to slip about. This can be an advantage for someone who paints with thinned – and thus quicker-drying – paint, and makes use of finely drawn detail, but is less suitable for thickly applied paint, as each successive layer will disturb the one below. You will certainly have to try several different supports before you can be sure which one suits you best, and even then you will probably find that different paintings call for different supports. The examples on pages 44 to 123 demonstrate the use of a great variety of types, and show how the artists have made use of particular surfaces to achieve the effects they wanted.

CANVAS

Canvases can be bought stretched and ready for use, but they are very expensive and it is much cheaper to stretch and prepare (prime) your own. Unprimed canvas can be bought by the metre in artists' suppliers, as can stretchers, which are sold in pairs so that any size can be made up. The illustration shows some different types of canvas, ranging from fine weave to very coarse. Generally, a coarse weave is suitable for broad, heavy brushwork, while a finely woven texture is best for finely detailed work. Linen canvas, which is undoubtedly the nicest surface to work on, is expensive and could be an unwise choice for a first attempt. Cotton canvas is much cheaper, and perfectly adequate. Cotton duck, in particular, stretches well because it has a tighter weave.

STRETCHING CANVAS

Stretching canvas is not at all difficult, and will save you money. To stretch a canvas you will need four wooden stretcher pieces – one for each side of the frame. In addition you will need 12-mm (½-in) carpet tacks to attach the canvas to the frame, a hammer and a pair of sharp scissors.

Assemble the stretchers, making sure that the assembled stretcher is square by measuring the diagonals – they should both be the same length. Then cut the canvas about 4 cm (1½ in) larger than the stretcher all round. Lay the stretcher frame on the canvas, then turn one edge of the canvas over the frame and tack or staple it in the centre of one side. Pull the opposite side of the canvas as firmly as possible and tack it at the centre of that side. Repeat this process on the other

ABOVE Stretchers can be bought in a wide variety of sizes. They are sold in pairs, which are then fitted together to form rectangles.

TOP Types of canvas. From left to right, top row: inexpensive cotton; good-quality cotton, which is similar to linen. MIDDLE ROW: hessian, very coarse and thus unsuitable for thinly applied paint or fine work, and linen. BOTTOM ROW: a different weave of linen and a ready-primed linen, suitable for most work and available from the larger artists' suppliers.

RIGHT Three types of canvas, as bought on the roll from an artists' suppliers.

two sides, and continue tacking or stapling, working from the centre outwards, and placing the tacks about 2.5 cm (1 in) apart. Then fold in the corners and tack one over the other. Finally, tap in the wooden corner wedges (normally sold with the stretcher pieces) as far as necessary to tauten the canvas thoroughly. (These can be tapped in again later if the canvas loosens while you are working.)

An inexpensive method of stretching canvas is to stick it down on hardboard with glue size. This is rather a messy job, and does not provide such a pliable surface as stretched canvas, but it has one considerable advantage in that flat pieces of hardboard are much easier to store than canvases – an important consideration for anyone who has a space problem. There are two types of size, that sold in builders' merchants for preparing walls and so on, and animal-skin size, sold in most large artists' suppliers. The latter is the best choice, as it will probably be needed in any case for priming (see below), but it has slightly less sticking power than glue size. Cellulose and other adhesives should not be used as they could react with the oil paint. To prepare the size, which is sold in crystal form, first mix it with cold water in a proportion of about one of crystals to seven of water, and leave it for a short time until it has doubled in bulk. Heat it gently in an old saucepan or double-boiler (not one you will use for cooking) until all the crystals have melted thoroughly. Glue size can be allowed to boil, but animal-skin size should not, as this weakens it.

Cut the canvas to about 2.5 cm (1 in) larger all around than the hardboard, apply the hot size to the smooth side of the hardboard, lay the canvas on top and then go over it with a small, hard roller of the type sold for lino cuts to smooth out any creases. To fix the edges, simply turn them over the back of the hardboard and stick them down with more size. (This is the messiest part, as it must be done while the size is still warm and sticky.)

Any left-over size can be reheated and used again. This method is most suitable for the lighter types of canvas, as heavy linen will not stick thoroughly, and it can also be used for materials not actually sold for painting purposes, such as muslin or cotton lawn.

BOARDS AND PAPER

Hardboard is an inexpensive, strong yet lightweight support which you can buy from any timber yard or builders' suppliers. Either the smooth or the rough side can be used, the latter being suitable only for those who like to use their paint thick. Its disadvantage, which applies also to the canvas-covered hardboard described above, is that it warps, but if you are framing your work it can be straightened out at this stage by battening the back (sizing both sides of the board also helps to reduce warping). For a large painting, the hardboard can be battened first by either sticking or screwing two pieces of hardwood battening across the back. (If using screws, take care they do not come through to the front, as hardboard is quite thin.)

Prepared canvas boards can be bought from artists' suppliers in a variety of different surfaces, the more expensive ones being the best. The cheaper ones tend to have a rather coarse and greasy surface, but are probably adequate for a first attempt. Such boards are also prone to warping.

Paper and cardboard make perfectly satisfactory supports for oil painting as long as they are primed (see below). They are excellent for small, quick sketches, as the paper, being slightly absorbent, allows the paint to dry quite quickly. If using paper, buy a good-quality, heavy water-colour paper, as a thin paper will buckle when primed. Specially prepared paper, called oil sketching paper, can be bought, usually in pads. Some people get on well with this, but others find its surface greasy and unpleasant to work on, like that of the cheaper painting boards.

SIZING AND PRIMING

The conventional method of priming all supports is first to apply a coat of the animal-skin size described above, and when dry to apply a coat (or sometimes two) of oil-based primer. You can use ordinary household undercoat for this, but special oil primers are sold by artists' suppliers for the purpose, and are probably the wisest choice. However, oil primers do take a fairly long time to dry. An alternative is to use emulsion paint, which dries quickly, or the acrylic primer sold under the (incorrect) name of gesso, which is compatible with oil paint. Acrylic primer should always be applied direct to the canvas, without the preliminary coat of size, and two coats will usually be needed.

The purpose of sizing and priming is to provide a protective layer between the canvas and the oil paint. Some contemporary artists, among them the English artist Francis Bacon (b.1910), do paint on unprimed canvas in order to achieve special effects, but this should never be a general practice. The oil paint will eventually rot the canvas or other support, and the paint itself will dry out and flake off as all the oil will have been absorbed.

EASELS

An easel is a necessity. You may manage to produce one small painting by propping up your canvas on a table or shelf, but you will very soon find out how unsatisfactory this is. Without an easel you cannot adjust the height of your work – essential if you are doing a painting of a reasonable size, as you must be able to reach different areas of it easily and comfortably – and you cannot tilt the work, which you often need to do either to avoid light reflecting on its surface or to catch the best light for working.

There are several different types of easel on the market, from huge, sturdy studio easels to small sketching easels that are light and easily portable. Your choice will be dictated by the space in which you are working, whether you intend to work mostly indoors or outdoors, and by the size of your work and the type of painting you are doing. If you intend to work out of doors frequently you will need a sketching easel (though small sketches can be done by propping the canvas or board against the open lid of a paintbox). If, on the other hand, you know you are unlikely to paint anywhere but indoors, the heavier radial easel could be a good choice, but this cannot easily be dismantled and put away, so you might choose a portable easel for space reasons.

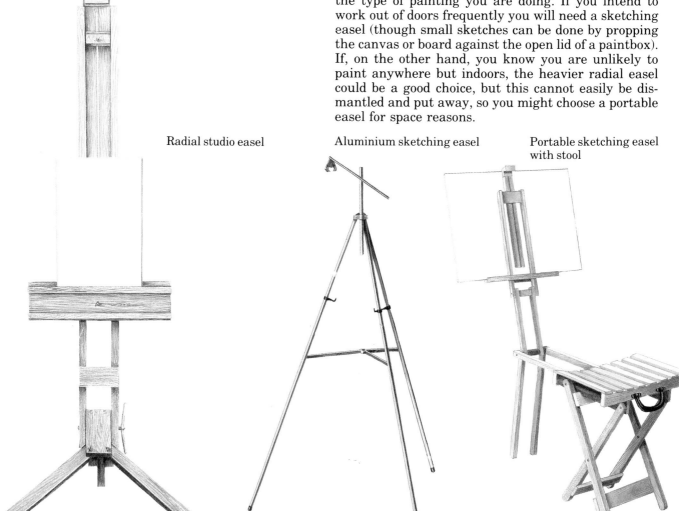

Radial studio easel

Aluminium sketching easel

Portable sketching easel with stool

There are three main types of sketching easel, the box easel, the wooden sketching easel and the aluminium sketching easel. The first type combines an easel and a paintbox, and can be folded up into a case for carrying. These were at one time very expensive, and the best ones still are, but cheaper versions are now appearing on the market, and for an outdoor painter they are a good choice, as everything can be carried in one piece of luggage.

Wooden sketching easels are inexpensive, but are not recommended, as the blocks which slide up and down in slots to enable you to adjust the height of the work tend to become warped, so that they either do not slide at all or are impossible to fix in position. There is nothing more infuriating than having to fight your easel, which often involves knocking it over, just when you want to work particularly fast because the light is changing.

The metal sketching easel, on the other hand, is excellent, and suffers from none of these disadvantages because metal cannot warp. It is easy to adjust, holds the work firmly, and has the additional advantage of being adjustable to a horizontal position for watercolours (you may find that you want to experiment with other media from time to time). It is also quite adequate for indoor work, providing you are not working on a vast scale, and can be tucked away unobtrusively in a corner when not in use.

The problem with all sketching easels except the heavier version of the box type is that because they are light, and thus easy to carry, they are also vulnerable to gusts of wind, the canvas or board acting as a most effective sail! Some artists manage to anchor their easel by pushing tent pegs into the ground and tying the easel legs to them, or by hanging a heavy stone from the centre of the easel.

THE WORKING SPACE

Few non-professional painters are fortunate enough to have access to a studio; nor indeed are all professional ones. Most people have to make do with a small, under-equipped room or just a corner of a room used by other people for other purposes. This can create problems, but these are surmountable with a little organization.

One problem is that oil paint is a messy medium and has an almost magical way of appearing on objects that seemed to be nowhere near it when you were painting. You get it on your hands without noticing, then you go and make a cup of coffee and it will be on the kettle, the mug, the spoon, and so on, ad infinitum. If you are working in a corner of a room, clean up as often as you can, including wiping your hands, never wander about with a loaded paintbrush, and cover the equipment table with plenty of newspaper.

A more serious problem is lighting. The best light for painting is, of course, daylight, but daylight is unpredictable and changes all the time, not only in variable weather conditions but also according to the time of day. If you have a north-facing window you are lucky, as north light (or south light if you live in the southern hemisphere) changes much less, but many rooms face east or west, in which case you will sometimes have the sun shining directly on to the work and reflecting off the paint surface, while at other times you will have almost no light at all.

Always try to position your easel so that the light source is behind you and coming over your left shoulder if you are right-handed.

Good light is vitally important: if you look in a good light at a painting done in a poor one you will see why. What were intended to be subtle gradations of colour and tone now appear as crude mixtures of bright colours and dingy ones, while what you thought of as nicely-blended, unobtrusive brushwork is actually quite clumsy and obvious.

One way of coping with this problem is to use artificial lighting which, while not as perfect as northerly daylight, is at least constant. The best lights for painting are the fluorescent 'daylight' ones, which can be bought either as ceiling lights or as lamps which can be fitted on to a shelf, table or windowsill. Look carefully at what is available before buying, as mistakes are expensive, and work out where the light source should be placed so that it does not reflect off the paint. One method is to fix a lamp over the window so that it boosts the available light, but a certain amount of trial and error may be involved before you arrive at a satisfactory solution.

Box easel

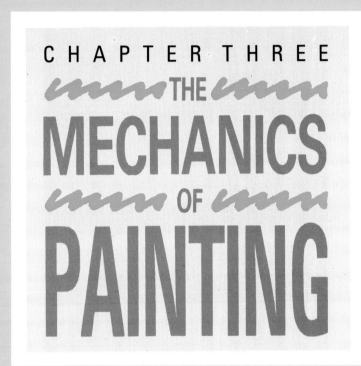

CHAPTER THREE

THE MECHANICS OF PAINTING

TOP, ABOVE AND RIGHT This painting was begun with a monochrome underpainting in dilute cobalt blue, an unusual but deliberate choice of colour, as the blue is repeated throughout the picture. The flowers and drapery were then built up in thicker paint, the method known as 'fat over lean', the background and foliage being left quite thin.

ALTHOUGH there are really no hard-and-fast rules in oil painting, it is helpful to have an idea of the various ways in which artists go about things so that you can experiment with different techniques, colour schemes and compositions as you evolve your own particular style. Rules are often useful in a negative way: once you know a rule you can break it for reasons of your own, or 'bend' it, as many artists have done with the rules of perspective. Constable and the French Impressionists broke the rules of their times, thus freeing painting from the very rigid set of procedures to which artists had previously been forced to adhere, but their knowledge of all the theories of painting was very thorough indeed.

GENERAL PAINTING TECHNIQUES

If you are painting a very simple subject, such as an empty landscape with a wide expanse of sky, there is often no need for an underdrawing or underpainting, except perhaps a line or two to delineate the horizon. However, for a more complex subject such as a figure study, or perhaps a landscape including people or buildings, a preliminary drawing on the canvas is usually advisable. This enables you to work out the composition and the position of the main elements within it, and to plan the balance of dark colours and light ones. For a portrait or figure painting you will need to establish how you want to place the figure in relation to the background, and you will need to get the proportions of the figure right. If you start an ambitious painting with inadequate drawing you will be forever altering parts of it, which will not only spoil your enjoyment, but will also produce a laboured and overworked painting. Careful planning at the start enables you to be more spontaneous later.

Underdrawings can be done either in pencil or charcoal, the latter being preferable, as it is a broad medium, easier to use freely. To avoid loose charcoal mixing with the paint and muddying it, brush it down lightly with a rag before starting to paint – you will still retain the main lines of the drawing.

Underpainting – another form of drawing but done with a brush – can be made either in monochrome or an understated version of the finished colour scheme, in both cases using paint well thinned with turpentine. If you find a blank canvas somewhat intimidating, you will find that an underpainting overcomes the problem by providing a 'stepping-stone' from which you can build up the succeeding layers of colour with confidence.

A monochrome underpainting should concentrate on the main masses of light and shade, as in the example illustrated, and a coloured one should avoid bright and light colours, as you will want to build up to these as the painting progresses. Nowadays artists often use acrylic paint for underpainting, as this dries much faster than even thinned oil paint, enabling the next stage to proceed immediately.

A good general rule for oil painting – and a very old one – is to work 'fat over lean'. This simply means that in the initial stages the paint should be used fairly thin (diluted with turpentine only) becoming thicker and oilier as the painting progresses. Working in this way reduces the risk of the paint cracking as it dries out. If, however, 'lean' paint is brushed over a layer of 'fat' paint (containing a greater proportion of oil) what happens is that the lean layer dries first, and when the fat layer beneath it eventually starts to dry it contracts, causing the dry layer on top to crack.

Not all paintings, however, are done in stages in this way; many are completed at one sitting, with a minimum of drawing or underpainting or even none at all. This is known as *alla prima* painting, and is much used for landscape or quick portrait studies where the painter wants to record his impressions rapidly in a free and spontaneous manner. The paint is used thickly, with each colour laid down more or less as it will finally appear. When oil paints are used in this way, the colours blend into each other, particularly when one is laid on top of another. This is a feature of *alla prima* painting, known as working 'wet into wet', and was much exploited by the Impressionists, particularly Claude Monet (1840-1926) in his outdoor paintings. For anyone who has not used oils before, *alla prima* is a good way of starting, as it will give you an immediate 'feel' for the medium and force you to work fast without being over-conscious of each brush-stroke.

SPECIAL PAINTING TECHNIQUES

As has been mentioned, there are many different ways of applying oil paint to create particular effects. Some of these are used almost unconsciously, when the painting seems to demand a particular approach, while others are the result of careful planning.

The method called *scumbling* comes into the first category and simply means applying semi-opaque

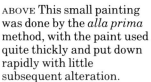

ABOVE This small painting was done by the *alla prima* method, with the paint used quite thickly and put down rapidly with little subsequent alteration.

The photograph (RIGHT) shows colours being blended into one another by working wet into wet. ABOVE a thin layer of transparent red paint is being laid over a dry layer of yellow. This is the technique called glazing, which gives an effect quite unlike that of one layer of thicker paint, as the colour below reflects back through the glaze, giving additional brilliance.

FAR LEFT The paint surface here is an important part of the painting, the broken patches and restless texture of the thickly applied colour enhancing the vividness of the subject. The paint was applied with a knife alone, and the detail, (LEFT), clearly shows how different is the effect from that of traditional brush painting.

LEFT Rembrandt used both glazing and impasto in his paintings. In *Woman Bathing,* the delicately glazed areas of flesh contrast with the bold brushstrokes and thick paint of the garment.

RIGHT Here scumbling was used to suggest the texture of the chalk cliffs. The paint was scrubbed on with a brush over dry paint below, and in places was worked in with the fingers. The foreground was put on rather dry.

paint on top of another dry or semi-dry area of colour in an irregular way. Part of the layer below will show through, so that a 'broken' colour and texture is created. This can be very effective for particular parts of a painting, such as skies, rocks, tree trunks, fabric and so on. Anything can be used for putting on scumbled paint – stiff brushes, a rag or even the fingers – and the paint can be dragged, smudged or stippled.

Areas of irregular texture can be made by laying a flat area of colour in opaque paint and then 'blotting' it, when semi-dry, with non-absorbent paper such as pages from a glossy magazine. As you peel back the paper, it drags at the surface layer of paint and creates a stippled texture. This technique is called *frottage.*

A way of creating another kind of texture is *impasto,* in which the paint is laid on thickly, often with a palette knife. In the past, artists such as Rembrandt combined impasto with areas of delicate brushwork, pointing up the differences in texture between, for example, flesh and clothing. Today many artists use impasto as a technique on its own, building up heavy layers of paint to make a raised and densely-textured surface. Special painting mediums are available which increase the bulk of the paint (see p. 15), and some artists even mix paint with sand for a rough, grainy surface.

Interesting effects can be achieved by drawing or scratching into a layer of wet oil paint to reveal another colour beneath or sometimes the white ground of the canvas, as in the example illustrated. The implement used can be anything pointed, such as the end of the brush handle or a knitting needle. This method is called *sgraffito.*

A technique that comes into the deliberate planning category is *glazing,* in which thin, transparent paint is laid over an area of already dry paint. Layers of glazes can be built up one over the other to create effects akin to the deep glow of wood that has been lovingly polished – but glazing is not a quick method as each layer must dry before the next is applied. Many of the rich, glowing colours used by artists of the past, such as Titian, were produced by laying thin glazes of brilliant colour over an underpainting, and the luminous quality of the landscapes painted by J. W. M. Turner (1775–1851) are the result of layers of glazing over thick, pale impastos.

ABOVE The artist scratches through the paint with a palette knife to reveal the white surface of the canvas. Where there are several layers in a painting, the technique can also be used to reveal one or more of the colours below.

LEFT The still life was given sparkle as well as additional definition by the use of the sgraffito technique.

These thumbnail sketches, of female figures in various poses against different backgrounds, illustrate the way in which some artists try out possible compositions for paintings. Such drawings, which can be done quite quickly and need be little more than scribbles, are an excellent means of working out the arrangement of the main shapes and the balance of lights and darks.

COMPOSING A PICTURE

The word 'composition' has a slightly alarming ring to it – it sounds as though it might be an intellectual exercise quite beyond the capabilities of the ordinary person. This really is not so: composing a painting is mainly a question of selecting, arranging and re-arranging, just as you might do when deciding on the decor for a room or when taking a photograph. A large, complex painting with numerous people and objects in it does, of course, need some thought; otherwise there may be too much activity in one part of the picture and not enough in another. But even here, it is less a matter of following a prescribed set of rules than of working out the balance of the various shapes, as in the case of planning a room – no one would put all the furniture crowded together on one side and leave the rest empty.

A 'good composition' is one in which there is no jarring note, the colours and shapes are well-balanced, and the picture as a whole seems to sit easily within its frame or outer borders. Even a simple head-and-shoulders portrait is composed, and a vital part of composition is selection – what you put in and what you leave out. In the case of a portrait you will need to establish whether the person should be seated, and if so on what, whether you want to include the chair, whether you want the hands to form part of the composition, and whether you want to use something in the background, for example part of a window frame, to balance the figure.

If you are painting a landscape you may think composition is not involved, that you are just painting what you see, but you will have chosen a particular view, just as you would when taking a photograph, and in choosing it you will have gone at least some way towards composing it. You may then find that you want to exaggerate or re-arrange some feature in the foreground, such as a rock or a tree, to provide extra interest, or alter the bend of a path to lead the eye into the picture.

There are some basic errors which should be avoided if possible. In general it is not a good idea to divide a landscape horizontally into two equal halves – the land and the sky – as the result will usually be monotonous. A line, such as a path or fence, should not lead directly out of the picture unless balanced by another line which leads the eye back into it. A still-life or portrait should not be divided in half vertically, while a flower painting is unlikely to be pleasing to the eye if the flower arrangement is placed too far down in the picture area, too far to one side, or very small in the middle, with a large expanse of featureless background.

In the case of interiors, portraits, still-lifes and flowers, backgrounds can be used as a device to balance the main elements of the composition. Use part of a piece of furniture behind a seated figure, for example, or a subtly patterned wallpaper which echoes or contrasts with the main shapes and colours in the figure. In landscape painting the sky is a vital part of the composition, and should always be given as much care and thought as the rest of the painting.

Even if you are working quickly, it is often helpful to make some drawings, known as *thumbnail sketches* (though they need not be small) before you start on the painting. These may consist of just a few roughly-drawn lines to establish how the main shapes can be placed, or they may help you to work out the tonal pattern of the composition.

A viewing frame is equally useful, particularly for landscapes painted on the spot. When faced with a large expanse of land and sky the problem is always how much of it to paint, where to start and finish, and how much of what you see will actually fit on the canvas. Anyone who takes photographs will be familiar with this problem: you raise your camera at a splendid view only to find that the small section of it you can see through the viewfinder is quite dull and featureless. A viewing frame is simply a rectangular aperture cut in a piece of card – a good size is about 11.5×15.25 cm ($4\frac{1}{2} \times 6$ in) – which you hold up in front of you to frame and isolate the subject. Once you have chosen the particular area of landscape that interests you, you can then decide how you want to

ABOVE The natural inclination when painting subjects like trees is to try and get everything in, but in this painting the artist has allowed the foreground trees to 'bust' out of the frame, giving a stronger and more exciting effect.

treat it and how much re-arranging is needed to make an interesting composition.

A useful aid for indoor work is a polaroid camera; several photographs of the subject taken from different angles and with different backgrounds will give you an idea of how you can best approach the painting, and they will also help you to work out the balance of colours and tones.

RIGHT In this painting the contrast between the dark and light tree trunks has been emphasised by the use of very thin paint. The solid foliage of the evergreens draws attention to the slenderness of the foreground trunks and provides a counterpoint.

COLOUR AND LIGHT

Colour can be a very complex subject indeed – whole books have been written on colour theory. Such theory is beyond the scope of this book, and in any case would be more likely to be a hindrance than a help to an inexperienced painter, but there are some basic guidelines which will help you to make a picture work, and there are also some terms which you will need to understand.

Colour has two main qualities, tone and intensity, the first being the darkness or lightness of a particular colour and the second being its brightness. If you take a black-and-white photograph of a landscape composed entirely of greens, you will see that some appear darker than others – proving that a single colour can have dark tones and light tones. In the same landscape, some of the greens will be brighter and more vibrant than others – in other words, more intense.

Colours which are opposite one another on the colour wheel, such as red and green, yellow and violet,

are called *complementary colours*. These can be used in a deliberate way to balance and 'spark off' one another; for example, a small area of bright red in a landscape could be used to enhance and intensify a large expanse of green. The Op painters of the 1960s used complementary colours in a highly intellectual way: by juxtaposing complementaries of the same hue and tone they created restless, 'jumping' effects.

Colours are basically either 'warm' or 'cool', and the warm ones will tend to 'advance', or push themselves to the front of a painting, while the cool ones will recede. In general, the warm colours are the reds, yellows, bright yellow-greens and oranges, while cool ones are the blues and colours with blue in them, such as blue-green. Some blues, however, are warmer than others, and some reds are cooler than others. You can see this by placing ultramarine or cerulean blue (both quite warm) next to Prussian or Antwerp blue (both cool), and alizarin crimson (cool) next to cadmium red (warm).

You can make use of the 'advancing' and 'retreating' qualities of warm and cool colours in modelling forms and in creating a sense of space and depth. In portrait painting, for example, use warm colours for the prominent areas such as the nose, chin and cheekbones, and cool colours for receding or shadowed areas such as underneath the chin. In landscapes, use warm colours in the foreground and cool, bluish tones in the background to emphasize the feeling of receding space (see below).

There is no colour without light, and the direction, quality and intensity of light constantly changes and modifies colours. This fact became almost an obsession with the Impressionist painter Claude Monet; he painted many studies of the same subject – a group of haystacks – at different times of the day in order to understand and analyze these changes. You can see the effects very easily for yourself if you look at any scene – the view from a window or a corner of the garden – first on a cloudy morning and then in low evening sunlight. In the evening everything will suddenly become golden and a brick wall which might have appeared a drab brown in the morning may now be a bright hue of orange or pink.

Light is vital to a painting, whether a landscape or a still-life or portrait study, and the way it falls defines the shape of objects and determines their colour. Both photographers and painters of landscape know that the high midday sun is their enemy, as it creates dense patches of shadow and drains the landscape of colour and definition. A portrait or still-life can also look flat, dead and colourless if lit directly from above, while a side light can suddenly bring it to life, creating exciting shadow areas of purple or green and vivid, sparkling highlights.

AERIAL PERSPECTIVE

This is a way of using colour and tone to give a sense of space in a painting, and to indicate recession. It is

particularly important in landscape painting. If you look at an expanse of landscape, such as one with fields and trees in the foreground and distant hills or mountains beyond, you will see that the colours become paler and cooler in the distance, with details barely visible. The objects in the foreground will be brighter and have much clearer areas of contrast, or tonal differences, which will become smaller in the middle distance and may disappear altogether in the far distance, so that the hills or mountains appear as pure areas of pale blue. It takes some experience to use aerial perspective successfully; if you accidentally mix a rather warm blue on your palette and try to use it for the distant hills you will find that they seem almost to jump forward to the front of the picture. The same applies if you combine a pale colour with a much darker one; there will then be a greater tonal difference than is actually present and the background will begin to vie with the foreground.

Aerial perspective can, of course, be either exploited or ignored. Sometimes, for instance, you might be more interested in creating a flat pattern or you might want simply to use areas of vivid colour.

LINEAR PERSPECTIVE

This, like colour theory, can be a very complex subject, almost a science. During the Renaissance, when the laws of perspective were first being formulated in a systematic way, artists vied with one another to produce more and more elaborate perspective drawings; for example Paolo Uccello (*c*.1396-1475) made a study of a chalice broken down into a series of separate receding surfaces which is quite breathtaking in its intricacy. However, unless your particular interest is architecture – you might perhaps want to make a series of detailed studies of the interiors of churches, for instance – it is most unlikely that you will need to understand more than the most basic rules, which are helpful when faced with the problem of how to make buildings look solid or how to indicate that they are being viewed from above.

Theoretically, you can make perspective work by just drawing what you see, and some art teachers believe that such rules should not be learnt, at any rate by beginners, as they have a stultifying effect. This is certainly true to some extent; too much careful pondering over the precise angle of parallel lines can

BELOW A scene such as this relies on some understanding of the laws of perspective or the effect of the high-perched buildings would be lost. When sketching out of doors, it is often helpful to mark in a horizon line so that the angles can be related to it; the eye alone cannot always judge such angles truthfully.

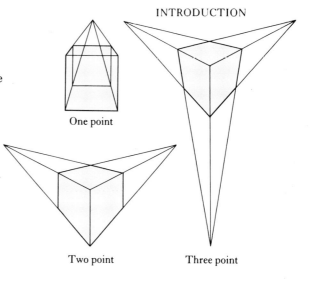

RIGHT One-, two- and three-point perspective. In the first, only two planes can be seen, and thus the parallel lines have the same vanishing point. When three planes are visible, two separate vanishing points are needed, and if the same cube is seen from above or below the horizon the sides will also converge at a third vanishing point.

INTRODUCTION

One point

Two point

Three point

horizon line

turn a painting which could have been fresh and immediate into one which is correct but dull. However, few amateur artists possess the enviable gift of being able to turn direct observation into drawing or painting with any degree of ease, and a knowledge of the basic rules can have a liberating effect rather than the reverse, as long as you don't allow yourself to become too bound up in them.

The primary rule, which many people learn at school, is that all receding parallel lines meet at a vanishing point, which is on the horizon. It is easy enough to learn such rules, but far less easy to apply them. A single building has several different planes, or sets of parallel lines, and a group of buildings, such as a farmhouse with barns and outhouses, has even more, as the buildings are often set at random angles to one another. Where, you may ask yourself, is this horizon at which they will all meet, and how is it determined? This is dependent on your chosen viewpoint. If you are high up, on a cliff or hilltop, the horizon will be level with you, so that you have very little sky and a large expanse of land or sea. You will be looking down at the group of buildings, and the

parallel lines receding from you will slope up to the horizon. If you are at a low angle, perhaps sitting on the ground, the horizon, still at eye-level, will also be low, giving a large expanse of sky. The buildings will be above the horizon and the receding parallels will slope down to it.

In the case of parallels running directly away from you, the vanishing point would be within the picture area, but for different planes at angles to them it will be a hypothetical one which can be some way outside the picture area to the right or left. If you are painting out of doors, the viewing frame previously mentioned is helpful in establishing where the various lines are leading to, or a small pocket ruler can be held up in front of your eye and lined up with a rooftop.

Of course, many artists choose either to ignore or to exaggerate the rules of perspective so as to create their own personal effects. For example, an artist who is more interested in the patterns suggested by a particular scene might paint the buildings quite flat, with no perspective at all, as a child would, while another might choose to 'see' a subject from above, with the horizon so high that there is no sky area at all.

CHAPTER FOUR
STARTING TO PAINT

IF you have never painted at all, or if you have not used a particular medium before, the idea of making a start can be quite daunting. If you are intending to go to a painting class, it is less alarming, as you will be painting what is put in front of you to paint, and a teacher will be on hand to advise, but if you are working at home there will be a great many decisions to make. For instance, what will you paint, what size will you work, and how will you actually begin? This chapter provides some suggestions and guidelines to help build up your confidence and so increase your enjoyment of painting.

CHOOSING A SUBJECT

Many people seem to feel that, just as there are 'proper' ways of going about a painting, there are also 'proper' subjects. This is quite untrue; as we have seen, there is no way of applying oil paint that is more correct than another, nor is there any one subject that makes a better painting than another. Nudes, still-lifes, flowers and landscapes are all types of painting hallowed by long tradition, but many artists have made fine paintings of just the corner of a room, a wall with a few flowers against it or a single tree. Vincent van Gogh made deeply moving and expressive still-lifes from such subjects as a pair of peasant's boots or a pile of books on a table.

Still-life did not exist as a painting subject until the Dutch artists of the 17th century 'invented' it. Nor was landscape, except as a background to a figure or group of figures, acceptable until the late 18th and early 19th centuries. In the past, the subject of a painting was largely dictated by the demands of patrons, but we have no such restrictions.

It should be said, however, that some subjects are more difficult than others, and it can be discouraging to find you have set yourself a task which your experience is not equal to. Portraits, for example, are particularly difficult. You have to cope with so many problems: how to render the colour of flesh, the texture of hair and clothing, the way the light falls on the planes of the face and, finally, how to 'get a likeness'. If your interests do lie in this direction, you could start with a self-portrait, as in this way you will have total control over your 'sitter' and can work at your own speed without feeling rushed and flustered. You will know your own face well already.

Still-lifes, flowers and landscapes all provide good starting points, depending on your particular interests. Subjects for still-lifes can be found in most people's homes or the nearest vegetable or flower shop, and you can choose your own arrangement, light it in any way you want and take your time over it. In the case of landscape, if the weather is not suitable for outdoor painting, or if you feel shy about it, you could start by working from a photograph (but beware of trying to 'copy' it in exact detail) or you could paint the view from a window.

ABOVE AND RIGHT Domestic interiors have been a favourite subject with artists since the Dutch 17th-century masters. These two paintings, Van Gogh's Yellow Chair and Gwen John's A

Corner of the Artist's Room in Paris, although totally different in their treatment and handling of colour and paint, both give a strong feeling of serenity, just as the Dutch paintings did.

Lighting plays a vital part in the arrangement of a still life, flower painting or portrait, and a subject can change quite dramatically according to the way it is lit. Back lighting (TOP LEFT) can be very effective for flowers, as the light will shine through the petals in places, giving a brilliant sparkle, with the front foliage and vase appearing very dark. Front lighting (ABOVE LEFT) tends to make any subject seem flat and dull, while side or diagonal lighting (TOP AND ABOVE RIGHT) will define the forms more clearly.

CHOOSING A SHAPE AND SIZE

This may seem trivial, but in fact both shape and size have an important part to play in the composition and treatment of a painting. A panoramic landscape, for instance, may suggest a wide horizontal shape which will enable you to show the broad sweep of the land as well as giving a sense of peace and tranquility. A single tree might call for a narrow vertical painting, while a still-life with a lot of objects in it could suggest a rather square one.

Size is a very personal matter: some artists work on vast canvases too big to fit in most living-rooms, while others produce tiny, detailed work on supports no larger than the average photograph. If you are working at home you are unlikely to want to work on a very large scale, and it is not usually a good idea to start very small. A good starting size is about 51 × 40.6 cm (20 × 16 in), a standard one in which you can buy both boards and canvases.

Painting is rather like handwriting – people with large writing feel constricted if for any reason they are forced to write small, and if your 'natural size' for painting is much larger than the support you have chosen you will soon find out, as your painting will seem to spread of its own volition beyond the edges. Until you have established a size which suits you, it is wise to use an inexpensive support, such as a piece of primed paper or cardboard, oil sketching paper or 'canvas board'. Hardboard is not recommended for early attempts as it has a slippery surface which can give a messy and unmanageable paint surface.

AVOIDING DISCOURAGEMENT

If your painting goes wrong at an early stage you are bound to feel depressed and discouraged. Various suggestions are given here which will help you to avoid or overcome the more common problems.

TINTING THE GROUND

Starting to paint on a glaring expanse of white canvas can be quite daunting, but even more important is the fact that a white surface is also 'dishonest', as it prevents you from judging the tones and colours correctly. There is very little pure white in nature, as white, like any other colour, is always modified by the light or shadow falling on it. Also, no colour exists in a particular way except in relation to the colours surrounding it. Thus, if you start a flower painting by putting down a bold brushstroke of pure cadmium red on a white canvas it will almost certainly be wrong, as the red you are seeing is actually given its quality by its relationship to the background, which may be neutral or even dark.

A method often used by artists is to tint the canvas in a neutral colour, usually a warm brown or grey, before starting the painting. This can be done either by mixing pigment in with the primer or by putting a wash of oil paint, such as raw umber, heavily diluted

ABOVE Although still-life and flower arrangements need not be elaborate, some thought is needed in the initial setting up if the foreground and background are not to become dull and featureless. Thumbnail sketches and polaroid photographs are useful aids in setting up an arrangement.

ABOVE The subject of this simple still-life was the artist's collection of assorted bottles, with the fruit used as a balance to the colours and texture of the glass. The lighting was entirely natural, simply the side-light coming in through a window, but the objects were set up with care so that the shadows fell pleasingly.

ABOVE These drawings show the different elements of a still-life arranged in a variety of ways. A symmetrical arrangement (LEFT) tends to be monotonous, but the arrangement, with the flat plane of the table angled away from the eye and a more varied grouping of the fruit (CENTRE), has considerably more visual interest. The drawing of the flower and fruit with draperies (RIGHT) provides more linear contrast and a busier background.

with turpentine, over the white ground. Acrylic paint can also be used for this since it dries much faster than oil paint, and you could buy a single tube just for this purpose. But remember that acrylic paint should not be used over an oil ground; oil can be used over acrylic, but acrylic cannot be used over oil.

PREPARATION

Always start with an adequate drawing or underpainting (see p. 24) in order to place the main design elements in the way you want them. Even a simple subject such as bowl of fruit can go very wrong if you fail to judge correctly the size of the fruit in relation to the bowl, or the bowl in relation to the table it is standing on. You may be impatient to start on the real business – the laying on of paint – but it does pay to take your time at this stage, for it will avoid a lot of frustration later.

KEEPING THE PICTURE MOVING

Try to avoid working in detail on one part of the painting at the expense of others. This approach can lead to a disjointed-looking painting, since you are more likely to tire of it half-way through. Generally, it is better to work on all parts of the canvas at once, so that you have a better idea of how one part relates to another in colour, tone and texture.

Some artists, such as the English painter Stanley Spencer (1891-1959), successfully reversed this process by starting with a careful and detailed pencil drawing and then painting area by area. There is theoretically nothing wrong with working in this way, but an inexperienced painter is unlikely to have the very clear vision of the finished painting which is required for such an approach.

In general, it is easiest to build up oil paint light over dark, as white is the most opaque colour; so keep to dark and middle tones in the early stages, working up gradually to the light and bright tones and colours. Always try to see the background as part of the painting, not just as an unimportant area; even a plain white wall has colours in it, and a totally flat background can be used as a shape, to form part of the composition. Avoid getting bogged down in detail too early; fine lines, such as the stems of flowers or small facial details in a portrait, are best left until last.

PROBLEM-SOLVING

Even paintings by professionals go wrong, but the beauty of oil paint is that they can so easily be altered. If you suddenly notice that your drawing is incorrect and that you have quite misunderstood a shape or colour, the best course is not to try to overpaint, but to scrape off the area with a palette knife and then repaint it. You may even decide to scrape down the whole painting and start more or less from scratch – this is often more satisfactory than trying to alter each individual area only to find that something is still not right. If you find that the surface of the painting has

Different artists have different methods of making sketches, according to their individual style and what particular aspect of a scene they want to note and remember. Some do detailed drawings in pen and ink or pen and wash, some make rough pencil sketches with colour notes, while others use oil paint, which is an excellent sketching medium because it can be applied so quickly.

become so overloaded with paint that you are just churning it up by continuing to add layers, there is a useful method, invented by a painting teacher called Henry Tonks and named *tonking* after him. This is done by laying a sheet of absorbent paper, such as newspaper, over the painting, rubbing it gently and removing it; this takes off the top layer of paint, and leaves you with something similar to a coloured under-painting.

USING REFERENCE MATERIAL

Painting is about looking at things – a good painter is constantly assessing objects and scenes with a view to translating them into paintings. This kind of analytical vision is largely a matter of habit and training – the more interested in painting you are the closer you will look and the more you will see – but few people have perfect visual memories, and for this reason artists often make visual references to use later on. Normally these take the form of sketches, and art students are always urged to carry sketchbooks at all times. Even a small, rough pencil sketch, sometimes with notes made about the quality of the light and the colours in the scene, can be turned into a complete landscape painting, or sometimes several sketches are made for different parts of a planned painting. For instance, a view of boats in a harbour might call for a rough overall sketch and some additional, more detailed drawings of individual boats.

It is certainly a good idea to carry a sketchbook – it is good practice if nothing else – but it takes some degree of skill to produce drawings which are good enough to provide all the information you may need and it takes experience to know what it is you actually want to make such 'notes' about. Photographs are now much used for this purpose, either as alternatives to sketches or as additions to them, and some artists even use picture postcards, either to suggest a theme for a painting or to remind them of some forgotten detail. One advantage of photographs is that they can record fleeting impressions, such as the sparkle of light on water, or a dramatic purple-grey sky just before a storm. They are also very useful for portrait painting, since few people are able to stay in one position long enough for a complete painting to be done.

However, photographs should be used with caution, and treated as aids to painting rather than models to copy. Straight copies of photographs, either of landscapes or people, can look very dull and dead, missing either the sparkle of the original scene or the character of the person. If you are using photographs for landscape painting, try to use several rather than just one, combining elements from each. Make a rough sketch from them and work from this rather than direct from the photographs. For portraits, they are generally used as a back-up, with the initial stages of the painting being done from life. The photographs can then be used for details, such as hands and clothing, with perhaps another live sitting for the final stage.

CHAPTER FIVE

OUTDOOR SUBJECTS

A LL the paintings on the following pages, although very different from one another, fall into the broad category of landscape, a term which can really be used to describe any subject that is located outside the walls of the studio or home, even if it is a painting of a building or a single tree. Outdoor subjects such as these need not actually be painted out of doors – indeed many fine landscapes are painted in a studio – but at some stage in the inspiration and evolution of a good landscape, close observation of the outdoor world is vital. Outdoor subjects thus present challenges and problems very different from those of still-lifes or portraits: the painter of landscapes cannot arrange the subject and lighting as he chooses; he can only decide on a scene and then select what he wants to show and what he will leave out. One painter, for instance, may be particularly interested in the way the light falls on a particular scene, or in the ever-changing shapes and colours of the clouds, while another will ignore these aspects in favour of shapes or flat patterns.

1

2

THIS painting was done from one of several sketches made on the spot. As you can see, the sketch is quite a rough one, but it provides all the necessary information as the subject is fairly simple and has been treated broadly, with little detail. When doing sketches specifically for paintings, rather than just sketching for its own sake, it is necessary to have some idea of how the finished painting will look, or you may find you have not made the 'notes' you will need. For example, if the artist had intended to treat the buildings in a much more precise and detailed way he probably would have needed to make more sketches of particular aspects of the building.

The composition has been somewhat altered in the painting, to make the path more central, and the gatepost has been exaggerated to create a sense of space between it and the farmhouse. The composition is simple and effective, with the curves of the lane and fence leading the eye in to the buildings, which are the focal point of the picture. This compositional device of a curve leading in to a central point is much used by landscape painters. The horizon is quite high, with the sky broken up into a rough triangle by the lines of the trees descending on each side of the building, and the sky itself echoes the line of trees on the right.

The painting was done very quickly, almost as it might have been if done on the spot, and the hardboard used as the support was first tinted with thinned acrylic paint in a shade of yellow ochre. This coloured ground has been allowed to show through in places in the finished painting, giving it a warm glow. This could not have been done on a white ground, as patches of white showing would be distracting and would throw all the colours off balance. Yellow ochre was chosen in this case because the painting was planned in shades of yellow and warm green, but for a different subject, a cool seascape, for example, a blue or grey ground might be used.

A charcoal underdrawing was done first to establish the main lines of the composition, after which thinned paint was used to block in the main areas. The paint became thicker as the painting progressed, with each area being worked on at the same time, so that the picture quickly began to emerge as a whole rather than as a series of bits – sky, foreground, middle distance and so on. When painting the buildings, the artist applied paint that was only roughly mixed on the palette, so that each brushstroke actually contained several colours. (Buildings can look flat and unreal if painted in too regular a way.) In the case of the trees, wet paint was applied on top of another still-wet layer (known as 'wet into wet'), thus modifying the colours and giving an impression of leafy texture. Quite a limited palette was used: three greens, three yellow-browns and one blue, plus black and white. Some artists disapprove of black and do not use it at all, but it is useful in landscape painting as it can be mixed with yellow to produce particularly rich greens.

TOP **1** A rough underdrawing was done with charcoal to establish the main lines. Pencil could have been used instead, or similar lines drawn with a brush and diluted paint, but pencil tends to mix with and muddy the paint, while a brush drawing takes a while to dry sufficiently to enable the first layer of paint to be put on. Charcoal can either be sprayed with fixative before the paint is applied or 'knocked back' by gently flicking with a rag to remove the surplus.

BELOW OPPOSITE **2** AND RIGHT **3** The main areas of colour were quickly blocked in with thinned paint and a medium-sized flat brush. This shape of brush should not be used for scrubbing on paint – a round one is best for this – but for more sweeping strokes.

BELOW **4** The picture began to emerge as a whole entity, as paint was applied loosely all over the surface at the same time. The colours used became slightly modified and defined as the painting progressed, but the basic balance of lights and darks was established at this stage.

3

4

5

6

ABOVE **5** AND RIGHT **6** The paint was used more thickly as the painting progressed, the steps at the side of the house being put in last with thick paint and a small brush. Details such as this, and the fence and gatepost, were left until the final stages, and add a crisp definition to the painting. Note how the yellow ground has been allowed to show through the loosely applied paint behind the house, echoing the golden colour of the path and giving a unity to the whole picture.

MATERIALS USED

- Support: hard-board 60.7 × 91.4 cm (24 × 36 in) primed with acrylic primer and tinted with acrylic yellow ochre
- Brushes: flats and brights, numbers 5, 7 and 10
- Colours: ivory black, titanium white, permanent green, sap green, chrome green, yellow ochre, raw sienna, burnt sienna and ultramarine

THE HEADLAND

THIS painting shows oil paint being used in a way more often associated with watercolour – in very thin washes. The paint was diluted so much that it was virtually transparent, and each wash was allowed to dry before the next was applied. Since oil paint mixed with a medium such as linseed oil can take a very long time to dry, turpentine was used in combination with the fast-drying alkyd medium, Liquin, which binds the pigment as well as thinning it; if turpentine had been used alone the paint would simply have dribbled down the surface.

If you look at the photograph of the scene you may see why the painter has chosen to work in this way; it is an extremely linear and angular subject, with the group of trees starkly defined against the sky and the very distinct lines of the cliffs converging at the bottom. Using paint thickly, in a more conventional manner, would have given an effect much softer than the one created in this picture.

Using oil paint in this way requires a rather deliberate approach – again much more like a watercolour technique – and the painting was begun with a very careful drawing in pencil. The colour scheme is deliberately sombre, with only six colours being used in all, but although the palette is so limited the colours are neither dull nor muddy, with the blue of the sea appearing quite bright in the context of the surrounding greys and greens. The sky, which the photograph shows as containing two distinct areas of tone, has been painted almost, but not quite, as a flat area, thus allowing the eye to concentrate on what is really important – the cliff itself. Painting the clouds as they actually appeared would have detracted from the effect rather than enhancing it. This kind of selection and rejection of elements is an important part of landscape painting.

The support chosen for the painting was a tall, narrow one, which suits the vertical emphasis of the subject. The surface of the canvas board shows through in places, and additional texture has been introduced by drawing with a pencil on top of the paint to define the lines of the cliffs, by scratching into the paint with a scalpel and by spattering thinned paint on to the board to suggest the appearance of the shingle beach.

1

ABOVE **1** A detailed and precise underdrawing was made with a sharp 3B pencil, after which the first diluted wash of olive green paint was carefully laid down on the area at the top of the cliff.

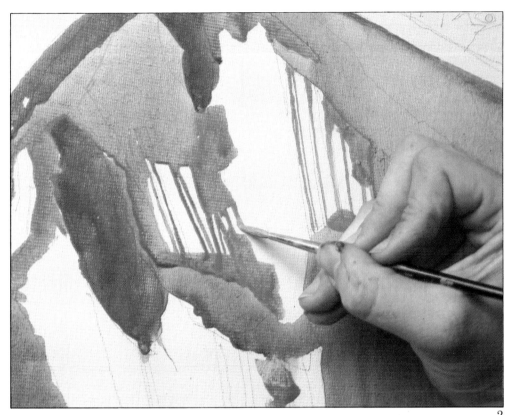

LEFT **2** More thinned paint was applied with a fine, soft brush, with areas of white being left uncovered. The lines were painted very carefully as this technique does not allow changes to be made. The pencil lines of the original drawing show through the thin paint, but this is not a disadvantage as in this case it adds to the effect.

BELOW RIGHT **4** The same pencil used for the original drawing was now used to draw into the paint to create the effect of the rocky fissures in the cliff face. As the paint is so thin the pencil lines are quite distinct; pencil marks in thicker paint would create indentations similar to those made by scratching with a knife.

2

4

LEFT **3** The trees and the wall below them were painted almost as flat areas with a fine sable brush. The painter could safely rest his hand on the painting while doing this detailed work as the paint in that area was already dry.

3

6

7

5

MATERIALS USED

- ● Support: fine-grained, ready-primed canvas board 76.2 × 50.8 cm (30 × 20 in)
- ● Brushes: number 6 sable and a number 6 soft synthetic as well as two flat bristle brushes, numbers 4 and 7
- ● Colours: titanium white, ivory black, cobalt blue, Payne's grey and yellow ochre, thinned with turpentine and Liquin

8

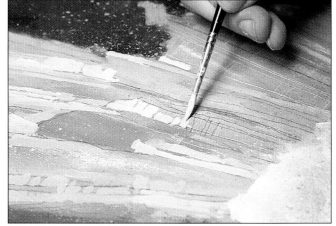

9

TOP LEFT **5** The support has now been fully covered, but areas of white have been left unpainted, to be treated in a different way in the final stages. The edges which separate each area of colour from the next are sharp and clearly defined at this stage; no blending has yet been done.

The detail (TOP RIGHT **6**) shows wet paint being applied to the dark area below the cliff. A crumpled tissue was used to create texture.

CENTRE RIGHT **7** To suggest the shingled beach, diluted paint was spattered on to the support with a stiff brush.

ABOVE LEFT **8** A scalpel was used to scratch into the paint, allowing fine lines of white to show through, a technique known as *sgraffito*.

ABOVE **9** This detail shows thicker paint in a mixture of white and Payne's grey being used for highlights. The paint was then blended with the finger.

THIS painting of a corner of a town garden, while falling within the general category of landscape, is actually more of an 'outdoor still-life', and it illustrates very well the statement made earlier that subjects for paintings can be found virtually anywhere. If you put two or three people into the same garden and told them to do a painting of some aspect of it, they would probably all choose quite different ones, depending on their particular interest and way of looking at things. This particular artist chose a subject which was literally under his feet, because he was attracted to the colours and patterns of the flagstones, the lines of the pot and stakes, and the texture of the foliage.

The painting was done out of doors in circumstances of some difficulty – the weather, and therefore the light, was changeable – and the painting had to be completed under an umbrella. A comparison of the finished painting with the photograph shows two things: firstly how the camera flattens out both colour and perspective, and secondly how various selections, rejections and adjustments have been made by the artist in order to make a satisfying composition. The foliage in the background, for instance, has been reduced to a few telling brushstrokes (if treated in more detail they could have detracted from the foreground); the colours of the flagstones have been altered and lightened to allow the foreground foliage to stand out, and the line of the stake has been altered so that it neither cuts the pot in half nor conflicts with the lines of the flagstones.

The painting had to be done quickly as the weather was so unpredictable, and the composition was established rapidly by blocking in the main areas in thinned paint. This degree of certainty about the way a finished painting should look is largely the result of years of observation and practice, but even professional artists sometimes change their minds, and as the painting progressed it became necessary to make some alterations. In the first detail you can see that the line of the stake ran exactly parallel to the line of the flagstone on the right, and led the eye of the viewer out of the picture, which should always be avoided. Thus the artist decided to change it, bringing the stake further over. Once this alteration was done, the paint was built up more thickly over the original thinned colour – in one place it was even smudged on with the fingers – and the paint surface in the finished picture is richly textured, particularly in the foreground area, where the brushstrokes have been used in a directional way to suggest individual leaves.

Paint surface is extremely important and plays a more vital part than many people realize in the finished effect of a painting; however well-chosen the colours and however good the drawing and composition may be, an unpleasant, slimy or churned-up paint surface will detract from the picture and may even make it impossible to see its virtues.

1

ABOVE **1** No drawing was done on the support as time was so limited, and the main areas were blocked in quickly with diluted paint. It became obvious very soon that the line of the stake would have to be changed, and this was done with masking tape, a useful addition to the painter's tools. Two parallel lines of tape were laid down to define the new line, and colour was applied rapidly right over it. The tape was then removed, leaving a clear, well-defined line.

3

LEFT Once the underpainting
was complete, the picture
was built up with thicker
paint, and more colours were
introduced. The photograph
(ABOVE) **3** shows a thick
mixture of yellow and white
being used for one of the
flagstones over an
underlayer of pinkish-brown.
Other flagstones were
painted in shades of blue and
muted grey.

Thick paint is being applied
(BELOW LEFT) **4** to define the
rim of the pot, and the foliage
is being built up (BELOW) **5**
with areas of scumbled paint
and thick brushstrokes of
yellow-green.

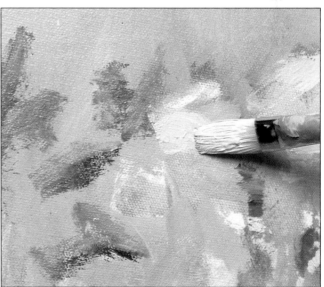

5

2

4

6

- Support: bought, ready-primed canvas 76.2 × 50.8 cm (30 × 20 in)
- Brushes: two flat hog's-hair, numbers 5 and 12, one number 12 soft synthetic
- Colours: titanium white, Payne's grey, burnt umber, raw umber, cobalt blue, cadmium red, Naples yellow, sap green, chrome green, viridian and chrome oxide

ABOVE **6** This detail of the foreground foliage illustrates the way in which paint and particular brushes can be used to create texture. The leaves here are suggested by short, curving brushstrokes, using thick paint over a still-wet layer beneath it so that the colour does not go on totally flat but is modified by the one beneath. No attempt has been made to define all the leaves, and some areas have been left quite loosely painted, adding to the spontaneous and free effect.

RIGHT **7** The artist uses his fingers to smudge in highlights.

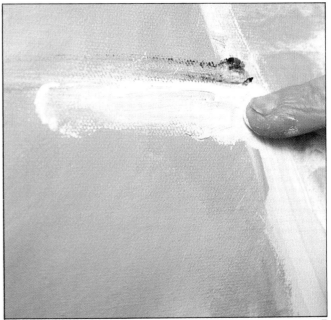

7

SEASCAPE OFF CRETE

THIS painting provides a contrast to that on page 51, as in this case the paint was used thickly on a very coarse-grained type of canvas called scrim. This is too flimsy to be stretched in the conventional way; so it was stuck down on a piece of hardboard with glue size.

The inspiration for the painting came from some photographs taken on holiday in Crete in blustery autumn weather. The painting set out to recapture the look of a harbour in late evening in far from tranquil weather, and the way the paint has been used gives an added drama and immediacy, so that it looks as though it could have actually been painted quickly on the spot. The particular photograph used as a reference is quite dull, but the painter has drawn on his own recollections for the colour scheme and composition.

The composition is a simple one, with the sea, the foreground and the background all being similar wedge shapes, relieved by repeated horizontal lines at irregular intervals. The buildings, little more than suggested shapes treated broadly and boldly, provide interest without in any way detracting from the focal point, which is the sea, shining with the reflected evening light.

Because scrim is such a coarse surface, it absorbs a good deal of the paint, which has to be applied thickly to cover it. Also, the paint covers such a surface unevenly, catching on some parts and sinking into others, effects which have been exploited in this painting to create an interesting, lively paint surface. Other effects have been used too: when painting the sea the artist squeezed white paint on to the support direct from the tube and then used yellow oil pastel in blobs on top of a layer of blue paint. The buildings were defined by drawing on to dry paint with a pencil, and some of the paint in the foreground area was wiped on with a rag. This is an excellent demonstration of the way in which different techniques and media can be combined to good effect. Some people feel inhibited about mixing media, believing that it is not 'proper' painting, but it is a mistake to feel restricted to the contents of your paint box – if you want to mix paint with sand and apply it with your fingers, and it seems to work, then do so.

ABOVE **1** Paint was applied thickly with a loaded brush and scrubbed into the surface. The colour used here was a mixture of white and cerulean blue, and the way in which the warm colour of the ground has been allowed to show through in places enhances it, whereas if the ground had been white it might have detracted from the effect of the blue.

BELOW **2** The basic composition of the picture – interlocking wedge shapes – can be seen very clearly at this stage, when the hills in the background have not yet been painted. The sea has been blocked in roughly, with a modified version of the same colour repeated in the sky.

3

4

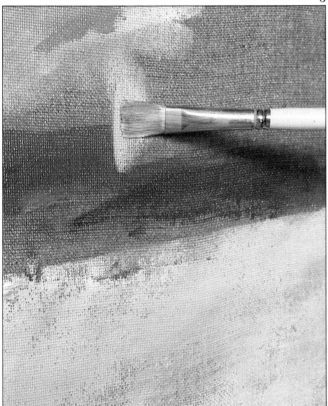

5

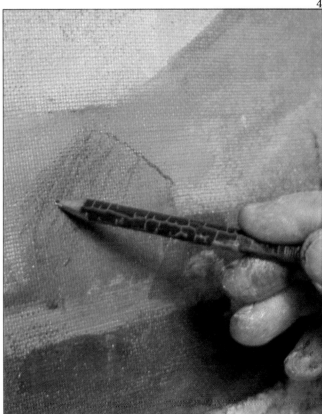

6

TOP LEFT **3** This detail shows yellow oil pastel being dabbed into the blue of the sea. This enhances the blue, since blue and yellow are complementary colours, as does the golden colour of the ground showing through.

TOP RIGHT **4** For the foreground, a mixture of black and raw umber was applied with a rag in broad sweeps. Here, too, the golden colour of the ground has been allowed to show through in places, modifying the darker layer of paint.

BELOW LEFT **5** The artist has allowed the colour of the support to show through the blue for the sky by applying the paint quite thinly.

ABOVE **6** In the detail a pencil is being used to redefine the buildings, which had become rather amorphous in shape. The pencil also modifies and darkens the colours beneath, in the same way as would applying a dark glaze to a lighter colour beneath.

7

MATERIALS USED

- Support: scrim-covered hardboard prepared with size but no other ground
- Brushes: number 12 flat only. Paint was also applied with a rag, and a yellow oil pastel was used on top of the paint in places.
- Colours: titanium white, ivory black, cerulean blue, Mars yellow, Naples yellow, burnt sienna, raw sienna, raw umber and ultramarine

ABOVE **7** The details show white paint being squeezed on to the support straight from the tube and then smeared with the fingers to blend it into the surrounding areas. The effect of direct application like this onto a coarse-grained support can clearly be seen in the finished painting (OPPOSITE).

AUTUMN MISTS

1

THIS painting, done on the spot on a grey autumn day, has a quiet harmony that captures the quality of both the type of landscape and the lighting. The light on days like this tends to have a flattening effect as there is no sunlight to cast shadows and create dramatic tonal contrasts, and distant objects look nearer for this reason – on a bright day this particular landscape would have had a totally different appearance. A grey sky and muted light can, however, provide a subtle but glowing range of colours, which have been fully exploited here; even the background was painted in pure, clear blues.

When painting out of doors, you may be tempted to ignore composition or think it is irrelevant – you are just 'painting what you see', after all. This is not really the case, as composition is always important; indeed you will find you are almost subconsciously composing as soon as you start to put a line on the canvas, by selecting some elements, exaggerating others, placing the horizon in a particular position, and so on. Here the composition is simple but effective, and was established at the outset by a sketchy line drawing. The curves of the path, dividing the foreground into a series of triangular sections, lead the eye to the strong horizontal line at the base of the tall tree, and from this point the main lines are the vertical ones of the trees reaching up to the sky. All the compositional elements are important: the tree on the left, going out of the frame at the top, is balanced by the one on the right, while the gentle diagonal at the base of the right-hand tree breaks up the broad horizontals elsewhere in the painting. An interesting exercise is to block out one part of a picture and note how it alters the whole balance. If, for instance, you block out the right-hand tree with your finger you will see that it results in an unbalanced, uneasy composition, where the eye has 'nowhere to go'.

The painting was done rapidly, the main areas being initially blocked in in shades of ochre and grey to establish the middle tones. Quite a small range of colours was used – one green, one blue, one bright yellow and four browns and ochres as well as white, as this subject did not require a great range. When working out of doors, it is a good idea to restrict your palette in this way, as otherwise you will be tempted to use too many colours, which can often spoil the unity of a painting.

LEFT **1** The broad outlines were drawn in with a fine sable brush and cobalt blue paint very much thinned. This type of painting does not require a detailed underdrawing, but it is essential to establish the main elements of the composition.

BELOW **2** As the effect of the painting depends on the relationship of the various broad masses of colour, the artist began to apply colour immediately, working all over the painting and placing the cool and warm middle tones in relation to one another. These, once established, provide a key against which the darker and brighter colours could be assessed.

3

ABOVE **3** The dark masses of the trees were painted next, followed by the relatively vivid green of the path (RIGHT) **4**, which was carefully related to the rich ochres of the rest of the foreground.

2

4

5

MATERIALS USED

- Support:
  fine-grained
  canvas 76 cm (30
  in) square, primed
  with animal-skin
  size and an oil
  ground
- Brushes: numbers
  2 to 8 in both flats
  and rounds, with
  a number 4 sable
  for the initial
  drawing and the
  final details
- Colours: titanium
  white, lemon
  yellow, yellow
  ochre, burnt
  sienna, raw
  umber, alizarin
  crimson, cobalt
  blue and viridian

ABOVE 5 The colours of the
background were modified
and 'cooled' to increase the
sense of space by making the
background appear to recede.

RIGHT Finally, a small sable
brush was used to paint the
details of the distant trees,
and the area at the base of
the right-hand tree was
darkened and defined.

GREEK VILLAGE

THIS painting was not done on the spot, but it is the result of much sketching and observation of a particular part of Greece, where the painter frequently spends holidays, and it captures the sun-soaked Mediterranean atmosphere very successfully. A series of drawings was made for the painting, together with colour notes and photographs, so that the composition and colour scheme could be planned and worked out from a wide range of reference material.

The painting shows a view from a window, a subject which often makes an interesting composition as the viewpoint is higher than the usual street-level one and tends to include more varied elements. In this case, the bird's-eye view of the rooftops provides an attractive contrast to the smaller rectangles of window frames and doors, and the straight lines of the buildings are balanced and enhanced by the curves of the trees, foliage-covered walls and the vegetable patch in the foreground, which lead the eye into the picture. The taut diagonals of the two rows of steps give an effect of movement and rhythm to the whole composition, which is full of interest and detail without being in any way fussy – even the small figures and the chairs and tubs on the balcony play a part in the scene, but are never allowed to dominate it. The balance of lights and darks is particularly important in this painting, as the artist wanted to capture the effect of the bright Mediterranean light, which creates strong tonal contrasts.

The painting was completed in one day. The paint was used quite thinly to begin with and built up to a thicker and richer surface as the work progressed (this is the classic oil painting method known as working 'fat over lean'). The quality of the brushstrokes is an integral part of the painting, and has been used in places to create textures and suggest forms, such as in the tree and the vegetable patch in the foreground.

The support was a fine-grained canvas, particularly suitable for a painting with areas of small detail and sharp straight lines, which would be more difficult to achieve on a very coarse canvas.

1

ABOVE **1** An underdrawing was done on the support using a small brush and cobalt blue paint heavily diluted with turpentine. Although the drawing itself was not very detailed, the painting had already been carefully planned, a necessary preliminary for a subject as complex as this one with its many contrasting shapes and tones. The artist then proceeded to block in the mid-tones, using thinned paint. Once these were established they provided a key for the lighter and darker tones. Another artist might have worked in a quite different way, doing a monochrome underpainting or charcoal drawing to establish the lights and darks first.

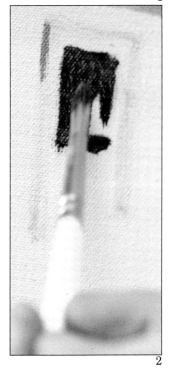

2

ABOVE **2** With the mid-tones established, together with the main lines of the drawing, the architectural details could be drawn in with dark paint.

RIGHT **5** The areas of foliage were then developed using viridian and raw umber for the dark tones and lemon yellow and cobalt blue for the lighter ones.

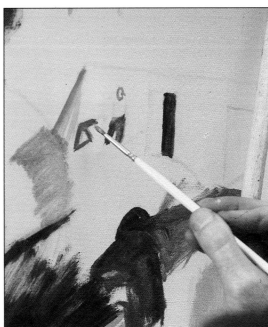

FAR LEFT **3** The artist rests his hand on a mahl stick to steady it while he draws a precise curve. The mahl stick is held in the non-painting hand with the cushioned end resting on a dry part of the canvas, or on the edge of it if the paint is wet. In a painting like this, careful drawing is essential – an inaccurately placed window frame or a crooked roofline would have a jarring effect, and spoil the overall harmony of the picture.

LEFT **4** A small round bristle brush was used to paint in the figures, giving detail without being over-meticulous.

3

4

5

6

MATERIALS USED

- Support: finely woven, ready-primed canvas 91 × 122 cm (36 × 48 in)
- Brushes: a selection of hog's-hair rounds ranging from numbers 6 to 10, with a number 4 sable used for the underdrawing
- Colours: titanium white, lemon yellow, Naples yellow, yellow ochre, burnt sienna, raw umber, cadmium red, alizarin crimson, cobalt blue, ultramarine, viridian and sap green. The painting mediums were linseed oil and turpentine

ABOVE **6** AND RIGHT At this stage, with all the main tones and colours established, the painting has emerged as a complete entity, whereas previously it had been a series of disparate elements. The feeling of warmth in the greys and shadow areas was achieved by mixing alizarin crimson into the cooler colours, while mixtures of white, yellow ochre, Naples yellow and burnt sienna were used for the warm browns and yellows. The colours were then modified and some areas developed and clarified, with the paint applied more thickly, and the final details such as the chairs on the balcony were added.

1

A PHOTOGRAPH provided the main reference for this painting, and in this case it was quite adequate, as the shapes are all quite bold and clearly defined. However, the photograph is noticeably dull in comparison with the painting, which reflects the artist's interests and ideas in a highly personal way. The paint has been used in a way which creates its own excitement and drama, enhancing the spikiness of the trees in the foreground and the angularity of the cypresses.

One of the most striking features of the painting is the sense of depth and recession which the artist has managed to convey through the use of aerial perspective (see page 31). The mountain in the background is painted in pale shades of grey with rather thin paint, while the foreground has much more tonal contrast, and the paint has been applied very boldly, with vigorous brushstrokes. Another device used to increase the feeling of space was to allow the main vertical shapes, the palm trees, to go out of the frame at the top and bottom of the picture, thus bringing them forward so that they exist on what is usually referred to as the 'picture plane', while the cypresses are clearly further back in space, in the middle distance.

The composition itself has departed from that in the photograph in seemingly minor, but actually vitally important, ways. The uncomfortable central placing of the two trees in the photograph has been changed to place the tall tree slightly further to the right, with the front tree to the left so that it balances the cypresses, while the tree at the far right has been brought just far enough into the picture for it to read as a tree rather than as an anonymous and rather dull shape. The detail of the middle distance has been considerably simplified, and the foliage at the top left given a more definite and pleasing overall shape. When working from photographs, always allow yourself to change the composition in whatever ways you feel will benefit the painting, even if you have taken the photograph specially with a particular painting in mind.

The paint itself has been applied in a way which creates an interesting surface, an important aspect of any painting. A variety of brushes was used to create a range of textural effects; thick paint was drawn into with the handle of a brush and scraped into with a knife (the technique known as *sgraffito*); and paint was flicked on with a painting knife to suggest foliage and the bark of the palm tree in the foreground. The palette itself was limited to only six colours plus white, an unusually small selection which has nevertheless produced a lively and varied colour scheme.

2

TOP LEFT **1** A rough pencil drawing was done on the canvas, after which the painting was begun with very diluted paint, each area being developed at the same time. Using paint thinned with turpentine and just a little linseed oil enabled the main shapes to be blocked in quite quickly. At this stage all the main areas had been blocked in and the canvas was completely covered, but the shapes were as yet treated only as broad, flat areas, and the foliage at the top righthand side had not been treated at all.

BELOW LEFT **2** The foliage was added when the paint for the sky was fairly dry, and a painting knife was used to flick on the paint. This gave an effect unlike any that could be achieved with a brush. It needs a sure hand to use a painting knife with confidence.

LEFT **3** The side of the painting knife was used to put on thick paint over a thinner layer below in a way that suggests the texture of the bark of the tree. Techniques such as this give a feeling of drama and excitement to a painting as well as creating areas of decorative texture. The thickly applied paint representing the trunk of the tall tree was drawn into with the handle of a brush (BELOW) **4** to suggest the spiky palm fronds.

3

4

- Support: ready-primed canvas board 76 × 61 cm (30 × 24 in)
- Brushes: bristle numbers 6 to 12 in both flats and rounds together with soft synthetic brushes for the finer details and a medium sized painting knife
- Colours: titanium white, ivory black, yellow ochre, alizarin crimson, raw umber, Prussian blue, Hooker's green, and the painting mediums were linseed oil and turpentine

5

6

LEFT **5** Paint was smudged on with the fingers and a small piece of rag in places where a soft effect was desired. The foliage was further defined by using a soft brush to work thick paint on top of the still-wet layer below. This is called 'working wet into wet'; the top layer will pick up some of the paint from the layer below, an effect which is exploited deliberately in paintings such as this.

LEFT **6** Texture was added to the tall tree and the mountain was defined with cool, pale greys to increase the sense of space (cool colours recede, while warm ones come forward). The cypress trees just in front of the mountain were added, being just suggested with one brushstroke each, working wet into wet so that the green was modified by being allowed to pick up some of the underlying grey.

DERELICT PIER

HIS subject is an ambitious one in which accuracy of drawing is particularly important; so several careful pen-and-ink studies were made before the painting was begun. (Rain came before the one illustrated was completed – hence the splashes.) The main lines of the pier, with its railings, seats, lamp-posts and buildings, were then drawn on to the support with charcoal. Note the diagonal line running through the tops of the lamp-posts, enabling the perspective to be plotted correctly. The drawing was tightened up and emphasized in places with thinned black paint and a small brush, after which the main colour areas were blocked in with grey, green and yellow ochre. The paint was initially used quite thinly, and applied with flat bristle brushes. Patches of the white support were allowed to show through in places, but the paint became thicker as the painting progressed, finally being built up into a rich scumbled surface which is extremely satisfying to the eye.

The composition is based on the relationship of the diagonal and vertical lines, with those of the railings leading in to the strong vertical formed by the outer edge of the building and then up to the opposing diagonal of the eave of the roof, which takes the eye back to the centre again. The curves – of the arches, lamp-posts and seat arms – act as a counterpoint to the taut, angular shapes.

The colour range is quite limited, but the colours nevertheless glow and shimmer with life, partly because of the way the paint has been physically applied and partly because of the way the colours themselves are juxtaposed. The building on the right, for example, could have been treated simply as an area of flat grey, but here rich colour has been introduced, with relatively bright patches of blue and yellow inside the arch, while blues and yellows recur on the front of the building, echoing the greens of the sea and the rich ochres of the pier top. Even the lamp-posts and seat arms have been warmed and enlivened by touches of muted yellow, which occur again in a stronger form in the area at the bottom of the railings, representing the reflected light from the sea.

ABOVE RIGHT **1** The main lines were drawn on to the support with willow charcoal. This was then dusted off and the lines were strengthened with thinned black paint applied with a fine synthetic brush. (RIGHT) **2** The lines of black have been overpainted very little, so that they are still visible as an integral part of the finished work. The artist worked from several sketches, but developed the painting further, so that it is not identical to any of them.

3

4

5

LEFT **3** AND BELOW **4** The sea was laid in first as a flat area of green, which was then given warmth and a feeling of light and movement by cross-hatching with brushstrokes of burnt sienna, white and red. There is a strong element of perspective in this painting, and the artist has used the railings against the large blocks of colour as a visual device to lead the eye of the viewer straight into the picture. The brushstrokes are very much part of the composition, and have been used in a directional way to strengthen the effect; those on the seat follow and accentuate the form (BOTTOM LEFT) **5** and those on the railings are worked round rather than along the forms. This has also helped to suggest the texture of the old metal.

- ● Support: smooth side of a piece of hardboard 60 × 75 cm (24 × 30 in), which had been sanded down before priming to remove the shine. Some of the sanding dust was left on the board to provide texture, and it was then primed with white gesso primer
- ● Brushes: Dalon synthetics, numbers 4 to 11, which the artist liked because they are less soft than nylon and give a good, fine point for detailed work
- ● Colours: titanium white, yellow ochre, light red, burnt sienna, ultramarine, sap green, cadmium green and lamp black, which is warmer than ivory black and gives deep, rich tones when mixed with ultramarine

ABOVE **6** The brushstrokes on the building are straight, following the vertical plane, and they have not been blended or worked together, so as to leave the paint surface clean and fresh. Although quite bright colours have been introduced here, they have been very carefully related to each other so that no one colour jumps forward or assumes undue importance. This is much more difficult than it looks.

RIGHT The final touches involved more work on the building and the addition of a scumbled texture over the whole painting, heightening the impression of old, crumbling metal.

CHAPTER SIX
INDOOR
SUBJECTS

ALL the paintings on the following pages, whether portraits, figure studies, still-lifes or flower paintings, have one thing in common – they have all been done under conditions which are in the control of the artists themselves. A portrait or still-life can be set up in whatever way you want – you can usually dictate what your model should wear and what the background will consist of, and you can decide what objects you want in your still-life or flower painting.

All this can be an advantage, as it means you need not feel rushed, but it can also be a disadvantage, as that very sense or urgency you feel when confronted with a subject that must be captured quickly can often produce a more interesting painting. One way of artificially creating this sense of urgency, and thus not allowing yourself to fall prey to the temptation of niggling away at a picture, is to set yourself a time limit. Take as long as you like over arranging and lighting a still-life or doing preliminary drawings for a portrait, but when you start the painting, decide that you will complete it in one or two sessions.

The only drawing for the portrait consisted of a few lines and outlines made with a number 3 bristle brush and thinned paint, **1** after which yellows, blues and warm red-browns were laid on, to be modified and defined later **2**. A rag was used to wipe off some paint from the forehead, cheeks and chin, **3** thus lightening the highlight areas. It was also used to smooth the previously roughly-applied paint in the background, removing some of the excess. **4** and **5** Shadows and highlights were built up in the face and hair,

PORTRAIT OF A MAN WITH A BEARD

THIS portrait was done quite quickly, in only two sessions, and has a fresh and spontaneous quality. Portraits often have to be completed in less time than the painter would perhaps consider ideal, since few sitters have either the time or the inclination to sit in one position for long periods of time. This particular portrait was actually done mainly from the photograph, which was freely adapted to convey the artist's own impression of the subject's colouring and character rather than being used as a 'copy' to be re-produced in paint. He could, of course, have taken much longer over the painting since he was not work-ing from a live model, but he preferred to simulate the conditions of working from life in order to avoid an overworked, tired painting. It is often a good idea to set yourself a time limit in this way, both with portraits and landscapes, and to try to rely on your original impressions of a face or scene rather than peering at a photograph and trying to find the exact shade or line you seem to see in it.

the paint being blended with a bristle brush and short, dabbing strokes. Because the painting was done on hardboard, which is not very absorbent, only turpentine was used as the medium at this stage, as the addition of oil would have made the paint too sloppy and caused it to dry too slowly.
6 Even so, by the sixth stage the paint had now become too thick and wet to work on satisfactorily, so the whole surface was blotted with newspaper, which removed the excess layer while still leaving a quite distinct image.

1

2

3

4

5

6

RIGHT **7** A piece of newspaper was applied, pressed lightly and lifted off, to remove some of the surplus paint. Blotting paper or towelling can also be used for this purpose.

7

BELOW **8** A rag was used to clean up the area on the face where the paint had become too thick.

8

The painting was begun with an underdrawing in neutral browns and blues, using thinned paint, after which layers of thicker paint were built up. The facial features were left quite undefined in the early stages, emerging only gradually from the broadly treated planes of the face, and the scarf was added later almost as an afterthought. All areas of the painting were worked on at the same time, the whole canvas being covered almost immediately, so that the relationship of the tones and colours could be assessed, balanced and altered where necessary. When the head was reasonably complete the artist decided to lighten the colours of the background, which also gave him an opportunity to correct and redefine the outline of the face. The tones and colours of the flesh were then adjusted in relation to the new background, and the relatively bright colours of the scarf blocked in to balance them. In oil painting, almost any such alterations can be made, but it is easier to work light over dark because white is the most opaque colour. If the painting had started with a light background, an attempt to change it to a dark one would probably have been unsatisfactory.

Because the painting was done quickly, there was no time to allow the paint to dry between stages, so a rag or a piece of newspaper was used from time to time to lightly blot the surface, removing the excess paint. A rag was also used to spread the paint in the background areas and to lighten the highlights in the early stages. Such techniques are particularly useful when working on a non-absorbent surface such as hardboard, which can easily become so overloaded with paint that successive layers stir it up and muddy it.

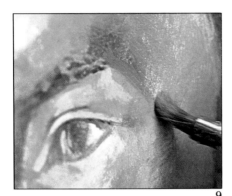

9

ABOVE **9** and RIGHT **10** Using a small brush, the artist begins to work on the more detailed areas of the painting to define the hitherto vague facial features.

- Support: primed hardboard 45 × 30 cm (18 × 12 in)
- Brushes: number 3 flat bristle and a number 5 round sable for the fine details
- Colours: titanium white, ivory black, cadmium yellow, yellow ochre, vandyke brown, cobalt blue, ultramarine, chrome oxide and vermilion, and the painting mediums were turpentine and linseed oil

10

11

12

ABOVE **11** and **12** When the painting was almost finished it became clear to the artist that it needed to be lightened in tone; so he overpainted the background, taking the opportunity to correct the outline of the face at the same time, and then adjusted the colours and tones of the flesh, blending the paint with light brushstrokes. He then altered the righthand side of the background again, so that from being the darker side it became the lighter one – almost white. The scarf, seen in the finished painting, was not originally planned as part of the composition, but the heightened tones and colours seemed to need a balance, and it was added as a final touch. This portrait provides an excellent example of the way in which oil paintings can be altered again and again without loss of quality.

OPPOSITE Earlier stages involved covering the face with a reddish glaze, giving a warmth and glow to the flesh. The effect of this is clearly visible in both the detail of the brow area and in the finished painting.

ANITA IN MINIATURE

THIS is a particularly interesting portrait because, although the treatment is bold and free, with clearly visible brushstrokes, the painting is very small, almost the same size as reproduced here. As this artist usually works on quite a large scale, producing a portrait as small as this presented something of a challenge, but she has met it with considerable success. It can be rather disturbing suddenly to change scale from a size which seems natural to one which does not, and this sometimes results in a different style being used, which the painter is not really at home with. In this case, however, the artist has managed to reduce the scale without detriment to her normal colourful and bold style.

As the portrait had to be completed quickly, a piece of cardboard was used for mixing the colours instead of the conventional palette, which had the effect of absorbing some of the oil and letting the paint dry more rapidly. Turpentine, used as the medium, also speeded the drying and provided a matt surface, which this artist prefers. Sable brushes were used in place of the more usual bristle ones in order to apply the paint carefully in small blocks, which were then blended lightly into one another. The colours have been considerably heightened and exaggerated, with the background appearing as an area of clear, bright blue and the face itself composed of separate, though related, patches of pure colour. This type of colour is known as high key, as opposed to low key, where all the colours are more sombre. An artist sometimes makes a deliberate choice to paint a particular subject in a particular key, but often it is more or less an instinctive thing. Some artists always paint in a low key, even when the subject is colourful, and others automatically heighten all the colours. The brightness of this painting was deliberate, and is enhanced by the use of a pure white support, with no underpainting; the white is reflected back through the paint, giving the colours extra sparkle and translucency.

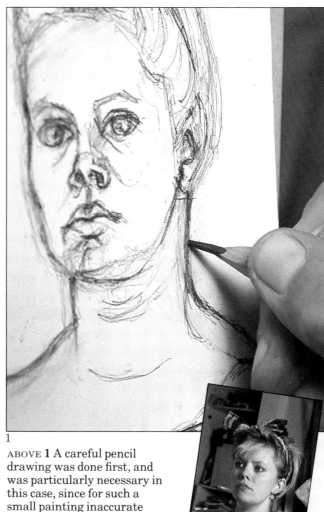

1

ABOVE **1** A careful pencil drawing was done first, and was particularly necessary in this case, since for such a small painting inaccurate drawing or a clumsy placing of the head in relation to the background could be disastrous. As you can see by comparing the finished painting with the photograph, the area of the pink blouse has been reduced to just two small triangles; these balance the bright colours of the flesh and lips. The area of background is greater on the left side of the face than the right, thus avoiding monotony. Even in a head-only portrait compositon this is important and should be planned at the outset.

OPPOSITE **2** The pencil lines, which were quite dense, were rubbed down lightly with a rag before the paint was applied, to prevent the graphite dust mixing with and muddying the colours.

The first flesh tints, mixed from a wide variety of pure colours, were then applied, and the planes of light and shade began to emerge. Note how the strip of cool, pale colour down the side of the face – the reflected light visible in the photograph – prevents the similar tones of the background and the shadow area of the face from merging together. The area of blue was blocked in at an early stage so that the flesh tones could be related to the colour of the background, and the artist put dabs of colour and tone on to the unpainted side of the face to help offset the effect of the glaring white canvas.

RIGHT **3** AND BELOW **4** The areas of pale flesh tones, mainly mixed from red, yellow ochre and white are being applied to the neck and taken right up to the background. The paint was used fairly thickly so that it was opaque enough to cover the blue and give a clearly defined line. The bright pink area around the eye, applied with a small brush, reflects the bright rose of the blouse, as does the shadow under the chin.

3

RIGHT **5** The only parts left to be painted at this stage were the lips, the headscarf and the hair over the forehead, with the hair being treated quite broadly and with little detail.

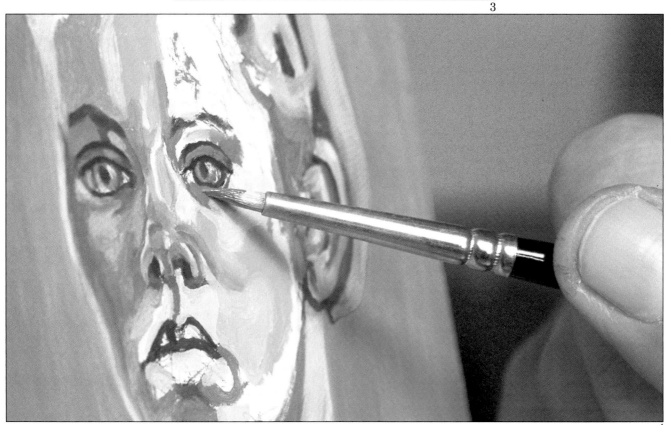

4

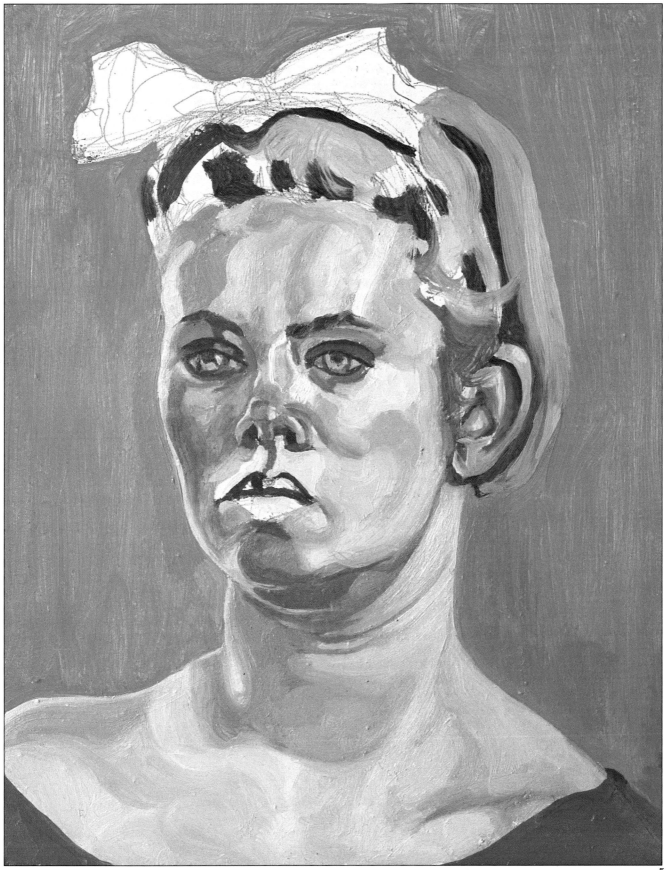

RIGHT **6** The lips were painted next, and then the patterned scarf, in which each colour was carefully related to those in the face itself. When painting in such a high colour key, much care and thought is needed to relate the colours to each other, otherwise there will be unpleasant discords. The hair was then modified in colour so as to emphasize the bright colours of the scarf, and the fringe was defined with free, bold brushstrokes.

OPPOSITE Note how the whole portrait is 'lifted' by the patterned scarf and red lips – all the colours suddenly appear brighter and the entire image is crisper.

MATERIALS USED

● Support: primed hardboard about 15.5 × 12.5 cm (6 × 5 in)
● Brushes: round sable numbers 2, 3, 5 and 8, and the paint was thinned with turpentine alone
● Colours: titanium white, yellow ochre, Naples yellow, cadmium yellow, cadmium red, alizarin crimson, Rowney rose, violet, cobalt blue, ultramarine, cerulean blue and terre verte

6

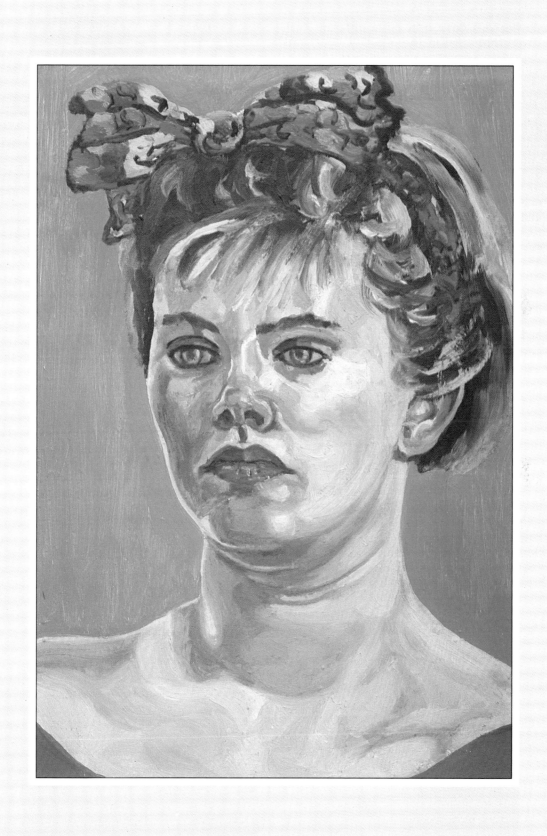

GIRL IN PROFILE

THIS painting was done in a quite different technique from that used in the other two portraits; the paint here is used very thinly, so that the early stages resemble a watercolour. The colours are also much less vivid, the emphasis being on the contrasts of lights and darks.

A profile is a difficult subject, and profile portraits are not often done, the three-quarter view being the preferred one. This is partly because a profile can look rather boring and unsubtle, and partly because, of course, it does not allow the eyes, the usual focal point of a portrait, to show. Here, an interesting composition has been made by placing the head to one side so that the back and top are cut off, with the line of the hair creating a bold curve to break up what would otherwise have been a stark vertical at the edge of the canvas. The artist has given the space around the head an importance of its own by painting it flat and allowing it to occupy almost as much of the total picture area as the profile itself. The picture can thus be seen as two interlocking areas (this is particularly noticeable if you look at it upside down). This concept is sometimes called 'negative space', and can form a very important part in a composition, the 'negative' space being used to balance the 'positive' image.

The luminous quality of the shadow area of the face has been achieved by *glazing,* a technique of applying thinned paint in layers, one over the other. Glazing is a slow process, as each layer must be dry before the next is applied, but it is a particularly suitable technique for painting flesh, and was much used by the early painters in oil, such as Jan van Eyck. In this case, linseed oil with a very little turpentine was used to thin the paint for the glazes, but linseed oil is not actually the best medium for this technique. A special alkyd medium called Liquin is now manufactured and sold specifically for the purpose; it dries fast and binds the pigment so that the glaze, however thin, will stay where it is put, instead of dribbling down the surface of the support, as can happen with linseed oil.

LEFT **1** A simple but accurate line drawing was done of the profile, including indications of the shapes of the highlights on the cheekbone, nose and chin. The background area was then blocked in with a thin wash of grey paint applied with a number 4 flat bristle brush, and a wash of burnt umber was used for the shadow under the brow.

TOP RIGHT **2** The warm tones were established next, using a mixture of yellow ochre and white for the hair, and burnt umber, cadmium red and titanium white for the face.

ABOVE **3** The shadows around the eyes were painted with a smaller bristle brush, a number 2, each separate block of colour and tone being carefully delineated.

BELOW **4** The skin tones were developed more fully by applying diluted paint in very thin glazes which allow light to bounce off the canvas and back through the colours. This produces a luminous glow which cannot be achieved with opaque paint. Glazes can also be laid over a layer of thick, impasted paint to modify the underlying colour, a method used by both Rembrandt and Turner. Here, however, all the layers are thin; in the detail the texture of the canvas is quite clearly visible through the paint.

OPPOSITE As a final touch, fine strands of hair were added above the forehead and beside the cheek and chin, using a very fine brush and a mixture of titanium white and yellow ochre. Note how these few lines 'lift' the whole portrait, hinting at the quality of the fine hair and breaking up the large area of background while allowing it still to exist as a definite shape.

MATERIALS USED

- Support: small, fine-grained canvas board bought ready-primed, 37.5 × 30 cm (15 × 12 in)
- Brushes: flat bristle, with a small sable for the fine lines
- Colours: titanium white, ivory black, burnt sienna, burnt umber, yellow ochre, cadmium red medium, scarlet lake and ultramarine. The mediums were linseed oil and turpentine, with a much higher proportion of linseed oil used for the glazing

4

1

2

3

NUDE AND SUNLIGHT

IGURE painting, like portraiture, presents a great many problems, not the least being that of getting the drawing right. When faced with a complex subject such as this, you will find your task much easier if you make the most important decisions *before* you start work. First, decide which aspect of the subject you are actually interested in and then how you intend to treat it. Some artists will be most concerned with attempting to convey the sheer beauty of the human body and the marvellous and varied colours of flesh and hair, while others will be interested in the pattern that might be created by a figure against a background. Another artist might not be concerned with either colour or pattern, and will aim at conveying the dynamic and sculptural qualities of the body, and the way the various planes and shapes relate to one another. Part of this decision will, of course, depend on the model. Some artists' models are beautiful, and cry out to be painted simply as lovely natural forms, while others are less conventionally beautiful but are interesting to a painter in more subtle ways.

This painting shows one particular approach to the subject; here the artist's main interest was not in the body as such, or the colours of the flesh, but in the interplay of shapes and the relationship of lights and darks. While being quite distinctly a 'figure painting', it is quite abstract in feeling, with the figure seen as just one element in the composition. The shadows – both that cast by the figure on the background and that cast on the figure by the window bars – have been given considerable importance, as have the shapes in the background. Another artist, whose preoccupations were different, might have played down these elements, or even excluded some of them, softening the shadows and painting the background as an area of space.

The painting was begun with a careful drawing in pencil, in which the figure was drawn in outline. This is not a method recommended for a beginner, as a drawing such as this, although it looks simple, is the result of years of practice and observation. But a good underdrawing in pencil, charcoal or thinned paint is important in a complicated subject, as without it you will find yourself having to make endless corrections,

ABOVE LEFT **1** A careful drawing was made with a sharp HB pencil, after which the shadow areas and outlines were strengthened with thinned black paint applied with a small brush. It is important to start with a good underdrawing or underpainting to establish the composition to your satisfaction. At this stage, you need to have a firm idea about how much of the figure you want to show, how it should be placed in relation to the background, and so on. It can also be helpful to make some small thumbnail sketches first, before you start to draw on the canvas, as this is often the best way of working out a composition. **2** As the prime concern of the artist was the relationship of light and dark shapes, he painted in the dark areas first so that they provided a 'key' for the rest of the painting, leaving the lighter and brighter areas white at this stage. **3** The shadow areas across the body were painted (with burnt sienna) before the flesh was blocked in, and all the other areas were then related to these.

which may ruin the composition you were aiming at as well as giving you a clogged and overworked paint surface.

The dark side of the figure was then outlined more distinctly with black paint and a small brush, after which the shadow across the body was painted carefully with burnt sienna. The flesh tones were related to this before the red-brown background, related in turn to the flesh tones, was blocked in. Each area of the painting was worked on more or less separately, the yellow patch of sunlight and the bright red patch in the foreground being added at a late stage. This artist had a very accurate idea of how the finished painting would look and so the method has been successful, but an inexperienced painter would find it hard to work in this way, as it would be difficult to assess the colour of the flesh, and the degree of tonal contrast within the body area, against the harsh white of the background.

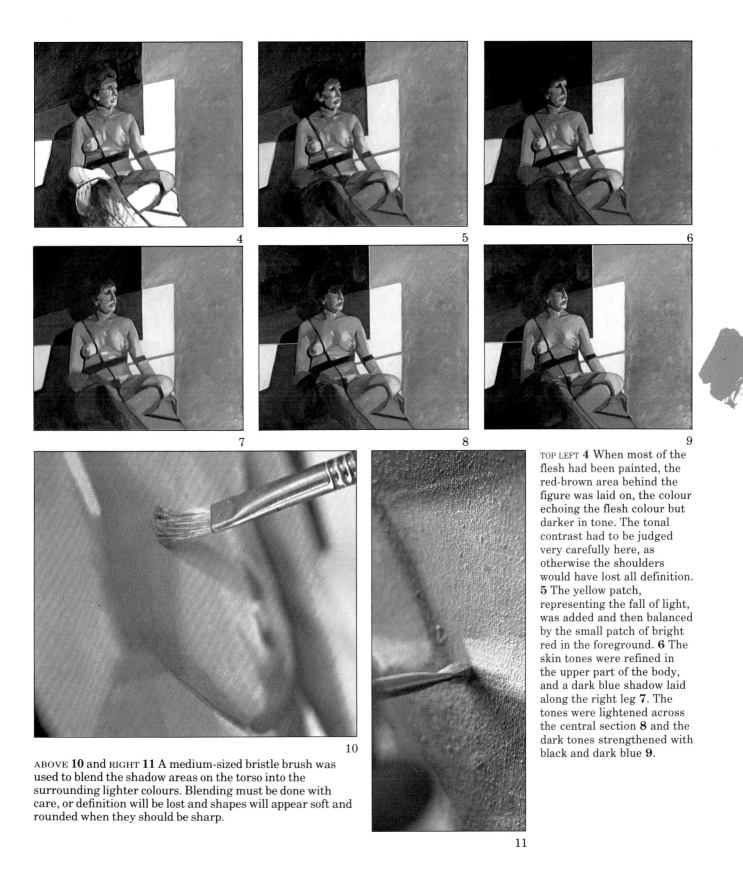

4

5

6

7

8

9

10

11

ABOVE **10** and RIGHT **11** A medium-sized bristle brush was used to blend the shadow areas on the torso into the surrounding lighter colours. Blending must be done with care, or definition will be lost and shapes will appear soft and rounded when they should be sharp.

TOP LEFT **4** When most of the flesh had been painted, the red-brown area behind the figure was laid on, the colour echoing the flesh colour but darker in tone. The tonal contrast had to be judged very carefully here, as otherwise the shoulders would have lost all definition. **5** The yellow patch, representing the fall of light, was added and then balanced by the small patch of bright red in the foreground. **6** The skin tones were refined in the upper part of the body, and a dark blue shadow laid along the right leg **7**. The tones were lightened across the central section **8** and the dark tones strengthened with black and dark blue **9**.

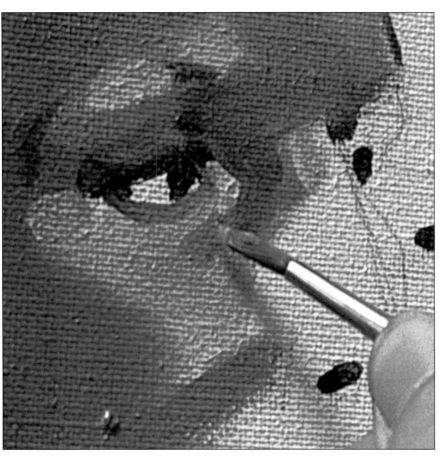

- Support: cotton duck, stretched and primed, 90 × 76 cm (36 × 20 in)
- Brushes: two number 6 bristle flats, a number 6 round sable and a 2.5-cm (1-in) housepainter's brush for the background areas
- Colours: ivory black, titanium white, burnt sienna, raw sienna, raw umber, burnt umber, cadmium yellow, yellow ochre, ultramarine and vermilion. The medium was turpentine alone

ABOVE AND RIGHT The highlight areas and facial details were painted with a fine sable brush and a mid- tone was blended between the shadow and highlight areas. Facial details should be left to a late stage in a figure painting, when you are quite sure no alterations have to be made to the drawing and composition.

DIANA

THIS full-length portrait, or 'clothed figure study', was done partly from life and partly from the photograph. A comparison of the finished painting with the photograph is particularly interesting in this case as it shows how much the artist has simplified the subject in order to deal with what he personally found interesting – the figure itself and the richly glowing blues, violets and orangey-browns. Another artist painting the same subject might have treated it in a quite different way, perhaps including the view through the window, the pattern on the sitter's blouse, and the details on the cupboard, thus making a much busier composition, but here all the emphasis is on the figure itself, with the background areas treated very sketchily so that they do not compete with the main image.

Colour is the dominant aspect of this painting, and the artist has started to place the colours immediately, with only the minimum of underdrawing, using thinned paint in shades of violet and cobalt blue. With the vivid violet of the blouse established, the canvas was then completely covered with thin paint, the colour of the background being more or less that which appears in the finished painting. The background paint was left thin, but the figure itself was built up in thicker paint, and in places the *sgraffito* technique – drawing or scratching into the paint with a knife or brush handle – was used to remove paint from the highlight areas, allowing the white ground to show through.

The composition is a simple one, as befits the subject, with the figure itself placed centrally but made to appear less symmetrical by the placing of the unequal shapes on left and right – the window and cupboard. The image has been given movement and interest by the diagonals formed by the bottom of the window frame, the skirting board and the top and bottom of the cupboard, the latter two leading the eye in to the figure. The angles literally point to the figure so that its central position, which might have resulted in an unfocused or flat painting, is quite acceptable. The bottom corner of the window and the top corner of the cupboard form a triangle with the light reflected from the top of the jeans, providing depth. If the background had been on a flat plane with the skirting board as a horizontal the effect might have been monotonous.

1

FAR LEFT **1** The artist began to lay the colour on immediately, using paint very much diluted with turpentine so that it would dry quickly. Marking in the vertical and horizontal lines for the cupboard and background helped him to position the figure correctly.

LEFT **2** As soon as the whole canvas was covered with paint the artist began to work on the highlights to define and sharpen the forms.

2

RIGHT **3** Here a painting knife is being used to scrape back to the white surface of the canvas.

BELOW RIGHT **4** The arm has now been more fully modelled, with a dark line of shadow down the outside, and a brush handle is being used to draw into it. Some of the purple colour of the blouse has been repeated on the inside of the arm and then scraped away, leaving just enough to suggest the reflected colour in the shadow.

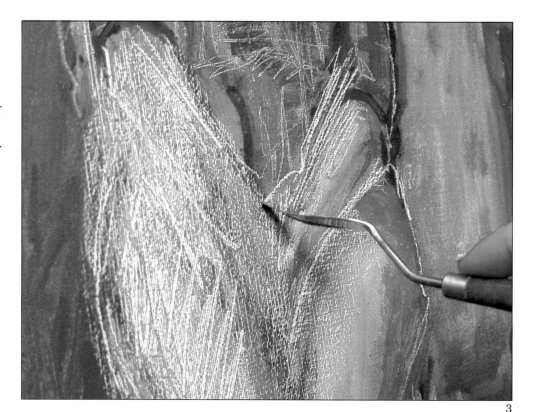

3

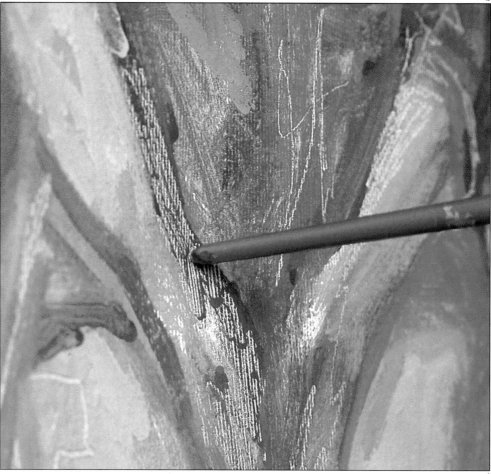

4

5

LEFT **5** The colour of the blouse and jeans is vitally important to this painting, and the artist has chosen to simplify by ignoring the pattern on the blouse (visible in the photograph) so that it stands as an area of vibrant blue. However, it was not applied as just one colour; mid and dark purple were used for the shadow areas and bright blue for the highlights.

BELOW LEFT **6** Shadows nearly always have a colour of their own rather than being simply a darker shade of the highlight colour.

6

RIGHT **7** The face, like the clothing, has been built up in thick paint, freely but carefully applied so that the features are distinct but not over-meticulous. Little blending has been done, but because the artist is working wet into wet the colours are modified by the process of laying one on top of another. The line of blue on the right, representing the reflection from the blouse, has been left quite distinct.

OPPOSITE The finished painting shows how the figure has been given solidity by the use of thick paint and strong tonal contrasts, while the background has been left as areas of quite thin and transparent paint. Although there is little detail in the background, it is not flat and uninteresting; different colours have been used to echo and harmonize with those of the figure itself.

MATERIALS USED

- Support: bought, ready-primed canvas 61 × 46 cm (24 × 18 in)
- Brushes: a selection of bristle and synthetic, a flat bristle being used for the background and small, round synthetics for the face and details of the clothing
- Colours: titanium white, cobalt blue, cerulean blue, cobalt violet, light red, alizarin crimson, yellow ochre, burnt sienna and raw umber. No medium was used except in the early stages, where the paint was thinned with turpentine

7

TEA-CADDY ON A WINDOW SILL

THIS small, quietly harmonious painting, with its limited range of colours and simple subject, provides a contrast with the one on page 112, where the approach is quite different. It also illustrates the way in which colour and composition can be used quite deliberately to create mood: here there are no jarring compositional elements and no bright or discordant colours, but the effect is far from dull – just pleasantly peaceful.

Most people have one or two items about their homes that seem to suggest an idea for a painting, and in this case the artist was attracted to the swelling curves of the pot and its decorative motif. In order to highlight these qualities, he chose to make the composition a geometric one, in which the horizontals and verticals of the window frame and shutter act as a foil for the curved and rounded shapes. The composition is very carefully balanced, with the strip of blue-grey in the foreground just slightly narrower than the window sill above, and the rectangle on the right large enough to be 'read' as the view through the window but not so large as to dominate the painting. The verticals of the window frame have been carefully planned so that they do not interfere with the dominant shapes of the pot and bowl, and the slanting shadows on the left, which appear in the photograph as very distinct areas of tone, are merely hinted at by a very slightly darker colour at the top left.

The paint has been applied very carefully and meticulously, with sable brushes used to build up thin layers, and the support, a fine-grained canvas, was chosen as particularly suitable for this kind of painting. For a picture like this it is important that the straight lines should really be straight – an accidentally slanting vertical line, for example, would provide just the jarring element the artist has been at pains to avoid – so masking tape was used to aid the process. At one time such techniques were considered rather 'mechanical', and frowned upon, but it is extremely difficult to draw a straight line freehand, let alone paint one with a brush, and there is no reason why masking tape or rulers should not be used.

The range of colours used was deliberately very small – just two blues, a green, grey, black and yellow. It can be a useful discipline to limit your colours in this way, choosing just one or two colours and their complementaries (blue and yellow, as here, or red and green) plus greys and browns. It may cut down your choices, but this can also be an advantage as you will have fewer to make, and you may find that your painting achieves a harmony and unity that it might not have had with a whole range of colours at your disposal. It will also teach you far more about mixing colours than reading a whole book on the subject.

1

2

TOP **1** AND ABOVE **2** As the composition is so simple, no underdrawing was necessary. Instead, the main elements were quickly blocked in, using thin paint and a sable brush, in more or less the colours that appear in the finished painting.

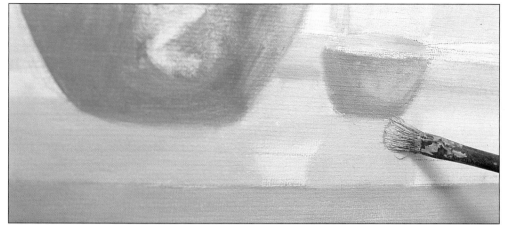

3

LEFT 3 At this stage a bristle brush was used, as the paint was rather thicker (though still relatively thin). The blue of the pot was built up using a mixture of ultramarine and white, with white and Payne's grey used for the window sill. Payne's grey is a useful and versatile colour, with a slight mauvish tinge. Here it appears quite warm in relation to the deep blue. A mixture of black and white would have given a much less 'alive' quality.

4

LEFT 4 Masking tape was applied to the line which separates the edge of the window frame from the little rectangle of landscape beyond. This allowed the paint to be applied quite freely on the window-frame area.

BELOW LEFT 5 The tape was then lifted off, leaving a clean, straight edge. To use this method successfully the paint must be quite thin and at least semi-dry; otherwise the tape, when lifted off, will take the top layer of paint with it.

5

RIGHT **6** AND BELOW RIGHT **7**
At this stage, several thin layers of paint had been built up one over the other, but the details, which give a crisp definition to the finished painting, had not been added. In the detail (RIGHT) a small sable brush is being used to paint the fine lines and small cracks at the bottom of the shutter. If you look at the finished painting you will see that this delicate diagonal line is actually vital to the composition, leading the eye to the pot and bowl, which are the focal points.

OPPOSITE The brickwork was painted in a mixture of Payne's grey, yellow ochre and white, with viridian and white used for the mini-landscape through the window. Great care must be taken with an area such as this; if the tonal contrast were too great or the colours too bright the landscape would 'jump' forward, assuming too much visual importance and conflicting with the foreground. Viridian, being a cool, rather blue green, is useful for receding backgrounds.

MATERIALS USED

- Support: small, ready-primed, fine-grained canvas only 30.5 × 25.4 cm (12 × 10 in)
- Brushes: small sable and a number 8 round bristle
- Colours: titanium white, ivory black, Payne's grey, yellow ochre, cadmium yellow pale, viridian, ultramarine and Prussian blue

6

7

STILL-LIFE WITH WATERMELON

THIS still-life, while very different from the one shown on page 105 in its use of thick paint and bright colours, has a rather similar atmosphere of simple, quiet harmony. One of the most difficult aspects of still-life painting is deciding on the initial arrangement; it is only too easy to buy up a greengrocer's entire stock and then find yourself unable to arrive at a satisfactory way of arranging the different elements, or to rush around the house collecting bowls, plates and vases which, when placed together, don't seem to add up to anything you want to paint. Here, as can be seen in the photograph, the artist has chosen a simple arrangement, but one in which the shapes are balanced very carefully.

The composition of the painting is based on a triangle with the point at the top left, and the circular shapes of the plate and half melon intersecting at different angles. The smaller piece of melon echoes the triangle, while the strawberries in the foreground both break up the area of white space and give a feeling of solidity by establishing the plane on which they rest. If you mask them out with your finger you can see how drastically the composition would be weakened and how the main elements would then appear to float in space. The artist has chosen to ignore the line created by the back edge of the table, treating the table top and background as a flat area of 'negative space'; treating the table and wall as separate planes would have detracted from the composition and reduced the importance of the main shapes, which appear almost as though 'carved out' of the space.

A variety of painting techniques has been used to create an interesting paint surface, the first step being a coloured underpainting in very washy paint, after which areas were built up and defined in much thicker paint. The watermelon was given texture by spattering paint on to the surface from a stiff-haired brush; a pencil was used to draw into the fruit; and the white background is very slightly textured with just-visible brushstrokes.

RIGHT **1** A faint underdrawing was done with pencil to position the main elements of the composition, which were then blocked in with heavily-diluted paint.

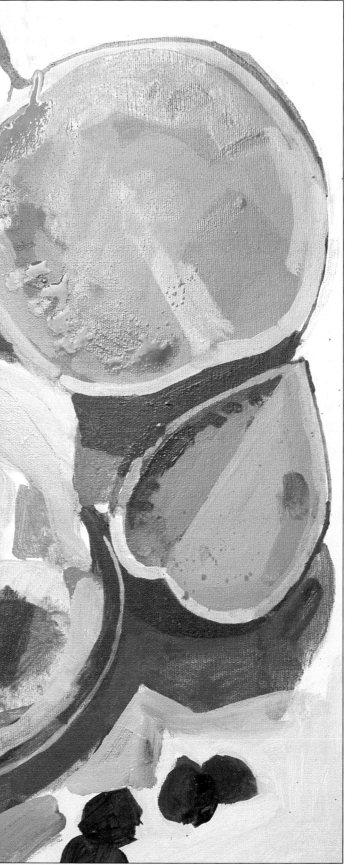

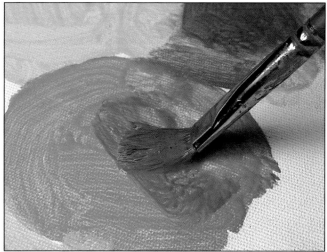

2

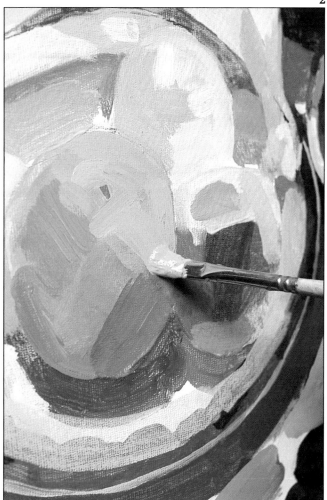

3

TOP RIGHT **2** AND ABOVE **3** As soon as the underpainting was dry the artist began to define the separate pieces of fruit, building up the highlights in thick, juicy paint.

The artist then drew into the dry paint with a pencil, OPPOSITE **4** a technique which has a dual function in this case as it gives texture and visual interest to the fruit as well as taking down the tones without the necessity for overpainting.

LEFT **5** Until now the strawberries had been left as just bold brushstrokes of dark red, but here the artist has given them shape and form, painting the highlights in a light pink and the leaves and stems in bright green.

BELOW **6** The final touch was to modify the shapes by working back into them with white paint and to paint the shadows in blue-grey, clearly outlined on the white background and establishing the plane of the table top.

5

6

RIGHT **7** The watermelon required special treatment, as the texture is an important element of the painting. The artist has chosen a technique he frequently uses – spattering paint from a stiff-haired brush (a toothbrush is often used for this purpose). In order not to splash paint on the rest of the painting he has cut a mask from newspaper, leaving exposed only those areas to be textured. Two tones were used for the spattering, one lighter and one darker than the mid-tone of the underpainting, the paler one echoing the highlights on the strawberries.

BELOW RIGHT **8** The tones and colours were chosen with great care as they had to be light or dark enough to show up, but not so sharply contrasting as to 'jump' off the surface.

7

OPPOSITE In the finished painting the pencil drawing is still just visible on the banana and the apple, and the same technique has been used on the smaller piece of watermelon and on small areas of the shadow under it and the plate. It is touches such as these that give a painting that special 'something', creating extra interest and liveliness; but they should never be allowed to become too important – special techniques are tools, not ends in themselves.

MATERIALS USED

- Support: bought, ready-primed canvas board 51 × 40 cm (20 × 16 in)
- Brushes: number 12 white bristle and a number 4 hog's hair, with a 2.5-cm (1-in) housepainting brush used for the spattering
- Colours: titanium white, yellow ochre, vermilion, cadmium red, cadmium yellow, sap green, cobalt blue and Payne's grey, a range consisting almost entirely of good, strong primaries

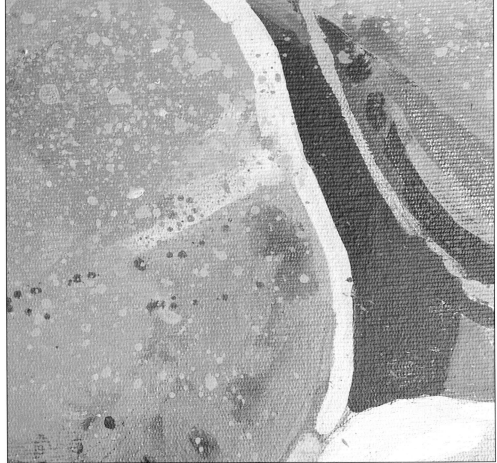

8

FLOWERS ON A WINDOW SILL

Aᴌᴛʜᴏᴜɢʜ you would not think it from looking at the painting, this is actually a very difficult subject, presenting a good many problems. The main one is how to deal with the picture planes – the foreground and the space beyond it – in such a way as to create a feeling of space and recession while still retaining the unity of composition which is the hallmark of a successful painting. If the background is allowed to recede too much it will run the risk of becoming dull, but if it comes forward too much it will overwhelm the foreground. The foreground itself has to be given much thought too; otherwise the vase of flowers, which is the focal point, could assume too little importance, and not be strong enough to balance the landscape beyond. Here the artist has solved all the problems very cleverly; the foreground has been given extra importance and interest by the inclusion of the window blind and curtain on one side and the top of a chair on the other, so that an interesting composition exists even without the buildings in the background. The hill village and mountains beyond have been allowed to recede just a little so that they read as a separate and more distant picture plane, but they are still very definitely part of the painting, a landscape in themselves, neatly framed by the verticals of the window. The artist has been lucky, as the hilly terrain has provided a landscape that fits the window; a flatter view would have necessitated a quite different treatment in terms of composition.

The colours used for the landscape echo the deep blues of the vase and cushion, but are slightly nearer one another in tone so that they do not come forward and fight with the foreground. As he worked, the artist had frequently to half-close his eyes, which makes it easier to assess tonal contrasts, and to make small adjustments. Although the colours are vivid and the tonal contrasts bold, the paint itself has been used fairly thinly, in a technique akin to that of watercolour, with small areas of unpainted white canvas left showing in the finished picture. This has given the painting a fresh, sparkling appearance, unlike that achieved by areas of applied white (though there are such areas too). This lively, spontaneous effect is enhanced by the quite rough and sketchy treatment of the window frame and sill, and it is interesting to compare this with the painting on pages 102 to 105, in which the window frame has been treated in a very much more detailed and deliberate fashion. These two paintings, indeed, illustrate very well the radically different ways in which two artists will approach a similar subject.

1

2

ᴛᴏᴘ **1** This is a complex subject, in which the correct placing of the verticals and horizontals is just as important as the bowl of flowers and the chair top; so a preliminary pencil drawing was made on the canvas to position all the elements in relation to each other. The main shapes were then blocked in in thin colour, the window frame being laid down first, with the bowl and chair painted over the resulting grid. This simple device of overlapping also serves to create depth. At this stage the background has been left as an undefined area of grey-blue in a mid-tone which will act as a key for the more specific tones and colours to be added later. The dark greens of the leaves (ᴀʙᴏᴠᴇ) **2** provide the key for the darker tones of the foreground.

3

LEFT **3** Once the tones of the foreground were established, the artist began to work on the buildings in the landscape, carefully relating the shapes and colours to those in the foreground.

Here yellow ochre is being applied thinly to the roofs, and the row of cypress trees has already been painted, echoing and balancing the leaves on the flowers.

4

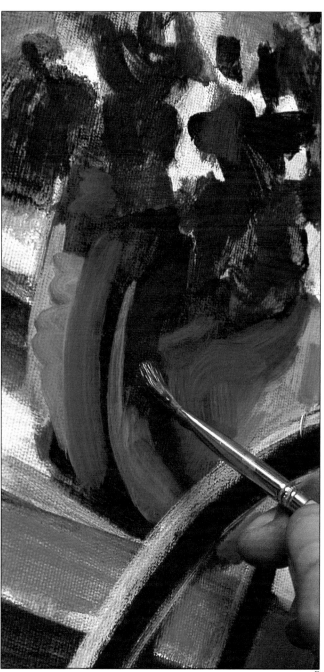

5

ABOVE **4** AND RIGHT **5** Now the artist works on the flowers, deepening the greens, heightening the reds and yellows, and at the same time deepening the blue of the vase. Small areas of the white canvas have been left unpainted, giving a sparkling effect to the leaves and flowers.

RIGHT **6** This detail of the flowers and leaves against the background buildings shows the way the greater tonal contrasts make the flowers stand out just enough to be read as being on a nearer plane. White paint has been applied to the tops of the flowers where they catch the light.

OPPOSITE The artist worked over all the areas of the painting at the same time, moving from foreground to background and constantly making small adjustments. The final touches were the fine lines of white to indicate the fold of the curtain on the left, and the addition of a cushion to the chair. This forms a triangle just intersecting the horizontal of the window sill.

MATERIALS USED

- Support: bought canvas board 51 × 40 cm (20 × 16 in)
- Brushes: bristle, number 12 flat and number 6 filbert. Turpentine was used to dilute the paint in the early stages
- Colours: titanium white, vermilion, cadmium red, cobalt violet, raw umber, Indian red, yellow ochre, chrome green, oxide of chromium, ultramarine blue and cerulean blue. (Vermilion is a very expensive colour, but is occasionally necessary for a subject like this, which relies on vivid and pure colours)

6

GERANIUM IN A POT

SOME people regard flower painting as a rather limited branch of art, but there is no reason for this attitude, as there are almost as many ways of treating a flower painting as there are of treating a landscape or portrait. Flowers can be painted outdoors as part of a landscape, indoors as part of a still-life, or simply by themselves, like the illustrations to natural-history books. In the previous painting, the flowers were only one element in a busy composition, while here one simple bloom in an undecorated pot forms the whole painting.

The problem with flowers is the same as with still-life – how to make an interesting and well-balanced arrangement that you can translate into paint without getting too bogged down in the minute details. Artists of the past, particularly the Dutch 17th-century masters, tended towards very elaborate arrangements with many different blooms, often in intricate and beautiful porcelain vases, which were really exercises in the minute depiction of fine detail, but this painting demonstrates how a simple subject can make an exciting painting.

As can be seen from the photograph, the artist has considerably exaggerated the angle of the flower head and the length of the stalk in order to give a diagonal emphasis to the subject, and has strengthened this by means of the slightly curving diagonal lines in the background and on the slanting edge of the skirting board. Placing the pot below eye-level has allowed the rim to be shown as a definite curve and the shadow to assume importance as part of the composition. The result is simple but pleasing; like most good paintings, this one looks deceptively easy.

The paint here has been used thickly, unlike that in the previous painting. Parts of the background were applied with a palette knife, with the side of the knife used to make sharply defined lines on the leaves. The flower heads were built up in thick impasto; in some places the brushstrokes themselves form the petals and in other places paint has been squeezed on direct from the tube, so that the painting has an interesting and varied surface. This is particularly important in a subject as stark as this, which might have looked rather dull and lifeless. A good artist plans the paint surface as carefully as the composition, so that it forms an integral part of the whole, rather than just letting it happen, but accidental effects can often be used to advantage also, and can frequently give rise to a new technique that can be put to use in a subsequent painting.

1

ABOVE **1** A few lines made with a sharp pencil served to place the main shapes, which were then quickly blocked in with bright colours. Even at this stage the paint was used quite thickly, as can be seen on the flower pot and the leaves at the top.

3

2

LEFT **2** AND ABOVE **3** The diagonal line for the edge of the skirting board was painted in next, together with an area of colour around the pot (ABOVE), acting as a key for the other colours. The photograph (LEFT) shows thick white paint being applied with a small brush to sharpen and define the edges of the leaves and stems.

LEFT **4** Here a medium-sized round brush is being used to apply thick paint to the flower heads so that the brushstrokes themselves form the shapes of the petals, and a special impasto medium was mixed with the paint to give it extra body. This is a good example of using particular brushes to create particular effects; a flat brush would not have been suitable for this purpose.

4

RIGHT **5** Here the flat of the painting knife has been used to apply thick white paint to an area of the background, giving a lively, rough-textured effect.

5

MATERIALS USED

- Support: canvas board 51 × 40 cm (20 × 16 in)
- Brushes: white bristle numbers 3, 4 and 6 (and a palette knife)
- Colours: titanium white, alizarin crimson, cadmium red, viridian, Prussian blue, raw umber and Payne's grey. The impasto medium, *Oleopasto*, was mixed with the paint in the areas where it was applied thickly

RIGHT **6** This detail shows the way the paint has been built up quite thickly on the highlight areas of the leaves so that they stand out from the areas of thinner, darker paint. The lines of dark green radiating from the centres of the leaves were made with the edge of a painting knife.

OPPOSITE The final touches involved more work on the background, foreground and shadow areas, so that the background is now perceived as an uneven piece of white fabric with folds and creases. There is just enough texture and detail to give interest to the painting without in any way detracting from the plant itself. The floor in front of the pot, previously painted flat, has now been broken up with short, stabbing brushstrokes, indicating an uneven fall of light.

6

INTERIOR WITH BROOM

THIS kind of painting, of familiar objects in a domestic setting, has always been popular with artists, and has its roots in the lovely, tranquil interiors of the Dutch painters of the 17th century. Probably the most famous of all such paintings in more modern times is Van Gogh's *Yellow Chair,* but the French artists Edouard Vuillard (1868-1940) and Pierre Bonnard (1867-1947), among others, also painted many exquisite interiors. Looking at such paintings, one often has the feeling that the artists were fortunate in having rooms that look so much more attractive than our own. This is, of course, sometimes well justified, since few people live in houses with fine views or with large shuttered windows, but this painting demonstrates what can be done with seemingly quite unpromising material – just a corner with a broom and a hat hanging on the wall. The artist has aimed at creating a feeling of quiet domestic intimacy by the choice of a subject in which there is no drama and no main focal point.

Here the artist had a very clear vision of how the painting was to look, and went about organizing it with this vision in mind. It is basically abstract in feeling, with no bright colours; so only a small palette was used. The main lines are vertical, with the diagonals at the bottom of the wall and door forming a zigzag line from left to right. What the artist had to consider was the balance of the lines and shapes and that of the lights and darks, all of which were planned with great care. Any change in the composition – for example, reducing the width of the door, removing the hat, or making the area of black floor larger – would upset the balance quite seriously.

Because the subject is such a stark and goemetric one, the artist has chosen to use his paint fairly thinly, to emphasize these qualities, and has created small areas of texture by drawing with a pencil and spattering the paint in places. He has also used masking tape to ensure that the vertical and diagonal lines are really straight and true, with clean, hard edges. In a painting like this, any deviation from a true parallel, however small, would completely destroy the effect.

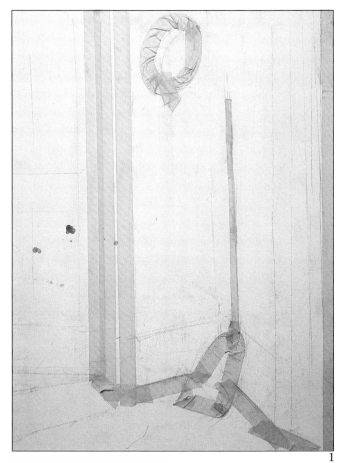

1

2

ABOVE **1** The first step was to make a very careful drawing, using a sharp pencil, a ruler and a set square. Masking tape was then placed over all the edges, so that the preliminary stage of this painting looks quite unlike the more conventional drawing or underpainting.

LEFT **2** AND OPPOSITE TOP LEFT **3** Paint was applied quite freely over the masking tape with a medium-sized flat bristle brush.

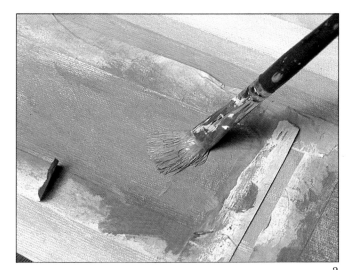

3

5

4

ABOVE **4** As soon as the tape was dry it was lifted, giving sharp, clean edges. Care must be taken when using this technique not to use the paint too thinly or it will seep under the tape.

6

ABOVE **5** The large area of the walls was covered with quite thick paint, a mixture of titanium white modified with small quantities of Payne's grey, raw sienna and cobalt blue.

LEFT **6** The underpainting was now complete, and the paint sufficiently dry to work on. Here the artist is using a small sable brush to paint small details of the hat and ribbon.

7

8

- Support: fine-grained canvas board 51 × 40 cm (20 × 16 in) (a surface particularly well-suited to this type of 'hard-edge' painting)
- Brushes: medium-sized flat bristle and a number 6 sable
- Colours: titanium white, Payne's grey, raw sienna, burnt umber, cobalt blue, viridian and cadmium red

FAR LEFT **7** By this stage all the canvas had been covered and the main areas were more or less complete, but the focus of interest, the broom, needed further definition and texture.

LEFT **8** The artist re-tapes the edges of the broom and places newspaper over the rest of the painting to protect it, leaving exposed the small area of skirting board around the broom. He then loads a bristle brush with thinned paint and spatters it with his finger.

9

10

ABOVE LEFT **9** AND ABOVE RIGHT **10** The bristles of the broom are suggested by firstly drawing into the thin, dry paint with a pencil and then by scratching the paint away with the handle of a brush.

OPPOSITE A comparison of the finished painting with the earlier stage clearly shows how important the final touches were. The eye is now drawn to the textured broom and spattered area of skirting board, whereas previously the painting had rather the appearance of a stage set waiting for something to happen, without a 'focal point'. The colours are muted, the atmosphere is calm.

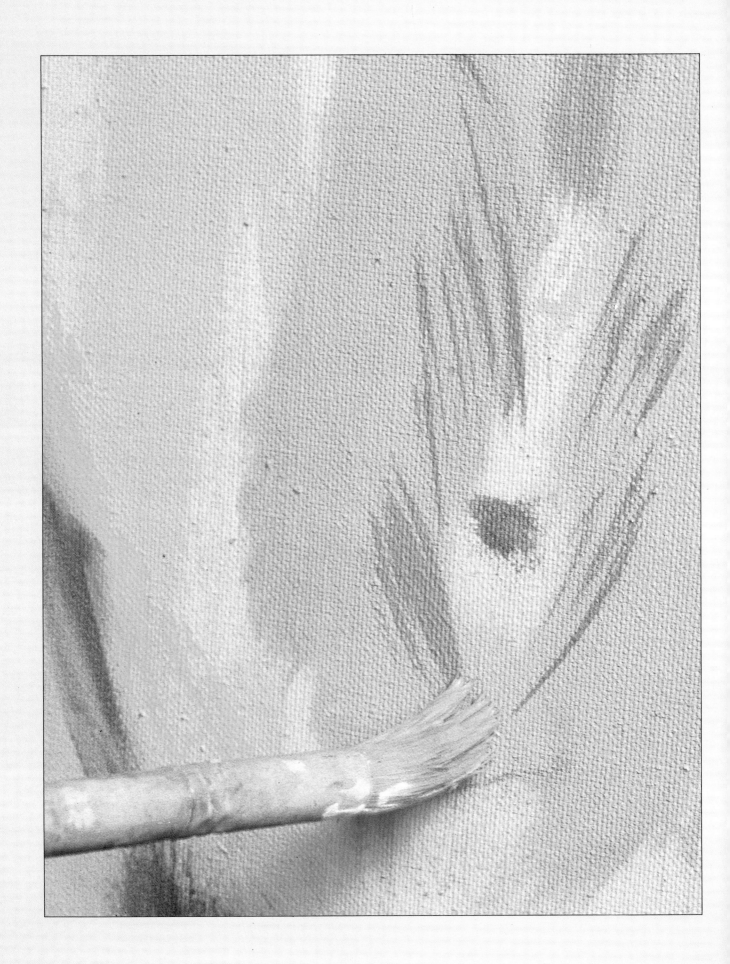

WHY ACRYLICS?

ACRYLIC IS a relatively new paint for artists, the first for nearly 300 years. During that time, painters and designers have used mainly oil, watercolour and tempera. In acrylic, we have a modern paint of enormous value to both artists and designers, whatever fields they are in – painting, illustration, graphic design, textiles, jewellery, mural and interior design, even sculpture.

THE NATURE OF PAINT

THE QUALITIES OF ACRYLIC are exceptional. It is certainly more versatile than most other paints. For one thing, it can stimulate almost exactly what they can do, in many instances better. It is clean to handle and has only a slight, pleasant aroma. No cumbersome equipment is needed, no special chemical knowledge to make it function satisfactorily. This alone makes it ideal for those who find oil paint somewhat messy, its smell unpleasant, its use arduous and something of a performance.

RIGHT ABOVE *Terence Millington,* Sofa.

RIGHT *Leonard Rosoman, Girl Lying in a Hammock.*

ADVANTAGES OF ACRYLIC

ONE OF THE ADVANTAGES of acrylic is its speed of working. It dries rapidly, in minutes if need be, and permanently. Alternatively, drying can be prolonged to suit individual working requirements. Acrylic dries throughout so thoroughly, it can be varnished immediately with either a matt (eggshell) or glossy finish.

Another advantage is that acrylic is both tough and flexible.

WHY ACRYLICS?

THEY ARE: SIMPLE AND clean to handle; flexible; water resistant; tough. Acrylics: can simulate other paints; smell good; need little special equipment; dry fast; can be cleaned; can be repaired; adhere permanently. It does not peel, crack or split, and it is water-resistant. The surface of dried acrylic can be gently cleaned should the need arise, and can be repaired easily if damaged.

Perhaps the most advantageous characteristics of acrylic are its adhesive qualities. It can be applied, without difficulty, to almost anything, and remain, permanently, without flaking or rubbing off. Unlike oil paint, which can damage the surface of certain materials if applied without

the appropriate priming, acrylic can be used without any special preparation if the situation demands.

Among other things, it will adhere satisfactorily to all kinds of wall surfaces, cloth, paper, card (cardboard), hardboard, wood, plastic – almost any object or surface suitable for painting or decoration.

BENCHES.I.BATTERSEA PK
FOR ALL FLESH IS AS GRASS.THE GRASS WTTHERETH

II.MEANWHILE ON TH
ENS.HARROGATE.FR
GARDENS.BOURNEM
EREST.GARDENS.TI
URNE.PT 3005.IN CI
OUTH.PGC.CO.C243S
BRIGHTON.LANSDOW
IN THE PARC.CEFN

Acrylic is a multipurpose paint; it can be used as a paste as well as a liquid, enabling a variety of surface changes to be carried out and explored. From the perfectly flat, or evenly gradated kind, to the highly modelled, textured surface that has sand, glass, wool fibre and tissue paper added to it. For among its many accomplishments, the acrylic medium is also a powerful glue.

It will especially suit those who delight in bold, bright, clear colours. Conversely it can be reduced to subtle tones and carefully gradated tints by the usual methods of mixing.

Acrylic's simplicity of handling is a major advantage, especially for beginners. The simple equipment needed

ABOVE Tom Phillips, Benches. This painting is based around a series of postcards. The artist has used a number of techniques (eg stippling and hatching) and a wide range of colours.

RIGHT The most convenient way to buy acrylics is in tubes.

ACE . PROSPECT . GARD
TE . 156 . IN . CENTRAL
DENNIS . P . 2082 . IN . TH
AN'S . WALK . SOUTHPO
GARDENS . BOURNEM
D . STEINE . GARDENS
5 . AND . REFLECTED
ANISHEN . PT . 28357

III . THE . SAME . A . YEAR . LATER

TOM . PHILLIPS . LONDON . IV . MCMLXX · XVI . IV . MCMLXXI

means less initial expense, a further encouragement to those who have never painted before.

Acrylic is uncomplicated to use, but it is important to learn how it behaves. Practice and experiment will teach you how to exploit the qualities of the paint. Experience with other mediums is not necessary; beginners are at no disadvantage to the more experienced painter in understanding acrylics, and the beginner may be less prejudiced and more adventurous than the painter skilled in other mediums. If you begin with a spirit of inquiry, you will soon grasp the potential of this exciting medium. Keep an open mind and persevere, and the results you will achieve will be rewarding.

CHAPTER ONE
ACRYLIC PAINT

ACRYLIC PAINT is made by mixing powdered pigment with acrylic adhesive. The adhesive looks milky when wet but becomes transparent when dry, revealing the true colour of the pigment. All the ingredients are carefully weighed and tested before use. It is this painstaking precision and control during the manufacture which enables thousands of tubes of paint of almost identical colour, consistency and quality to be turned out at any time.

THE NATURE OF PAINT

ACRYLIC IS UNLIKE ANY other paint, but it has affinities with all of them, since all paints contain the same ingredient: pigment. A pigment used in water-colour is identical to that used in oil and acrylic. The quality is equally high, its brightness and durability the same, and the care used in manufacture just as thorough.

The major difference between one paint and another is not the colour but something much more fundamental: the binder. The binder largely decides the character and behaviour of the various paints. Binders also play a large part in permanence and drying qualities, brilliance and speed of working. They also determine what kinds of diluents (also known as solvents) and varnishes may be used in conjunction with them. For instance, water is the diluent for watercolours and gouache, and turpentine for oil, because of the liquid binders used.

A brief look into the history and development of paint will provide valuable insight into what may be achieved when it is used with imagination.

The history of painting reveals that before the establishment of paint and equipment manufacturers and suppliers most artists made their own materials. They ground their own paint, prepared their own supports and primings, even made their own brushes.

In studios in the 15th century the apprentices who worked under the master ground the colours and made the supports. It was all part of the artist's training.

Irksome as it may appear to us today, for them it was a normal part of the process of painting to know how paints were made as well as how to use them. It gave them, in effect, an enormous respect for their materials and was instrumental in achieving a high level of craft which, in turn, richly enhanced the creativity of their work.

Today, happily, we can buy brushes and paint of a consistently high standard whenever we need them. And though we can buy every kind of support to suit all mediums, prepared for oil, tempera or acrylic – canvas, hardboard, card (cardboard), even paper for oil paint – we can, if we prefer, make our own with ready-to-be-assembled stretchers and prepare our own canvas or board with ready-made primings – not necessarily to save money, which it undoubtedly does, but for the satisfaction it will give.

PIGMENTS

PIGMENTS ARE the colouring materials of paint, and are usually made in the form of powders. From the earliest, pigments had to be bright and clear, and able to withstand prolonged exposure to light. Certain colours were apt to fade and did not produce the subtle tints and shades we would admire today, but were more likely to produce a dead or muddy effect.

Throughout history, bright colour was preferred for both practical and aesthetic reasons, having close associations with joy, celebration, pleasure and delight. To express these emotions, bright, rich hues were in constant demand, and the search for pigments that possessed these qualities has been constant over the centuries.

By the Middle Ages the range of colours was quite extensive, and put to complicated use on walls, illuminations, panels, in books and on woodwork. An all-purpose paint like acrylic would have suited them admirably.

After the Renaissance, pigments reached a peak of brightness and variety. Thereafter a more expressive and realistic style emerged and the medium more suited to this was oil paint. Realistic paintings moved away from bright colours to rich, sombre hues, which brought a new range of pigments into being. An interest in brighter colour returned again in the 19th century due, in part, to Constable and Turner, the designs of William Morris, and the Impressionists.

HOW ACRYLIC PAINT IS MADE

   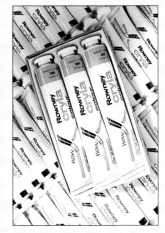

1 *The first constituent is the powdered pigment.*

2 *The pigment is mixed with acrylic adhesive.*

3 *The paint is then milled between steel rollers.*

4 *After it has been inspected, the paint is put into tubes.*

Delight in bright colour today means a wide range of pigments, and the list of those available is long. The names of pigments often echo places: burnt Sienna, Venetian red, Naples yellow, Prussian blue, Chinese vermilion; or recall the materials they are derived from: cobalt blue, rose madder, emerald green, ivory black, sap green, geranium lake and so on. Though interesting sounding, the names give little indication of the quality or behaviour of colours, and some are sold under two or three different names.

To simplify the situation, the names of absolutely necessary colours are listed further on, and you may want to look at a colour chart to see the full range. The number of colours needed to produce a variety of tones and tints need not be large. Pigments today are bright, durable (unless specified) and capable of a great deal of mixing.

Briefly the requirements for a reliable pigment are that: it should be a smooth, finely divided powder; insoluble in the medium in which it is used; able to withstand the action of light without changing colour under normal exposure; and it should be chemically inert and unaffected by materials with which it is mixed, or by the atmosphere. Moreover, it should possess the proper degree of opacity or transparency to suit the purpose for which it is intended, and should conform to accepted standards of colour and colour quality.

The raw materials used to provide the pigments are customarily classified as inorganic or organic. Inorganic materials are those of purely mineral origin such as the natural earths: ochres, raw umber, which can be calcined like burnt umber and burnt sienna, and the artificially prepared colours like cadmium yellow and zinc oxide, the basis of the famous 'Chinese white' which was introduced in 1837 by Winsor & Newton.

Organic pigments include animal and vegetable substances, as well as complex synthetic substances. Vegetable sources furnished colour like gamboge, indigo (now not available) and madder. Animal sources produced cochineal which was made into carmine, and Indian yellow was an incredible colour made in India from the urine of cows fed on mango leaves. It has now been replaced by synthetically made colours. Other artificially prepared organic colours include alizarin, or anilines (now largely discontinued for aritists' colours, but occasionally used as constituents of household paints and printers' inks).

Many of these organic colours are no longer produced, and have been replaced by newer and more durable colours that have been developed successfully over the years. Notable among these is the phthalocyanine range, the first of which was a very intense blue, known under the trade name of Monastral blue and a very suitable replacement for the less reliable Prussian blues, whose colour effects and pigment properties it closely resembles.

The range has now increased to include yellows, reds and greens, and a splendid violet, all of them available in oil, watercolour and acrylic. These colours are classed as organic and are derived by a chemical process from an organic dyestuff. They are very intense with a high degree of durability and, like acrylic paint itself, are a modern and flexible addition to the artist's means of expression.

PAINTING WITH PIGMENTS

WHEN PIGMENTS ARE SEEN as powders they are fresh and bright with a beauty all their own. When mixed with a small quantity of water a paste is formed that can be painted with. When the water dries the bloom returns, but so does the powder. In other words it reverts to its former state. What is needed is something to bind the coloured grains together to make them adhere. For this purpose some kind of glue or binder must be added to the powder before it becomes paint.

The paints that have the slightest amount of binder, so that the pigment is as pure as possible, are pastels. They are, in effect, dry paint, but though beautiful to look at and work with, they are very fragile. The finished work is easily brushed off unless properly fixed, which, of course, takes away some of the original freshness, and represents the major difficulty over the centuries: to bind the paint so that the colour is not impaired.

To repeat, the major difference between one paint and another is not the colour or the pigment, it is the binder. Understand the nature of binders and you are half-way to understanding acrylic. This is where the mystery lies.

BINDERS

■ GUM

The earliest form of binder was a gum, probably gum arabic, though gum tragacanth was supposedly used by the Egyptians. Gum tragacanth is used principally to bind pastels, and gum arabic to bind water colours and gouache.

The popularity of gum arabic as a binder is probably because it dilutes well with water and does not impair the brightness of the pigments. It can also be made into small cakes of paint that are compact and easily stored, and dissolve easily when needed. The only limitation is that watercolour has little body, and is best used transparently, in washes and glazes.

As soon as white is added to the pigment it becomes more opaque. This kind of paint is known as gouache (derived from the Italian word for gum) and dries matt and bright. It is very popular with designers and often referred

THICKENER

MATT MEDIUM

MODELLING PASTE

GEL MEDIUM

TEXTURE PASTE

to as designer's gouache or poster colour.

Gouache can also be bought in cake form, but is more practical in liquid form, in bottles and tubes. It is not waterproof and cannot be overpainted without picking up the colour underneath. Neither will it stand up to harsh treatment or exposure. Like watercolour, the only protection is to put it immediately under glass.

■ EMULSIONS

Any sort of paint that is bound with an emulsion that contains oil, but is mixable with water, is called tempera. The tempera most frequently used throughout the Renaissance contained the yolk of an egg. Other emulsions contained casein glue, wax and parchment size. The oil most often added to the emulsion was linseed oil.

Most of the paintings and decorations of that period, seen in museums and art galleries today, could be correctly assumed to be tempera paintings.

Egg tempera in particular, dries quickly, hardly changes colour, and is fairly waterproof – sufficiently so not to pick up when over-painted. It has a good surface that wears well, provided it is treated with care. It is by far the best of the mediums, but requires technical knowledge and expertise to handle it well.

There are other drawbacks: speed of working is slow, it does not cover large areas well and is therefore better confined to small panels. There is always the difficulty of making flat, even coats of colour on a large scale because the emulsion binder cannot accommodate huge amounts of pigment – something acrylic can do with ease.

Tempera lends itself to simple, images. For more realistic forms of expression, oil paint is more suitable.

■ OIL

The most common oil used to bind pigment is linseed, and gave the freest possible manner of working for over 300 years. In fact until the introduction of acrylic, an artist could work on a large scale with oil paint without the limitations imposed by tempera and fresco (a pure, but temperamental binder that only functioned well in hot, dry climates) and paint as realistically – or expressively – as vision dictated.

Pigment ground with oil is slow to dry and therefore slow to use, but it brought a softer, more delicate tonality to painting, and did justice to the visual delights of light and shade. Moreover, because of its consistency, it could exploit more surface textures than tempera.

Drying could be speeded up with the addition of siccatives, like copal, dammar and mastic, which in turn could also be used as varnishes. The addition of natural resin toughened the paint so successfully that all manner of objects and surfaces could be painted.

The practical application of oil paint outweighed its many disadvantages: that it darkens over a period of time, attracts dirt, is difficult to clean, cracks and peels, and is messy and smelly.

Oil paint has to be diluted with turpentine and brushes and palettes cleaned with white spirit and can be applied only to primed surfaces. It requires technical expertise and virtuosity and is not an easy medium to master.

ACRYLIC BINDERS, MEDIUMS, VARNISHES, RETARDERS AND SOLVENTS

THE LIQUID binders mainly used for oil paint, watercolour, gouache, tempera, fresco, wax encaustic and so on, were not intended specifically to bind pigments. Linseed oil, egg, gum, wax and lime are natural products with many other uses, and were adapted to make paint. Consequently all kinds of difficulties were apt to crop up to spoil or limit the full potential of the paint.

Acrylic binders are completely different. They are made specifically for the jobs intended for them. Chemically, acrylic binders are based on polymer resin, and classed as an emulsion into which pigments are mixed. It is, in short, a clear plastic, with great adhesive properties, and water-resistant – despite the fact that the diluent is water. For once the binder is dry, it becomes completely insoluble in water.

Acrylic binders (or more specifically, mediums) can be obtained in three consistencies. This alone makes acrylic unique. With oil paint, a number of alien products are needed to thin or thicken it. Acrylic thinners and thickeners belong to the same family. With them, not only are we able to achieve what other paints can, but a great deal more besides. These mediums, or binders, come as:

- ☛ liquid
- ☛ jelly (Gel)
- ☛ paste

They are milky-white in colour when wet, but after evaporation of water, they dry to a clear, transparent film, which is fairly tough and flexible. This also ensures maximum brightness of the pigment.

When these binders are used to exploit the possibilities of acrylic paint they become in effect mediums: liquid constituents of paint, in which the pigment is suspended, or liquids with which the paint may be diluted, without decreasing its adhesive, binding, or film-forming properties.

Mediums can loosely be described as paint additions to make the paint flow or dry more variously, or to produce different results for special kinds of work (impastos, for example, where the addition of a medium will give more bulk to the paint), or, as in the case of acrylic, to transform it into a modelling material. These additions can also thin or thicken to produce a variety of visual effects such as glazes, scumbles, impastos, etc.

Although you need not try them all immediately, you may want to know something about them and what they are capable of, to understand the possibilities of acrylic, and to experiment with them later.

■ ACRYLIC GLOSS MEDIUM

Acrylic gloss medium increases the translucency and gloss of acrylic colours while reducing consistency to produce thin, smooth paint layers which dry rapidly. This means that an unlimited number of glazes of exceptional brilliance, depth and clarity can be developed and exploited.

A few drops of the medium mixed with ordinary watercolour or gouache immediately transforms them into an acrylic paint, that is, they take on many of the characteristics of acrylic paint: quick-drying, water-resistant, capable of overpainting without picking up and a gloss finish.

The acrylic gloss medium is an essential part of the acrylic artist's paintbox, as essential as water itself, for nearly all the main tasks that acrylic is capable of are much better done with a few drops of the medium added to the paint or wash. This medium has a secondary function as a gloss varnish though there is a newer and more practical and versatile product in two finishes, gloss or matt, which can between them furnish a glossy, semi-matt or eggshell, or matt finish.

■ ACRYLIC MATT MEDIUM

The matt medium behaves in a similar way to the gloss, and everything said of the gloss medium also applies to the matt. It is a useful medium to have if you intend to paint matt, so that the tones of the colours can be properly mixed before painting. There is an appreciable difference in tonality between matt and glossy finishes. The pigment dispersed in either medium may be the same for both matt or gloss, but the light affects them differently. To allow for this during painting, the addition of a few drops of matt (or gloss) medium in the paint mixtures will ensure that, on drying, you get exactly the tone or tint you want.

■ ACRYLIC GEL MEDIUM

Gel medium is thicker than the gloss or matt mediums. As its name implies, it is jelly-like in texture and consistency, and like the gloss medium has two distinct functions.

First, it enables thick, highly textured impastos to be produced easily while maintaining consistency of colour, and second, the colours increase in translucency the greater the proportion of gel medium used. At the same time, the drying rate is retarded to some degree.

Glazes and impastos are an integral feature of acrylic painting and, because of its fairly quick drying qualities, acrylic has an advantage over oil paint, which is by comparison a slow drier, making glazing a long drawn out operation, in which it is hard to foresee the result.

Glazes are made by laying a transparent film of colour over another that has already dried. With oil it may take up to two months for a surface to dry out thoroughly for glazing to be done. With gel medium it can be done in a matter of minutes. Moreover any number of glazes can be overlaid, and not just one, as with oil paint. Glazing is a beautiful way of using colour so that its brightness and purity is exploited to the full.

Both the acrylic gloss medium and gel medium can be used to make glazes. The difference is merely one of consistency. The gel medium is much thicker than the gloss, and therefore can also be used for impastos. Nevertheless it will make beautiful glazes especially with a palette knife.

Impasto is thick paint that can be textured by the movement of the brush or by the edge of the palette or painting knife.

Impasto has been a particular characteristic of oil paint, and gives tremendous vitality to the expressiveness of the image. Gel medium can achieve this effect in exactly the same way as oil paint, with just as much vitality, and is less liable to crack. It dries much quicker than oil so is less easily spoiled or damaged during painting and, once dried, it becomes very hard to dislodge.

■ ACRYLIC TEXTURE PASTE

The thickest, and the most powerful acrylic binder, comes in a carton. Though more dense than the other two binders, it can be watered down without any loss to its adhesive powers.

It can be used to make those very heavy impastos that Vincent Van Gogh was so fond of; for this kind of vigorous brushstroke, large brushes will be needed, or a palette or painting knife will serve just as well.

Alternatively, instead of using this medium to make thick coloured impastos, it can be formed so that other materials, for example sawdust aggregate, may be pressed or embedded into it, to create richly textured surfaces.

Grumbacher, Winsor and Newton, and Rowney Cryla (2) are just a few of the acrylic paints on sale today. Rowney Flow Formula (1) is used for covering large areas with flat colour. The canvas should be primed with an acrylic primer (3) or gesso (4). Mediums are available in gloss (5, 7, 11, 13) or matt (6, 10) textures. Retarding medium (16) slows the drying time of the paint. Like mediums, varnishes can be matt (8, 9) or gloss. Acrylic varnishes are normally insoluble, but Rowney make a soluble gloss variety (12). Also useful are gel medium (15) and water tension breaker (14).

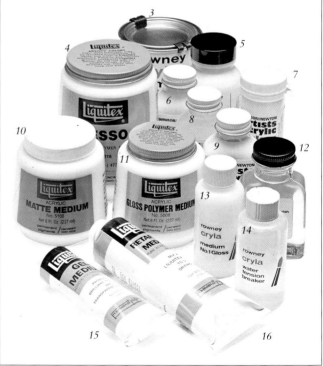

The Tepline paste medium has remarkable adhesive powers, and so presents numerous possibilities for design, one of which is the pleasant and simple assemblage known as collage. It presents many possibilities for design and can be used to model and, with the addition of sand, marble dust or other aggregate to strengthen it, it can be carved or cut and even sanded when dry.

■ ACRYLIC WATER TENSION BREAKER

The water tension breaker is a concentrated solution of a wetting agent, which is diluted with water before use. Water tension breaker can be added to water, or matt or gloss mediums, following manufacturers' instructions in quantities depending on the effect required.

Use of this additive allows easier, more rapid thinning of colours with minimum loss of colour strength. Staining effects of maximum intensity into difficult surfaces, such as unprimed canvas, are more easily attainable with colour diluted in this way.

The flow and ease with which the colour may be used are increased so that flat, even washes of colour can be applied to large areas of the work. This is ideal for hard-edge techniques, and for spraying acrylic colours.

It should also be very helpful for those who like to use acrylic in free-flowing washes (like watercolour for example). All that would be required is a few drops of the tension breaker in the container of water.

■ ACRYLIC GLOSS VARNISH

The main advantages of this varnish are that

☛ it is not prone to bubble formation (as the acrylic gloss medium tended to do if brushed vigorously).

☛ it is removable by an acrylic varnish remover (the gloss medium cannot be removed, as it becomes an integral part of the painting when used as a varnish).

☛ it has a remarkably good flow, which means that it will spread evenly over the surface, without leaving unsightly brushmarks.

This gloss varnish is water-based and dries to a flexible, transparent, extremely light-fast, glossy film. Two coats applied liberally are recommended since any parts that may be missed by the first coat will be covered by the second. On the other hand, the application of two coats necessitates waiting for at least two hours for the first coat of varnish to dry before the second can be applied.

Some manufacturers recommend slight dilution with a few drops of water to achieve good flow, but I have found that this varnish flows very evenly straight from the bottle. However, a few drops of water never does any acrylic material harm – on the contrary, it acts as a safety device for both paints and mediums to be so diluted.

The final varnish film is water-resistant and scuff-resistant and brings out the brilliance of the colours wonderfully. It both protects and enhances at the same time, which is the major reason for varnishing finished work. Varnishing consequently becomes the normal extension to painting, and should offer few problems if all these points are observed.

Acrylic gloss varnish can also be used to varnish prints and posters to protect and enhance them. The varnish

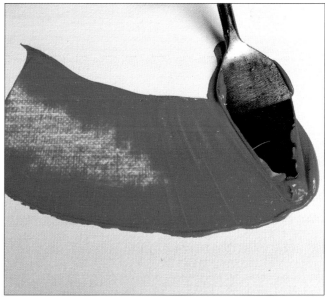

TOP *A painting knife is used to mix paint and gel in equal proportions.*

ABOVE *The consistency of the gel is thick, and so it retains the shape of the knife marks.*

should, however, be applied first to a small test area to assess suitability for use. It should also be pointed out that attempting to remove varnish film from prints is not recommended, as damage to the print may result.

Should cleaning of the varnish film be necessary, a soft cloth moistened with either water or weak soap solution can be used with complete safety to wipe the surface.

■ ACRYLIC MATT VARNISH

For very large works – murals, wall decorations, exhibition stands and so on – it is usually the practice to varnish with a matt finish, as a glossy surface on a large scale will reflect the light unevenly, giving an unwanted shine. Irregular shine will distort the image, or impair the visual effect which can be very irritating to look at. The only answer to this is a completely matt surface.

Similarly for those who prefer blonde or high-key colours, a matt finish will be more suitable than a rich glossy one. Be careful when buying the varnish to stipulate exactly the kind of varnish you require, and to check the label on the bottle. Acrylic matt varnish has similar qualities to the gloss varnish. It is also removable. One coat will be found to be adequate, but another may be given if necessary after two hours. It can also be used on prints and posters.

■ SATIN ON EGGSHELL FINISH

If you find that a glossy finish is too shiny, or a matt one too bland, there is a way of making an intermediate finish. Simply blend the gloss varnish with the matt in a saucer, or container, and brush on as directed. The resultant midway finish can be adjusted to suit individual preferences by adding either more gloss or more matt to the mixture. A prepared satin finish is also available in art supply shops.

TEN SIMPLE RULES FOR SUCCESSFUL VARNISHING

VARNISHING WITH acrylic matt or gloss varnish should present no difficulty provided these ten points are followed.

Varnishing can be carried out with undiluted medium, straight from the bottle, but it is a more practical, and safer, practice to pour a little medium into a clean saucer or container and add a few drops of water to thin it slightly. This slows the drying rate, enabling you to carry out the operation without haste.

Always varnish, if possible, with a soft brush. A hard brush may leave brushmarks, which will look unsightly. Wash brushes immediately after varnishing. Dried varnish is very hard to remove and if left may harm the brush.

To be quite certain of completely covering the surface with varnish, look obliquely along the work. Any untouched areas will be detected immediately because of the reflected light.

Discard any unused varnish and use a fresh supply each time.

Although the varnish has no smell to speak of, there is no reason for leaving the screw-cap off when not in use. The water in the medium will evaporate fairly quickly, and if it does, the varnish will no longer do its job properly.

The surface to be varnished must be absolutely dry – that is, dry all the way through – otherwise the varnish will pick up and spoil the look of the work. Acrylic paint dries fairly rapidly, and it should not prove too difficult to determine whether the paint is fully dry or not. Nevertheless thicker coats of paint, like impastos, may be deceptive. The best rule is to leave it for a week or so to make absolutely certain.

Ensure that the work to be varnished is clean. Specks of dust and other unwanted particles can appear from nowhere, so gently brush the surface with a clean, soft rag or soft brush prior to varnishing.

ABOVE *Texture paste is the thickest acrylic medium. Here, it is applied directly to the support.*

Always varnish in a clear atmosphere. Don't carry out the job, for example, in a room where any sawing, planing or sanding has taken place. Once grit or dust gets into the varnish it is difficult to remove without damage to the paint, and a great deal of time-consuming trouble.

Don't hurry the job; take plenty of time to do it properly. Put aside the work to be varnished until it can be done without haste.

Never under any circumstances use acrylic varnish over oil paint.

Varnishing is a normal part of painting with acrylic, and should offer few problems if these ten points are scrupulously observed. If in doubt, the best procedure is to try the varnishing exercise with the medium on any and every kind of expendable surface available. Paintings that have been discarded make a useful beginning; or splash some acrylic paint on a piece of card or paper, and experiment by varnishing them when dry. It should not take long to grasp the principle of varnishing with a soft brush.

■ ACRYLIC GLOSS AND MATT VARNISH REMOVER

If for some reason either of these two varnishes is to be removed before revarnishing, this varnish remover will do it successfully. The remover should be applied liberally to a soft cotton pad and then rubbed on to the varnish film. The varnish will begin to be removed almost immediately, and care must be taken to avoid excessive rubbing of the underlying acrylic paint. Any slight paint pick-up on the pad will indicate that complete removal of the varnish has taken place. Revarnishing can then begin.

■ SOLVENT FOR DRIED ACRYLIC COLOURS

There are always occasions when dried acrylic paint gets where it is not wanted: on brushes particularly, and on palettes and clothing. It is amazing what hot water can do to dried acrylic, by allowing it to float off certain kinds of surfaces such as china, glass or stainless steel. With more porous or absorbent material, however, dried acrylic paint is much more stubborn and difficult to remove.

This solvent therefore is a useful material to have when that kind of emergency arises. It should only be used in a well-ventilated room. Avoid breathing too much of the vapour, and refrain from smoking when using it.

The solvent softens the paint so that it can be removed easily. It can be used on brushes, palettes, clothing and paintings with perfect safety, provided the above conditions are observed.

■ RETARDERS

Retarders are available in both liquid and gel form. One retarder I used, which is slightly translucent and gel-like in consistency, retards the rate of drying considerably when blended with acrylic colours. Even on a very warm day, the colours I mixed with it remained wet for hours.

Gel-like retarders have the advantage of allowing textural effects and impastos to be achieved. Fluidity can be attained by adding a little water. However, mixing must be carried out thoroughly with a knife, the proportions being three times the amount of colour to one of retarder, and six times the amount of colour to one of the retarder for the earth colours (yellow ochre, raw sienna, light red, burnt sienna, burnt umber, and raw umber.)

Retarders are effective only if used with thick paint; water limits their performance, so you have to choose to some extent between diluting your paint and using a retarder.

No firm drying times are given, but it seems to stay moist for a considerable length of time, sufficient to do any amount of work required before drying.

■ OIL ON ACRYLIC

As a general rule, one may take it as axiomatic that oil and acrylic don't mix, except in one particular instance: oil paint may be painted over acrylic paint, preferably on a rigid support, like hardboard. Canvas is not recommended.

But acrylic must never be painted over oil. Oil rejects acrylic, and moreover dries in an entirely different way from acrylic, so the result will be little short of disastrous.

However, because oil can be overpainted on to acrylic, it means that one can paint backgrounds or underpaintings with acrylic before finishing with oil. This is somewhat like the methods adopted by the old masters of underpainting with tempera, because it dried quickly, and finishing with heavier, slow-drying oil, which had more texture and body, and which, because of its slower drying time, was capable of considerably more finish and fine detail.

Whether the method of overpainting acrylic with oil is preferable to painting throughout with acrylic, using a retarder for the parts of the work which need a slower drying rate, is open to conjecture. The answer can only be arrived at by personal experience, and a degree of experiment.

Paint is prepared on a palette or in a container before it is applied to a surface. If the paint is too thick, it can be thinned or diluted with a solvent, or diluent. If too thin, mediums can be added to give more body. If the paint dries too quickly, a retarder can be added to slow the rate down. The aim of these additions is to ensure that the paint will flow properly from the brush or knife. If it flows evenly there will be no strain or pressure needed.

Tools and equipment play a great part in painting, and must be properly looked after to perform their functions well.

Acrylic paints can be used very effectively in combination with oil crayons.

CHAPTER THREE

PAINTING WITH ACRYLICS

Next to watercolour acrylics are the simplest of paints to use. The minimum amount needed is a few tubes of paint, some brushes, a palette and water. This is not to say that watercolours or acrylics are the easiest paints to use because the equipment needed can be reduced to the bare minimum, but because of its basic simplicity, acrylic can give enjoyment from the very start.

MANY PAINTERS AND DESIGNERS make a practice of combining acrylic with other media like coloured inks, drawing or gouache. Acrylic seems to work well with almost any conventional medium, provided it doesn't contain oil.

The reason for including information on what must seem like so much equipment is that it can be used when needed should it be required. Those who have painted with oils will know how much basic equipment is needed just to begin. Happily this is not so with acrylics. Paints, paper, brushes and water are all that will be needed. With exerpience newer items will be added and others discarded.

THE INFRASTRUCTURE OF PAINTING

LOOKING AT A PAINTING or design is rather like looking at an iceberg. We only see the tip. We can't see what's underneath holding it up, as it were. We know, however, that a great deal of the iceberg is beneath the water – hence its strength.

The strength of a painting, too, lies beneath the surface – and has dangers for the unwary as well as delights. If this fact isn't understood, painting will forever be a mystery.

Actually the principle is very simple and quite easy to understand. It is this: paintings are built up in layers. Even watercolours are built up with layers of washes, one transparent film over another.

This layering of one coat of paint over another varies with the function of that layer. For example the function of the primer differs from the function of a glaze: the primer, because it is a sealer and a reflector of light, is thick and opaque; the glaze is thin and transparent because its job is to let the light, or another colour, come through.

For most household jobs, the paint layers would be fairly simple: sealer, undercoat, top coat.

For painting in oil or acrylic the number of coats or layers could be as many as ten. For example, starting from the bottom:

LAYERS OF A PAINTING

SUPPORT: PAPER, CARD, CANVAS, hardboard etc.
sealer: glue size or acrylic medium (optional for acrylic, necessary for oil)
primer: gesso, acrylic white, lead white etc.
wash or toned drawing
underpainting: blocking in the main areas of colour, usually thinly
middle layer
scumble
impasto
glaze
varnish

This is precisely what painting entails: a study of the layers of paint. The success of any painting depends on how they are amalgamated. Naturally only a few of them may be used on any one painting, but to get the best out of acrylics it is essential to be acquainted with them. Fortunately acrylic dries quickly, so the process of laying one coat over another can be speeded up, and takes much of the tediousness out of painting. Oil paint, being a slower-drying paint, hasn't this advantage.

The study of paint layers goes hand in hand with a study of colours and the way they interact with each other. Before that, we have to consider another important factor – water.

WATER

A NUMBER OF MEDIUMS have been suggested for use with acrylic paint to make it flow better, to give different finishes – gloss, eggshell or satin, matt – to produce every kind of impasto from medium, to thick, to very thick, and to retard the drying rate. But the most important of these, the medium that takes precedence over them all, is the diluent itself: water.

Acrylic paint is made up from three components: pigment, binder, water. Water plays a dominant part in painting with acrylics, not only for the vital process of thinning the paint to the required consistency, but also for cleaning brushes and palette. Without water, painting with acrylics becomes irksome, if not actually impossible.

Literally one must study the behaviour of water, for apart from its thinning and brush cleaning propensities, it must play its part throughout the whole of the work. Water is the life blood of acrylics, and though the other mediums extend the range of achievement, one can, at a pinch, do without them – as many of us did when acrylic paint was new and largely unknown. Consequently we were forced to examine just how much we could do with water alone.

By giving water the central role to play in acrylic painting, you learn that the amount used largely controls the rate of drying. It is essential to remember that once the water evaporates the paint hardens and cannot be redissolved with any more water (as it can with watercolour and gouache).

With experience and experiment you learn to add just the right amount of water to produce: the right consistency and the appropriate drying time to allow for working. This produces the simple rule: the more water used, the thinner the paint and the longer the drying time.

The four main forms of consistency are: thin, thick, transparent, opaque. Some of them can be amalgamated by the use of water alone: thin/transparent; thin/opaque. However, the only way to admix thick and transparent is by the use of a gel. Similarly the only way to get a really thick paint is by the addition of acrylic texture paste.

For the rest, water is sufficient.

Because acrylic is a water-based paint, it is always the practice to wet the brush before use, especially for mixing paint. As a general rule, never use a dry brush for anything pertaining to acrylic. A dry brush won't allow the paint to flow properly, will alter the drying times so that it will be harder to gauge, and won't do a sable brush much good. However if it does transpire that a dry brush has inadvertently been used, wash it out immediately afterwards.

(The exceptions to this rule will be seen in the section on scumbling, but here old brushes are recommended.)

This means acquiring, early on, the habit of constantly dipping the brush into water, and shaking out the excess, before beginning.

You can do the same with a palette knife – moistening it before use – though of course, the knife won't retain the water to anything like the same degree.

CHOOSING COLOURS

THE NEXT, AND MOST important, stage, is choosing colours, then mixing and applying them. The following colour exercises are very basic and, to get the maximum benefit from them, thin opaque paint, rather than thick or transparent paint, is recommended. The latter kinds of paint will be gone into later, and may be adapted to the exercises accordingly.

Choose a palette that will hold the paint well. Thin paint does have a tendency to slop about. Try the kind with wells or use a small saucer or two.

Another point to note is that once acrylic paint is mixed, it will last indefinitely so long as the water in it doesn't evaporate. Therefore any colour that has been mixed, and for any reason isn't needed right away, can be kept in a small jar or container so long as it is properly stoppered. For this purpose, I use discarded film cassette canisters, which are ideal for ready-mixed paint, and are useful for taking outdoors for working. A dab of the colour contained in them on the lid of the canister identifies them immediately.

Choice of colours is the very heart of painting and designing. The question is how to go about it? What are the rules, or principles, if any, that apply?

The overwhelming compunction on seeing a colour chart for the first time, is to want them all – and then give up because the choice is so wide, so it is refreshing to be told that the maximum number of colours needed to make up a palette that will do practically everything is FIVE.

FIVE ESSENTIAL COLOURS

WHITE IS ABSOLUTELY MANDATORY in any palette, for mixing tones and tints, for repainting prior to glazing or alteration, and as a colour.

Black is essential for tones, and as a colour.

Yellow – primary.

Red – primary.

Blue – primary.

The three primaries, yellow, red and blue can be mixed to make three further colours, or secondaries: orange, green and violet in the following way.

Yellow and red make orange.

Yellow and blue make green.

Blue and red make violet.

The secondary colours – orange, green and violet – can be bought in tubes ready-mixed which, if preferred, will make the basic eight-colour palette.

Whether you decide to have a five or eight palette,

mixing primaries to make secondaries must be carried out at some time for the experience of seeing what happens.

As an aid to choosing colours it is helpful to use a colour chart. Charts give the best information on the tone and range of the selection, the names of the colours, and a note or two on their use and permanence. Moreover charts are good to refer to for other reasons. By being the standard or yardstick of what pure colour looks like *before* mixing, they will aid mixing by being a reminder of what they were. With colour, the way to enhance understanding of them is to experience them often.

You can learn about colour by theory or by painting from nature: still lifes, landscapes, portraits, nudes and so on. Both methods have their respective value as a means of understanding colour. But for many students, especially beginners, studying colour directly from nature can be confusing, for the very reason that nature tends to get in the way. Degas once remarked to a student: 'If you want to learn to paint, don't study nature, study paintings.'

The colour-mixing exercises that follow take this observation one stage further, and concentrate solely on mixing and applying the paint. By so doing, you will experience exactly what colour does when mixed and applied. The exercises are fairly easy to carry out, and the results are immediate.

Begin with well-balanced and versatile hues. I would recommend yellow, red, blue. To these primaries I would add as secondaries orange, green, violet.

The ochres, umbers and siennas can be mixed approximately from the six-colour palette suggested. They may be added to the palette later, if required.

To explain why I have laid so much emphasis on the hues, the nature of colour temperature needs some explanation. Briefly, colours are either warm or cold depending on whether they are closer to one end of the spectrum or the other. *Warm* colours are those closer to *red*. *Cold* colours are those closer to *blue*.

Most colours have a bias one way or the other. Balanced colours, neither too warm nor too cold, are ideal for mixing secondaries from primaries.

Mixing primaries together to make secondaries is a delicate operation for those unused to mixing them, because the mixtures must be perfectly balanced. If the mixture is orange, it must not be too yellow or too red. With balanced primaries, it is much easier to judge.

COLOUR TEMPERATURE

Warm colours are those closer to the red end of the spectrum.

Cold colours are those closer to the blue end of the spectrum.

MIXING ACRYLIC

TO GET USED TO the way acrylic behaves, and to get the feel, as well as the visual impact of a mixture, a sound practice is to begin mixing each colour – both primaries and secondaries – with white first, and then with black. Then add black to white mixes, and white to the black.

Mixing white with a colour is referred to as a *tint*.

Mixing black with a colour is referred to as a *tone*.

All colours, whether pure or mixed together on the palette, can be toned or tinted with the addition of black or white. To grasp the range of tones and tints, and the extent to which they can be manipulated, all the colours that are available should be tried out at some time.

The point of this is that once the visual experience of mixing colours has taken place it will remain as a guide for future reference. Once seen, never forgotten. The more mixing that is done now, the more confident will be the results later. The results of these experiments should be kept, at least for a time, as a reminder.

COLOUR MIXING

EXERCISE 1 – LIGHT TO DARK

THE VERY FIRST EXPERIENCE with mixing can be with just white and black, before trying out the other colours. It is slightly easier to judge tones and tints of grey than the tones and tints of primaries and secondaries. This exercise is basic to all the colour mixing exercises. It will incorporate mixing, applying and experiencing the visual impact of tone, tint and hue.

Mixtures should be well integrated, on the palette, with a knife, and with enough fluidity to allow the brush to make a good, clean stroke.

For the kind of grid that will suit this exercise best, use six squares, about ½ in/1 cm in size, which can be conveniently filled with variegated tones of paint from light to dark, and from dark to light.

Method 1. Add black to white, to make a series of greys, from the palest to the darkest tints, in six steps. The grey of medium strength should occur in the centre of the scale.

Method 2. Reverse the process by adding white to black.

This exercise can now be repeated with all the colours, one by one, included in the palette, utilising Method 1 to make tones, and Method 2 to make tints.

Points to remember, observe and develop:

1. These exercises are fundamental. There is no need to paint them carefully, if your natural inclination is to paint them freely. The practice should be as enjoyable as possible. The only proviso is that care should be taken in the mixing of the paint, so that each change of tone, in its respective square, is as clear as possible.

2. There are no rules; and no end product to cause worry. The main point is, that when trying any new colour, do it this way before using it for whatever purpose you have in mind.

3. The aim of this exercise is to sharpen sensitivity, and give valuable experience not only in mixing colour, but to see what the colour looks like when mixed.

4. The exercises can be carried out in any order; size is optional, but for the best results, white paper or card (cardboard) is recommended, primed or unprimed. For a primed white surface one thin coat is sufficient.

5. The grid may be varied to accommodate more tones and tints, and more colours. As a variation, the tones and tints may be further mixed horizontally as well as vertically.

BELOW LEFT *The grid with separate tones.*

ABOVE *The horizontal and vertical grid.*

6. As an alternative exercise the mixing may be carried out without using white. The colours can be lightened by the addition of water to make them more transparent. This is the same technique as is used in painting with watercolours. It is a useful exercise, but needs more care than in using opaque acrylic, as the washes are more difficult to control. However, whatever result is obtained, practice in using colour this way is valuable, if only to experience the differences between using opaque and transparent colour. As a further experiment the exercise can be carried out on

different surfaces (as with watercolour) with both primed and unprimed paper.

7. Painting can be done with knife or brush. Try experimenting with them all, at some time or other, and become familiar with them at every available opportunity. This is the true meaning of practice.

8. Once confidence in mixing is acquired, any other acrylic colour may be tried out – the umbers, siennas, ochres, as well as the cadmiums, blues and greens mentioned earlier.

WHITE PAINT

WHITE PLAYS A MOST important role in painting and you will need more of it than any of the other colours. If possible buy the larger quantities. Large tubes will be less troublesome than small tubes which will run out very quickly. There is no good reason that I can fathom why one cannot use acrylic primer, if one does run short, as it is made of the same pigment, titanium white, and acrylic binder, as the tubed titanium white.

Titanium white is the only white pigment used, at the moment, for acrylic white paint, and is very powerful. A little goes a long way. So one has to be careful when mixing to add the white sparingly, or strong colours will be reduced to tints surprisingly quickly.

With jars of white, be very careful to keep the tops of the containers clear of dry paint, or the water will evaporate and the paint harden. A good tip is to sprinkle a few drops of water on the white to ensure that it doesn't, before putting the lid back on.

BLACK PAINT

MARS BLACK, WHICH IS absolutely permanent, is manufactured from artificial oxides of iron and is rather powerful so that, like white, it should be mixed sparingly with other colours. Although its use is suggested in the exercises, tones can be produced with many other combinations of colour – red and green, for example, make very good grey-blacks, as do blue and umber. Black is nevertheless a good utilitarian standby and an ideal colour for beginning the mixing of tones without too many problems.

EXERCISE 2 – DIRECT VISION

I HAVE MENTIONED BEFORE that learning about mixing and applying colours can be done directly from nature, but that the process can be confusing to those unused to the practice. As a bridge from mixing colours on a systematic chart basis as in Exercise 1 to the full examination of colour in nature which will lead to the painting of pictures, the following method is a simple and easy step in that direction.

Colour mixing and application are exactly as in Exercise 1.
1. Thin, opaque paint.

ABOVE The tonal scale runs from white to black. Every colour has a tonal equivalent on that scale between light and dark.

2. Primed or unprimed paper or card (cardboard), size optional but not bigger than 33×22 in/84×56 cm.
3. The choice of brushes is again optional.
4. Black and white paint are mandatory.
5. Three primaries only to begin with: red, yellow and blue; other colours can be added later for further experiments.

The aim of this exercise is to examine one colour at a time in all its variety, subtlety and visual impact by observing directly a group of objects all of the same colour.

To carry out this exercise, select a number of objects of the same colour: red, yellow or blue (omit green for the moment). Though only one of these colours is to be used at a time, the more varied the shades, the surfaces and the size that can be assembled the better.

If a particular colour is chosen, say red, to begin the experiment with, it will be immediately noticed that reds vary enormously. Some are warmer, others colder. Shiny reds will appear quite different from matt, some will be darker than the others and so on.

As an aid to selecting objects use this framework as a guide:
1. Size: large, small, cylindrical, cubic, round, triangular or concave.
2. Surfaces: smooth, rough, shiny, matt, textured, patterned.
3. Tone: light, dark, brilliant, faint, harsh, soft.

As a general rule three objects on a similar colour background are sufficient to begin with, arranged so as to make the maximum effect of the colour obvious.

The painting can be done either freely, in broad brushstrokes or flatly, in simple plain-coloured areas.

The object of this exercise, whichever way it is painted, is to mix different tones and tints of the same observed colour. The experience of Exercise 1 will be of great help here, and the painted charts can be referred to constantly if need be. The exercise will be helpful in making the eyes colour-sensitive to the gradations and variations of tones and tints that make colour so fascinating and elusive to control. This particular way of observing colour will enable you to grasp the essentials of manipulating colour.

The suggested method of painting to adopt is as follows:
1. Establish the large areas of colour first: this is usually the background, but if there isn't a great deal showing, begin with the largest shapes instead.
2. Use the brush to make deliberate marks of paint. Let the brush do the work. Avoid strain and above all avoid scrubbing. Load the brush with as much paint as can be held comfortably, and when exhausted replenish with fresh paint. Don't ever scrub with a dry brush. It will ruin the hairs, and make an unpleasant mark. Let the brush flow freely.
3. Build up the shapes of tone with crisp dabs of paint. Make no effort to make the painting look 'real'. Aim instead to examine the different areas of colour, and try to

state them as approximately as possible. Don't strain to make a picture, let the paint and the colour dominate instead.

This exercise should be repeated using all the primaries. It can then be followed by exploring the secondaries: green, orange and violet.

Variations on this theme can be made by:
1. changing the background to a different colour from the objects
2. introducing *one* object of an entirely different colour
3. introducing a white and black object to create a contrast
4. introducing *two* different coloured objects
5. painting on a coloured support
6. changing the background to *black*
7. changing the background to *white*.

COMPLEMENTARY CONTRAST

COMPLEMENTARY COLOURS ARE THOSE that lie opposite one another in the colour circle. As a follow up to the last exercises, and for further variations on colour combinations, here is the way in which complementaries work in contrast with one another. They make an interesting point about the way we respond to groupings of colours, and it is absolutely essential for designers to know what they consist of for future use.

Examples of primaries and secondaries consists of: yellow, violet, blue, orange, red, green. And in all these pairs primaries are always apparent – hence the necessity of mixing them together to make secondaries in the early stages. One gets to understand them better by doing so.

These colours are opposite yet require each other: they produce a vividness when adjacent, yet annihilate each other when mixed to produce a dark grey (useful as the basis for a neutral background, or underpainting to work on).

Another useful peculiarity of contrasting complementaries is that, though opposite, they have the remarkable ability to appear perfectly harmonious. This makes

using them an agreeable pictorial device for enhancing both paintings and designs. By utilizing the complementary chart, you have the beginnings of ready-made colour schemes that can be easily carried out with acrylic.

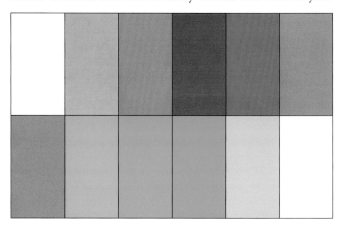

In the top row of squares move through yellow, orange, red, to violet, and the bottom row from violet, blue, green back to yellow. Begin with the primaries and secondaries directly over their opposite, and place the intermediate tones and tints in between in their correct order. The gradations of green should be placed under the appropriate gradations of violet above.

As an additional exercise, painting your own colour circle will give valuable experience in trying out colours straight from the tube without any mixing at all. Alternatively the secondaries can be mixed from the primaries to observe how possible it is to do so successfully.

Whichever method is adopted, it will remain as another interesting alternative in exploring the possibilities of colour.

Complementaries, and indeed, colour generally can be further studied with profit. Another simple experiment is to try painting on a coloured underpainting. Usually you begin on a white surface. Painting on a coloured surface opens up a great number of possibilities, too many to start with perhaps.

COLOURED SURFACES

COLOURED SURFACES AND SUPPORTS fall into two distinct categories: naturally coloured materials, such as wood, unglazed ceramic, metal, linen, hardboard etc; artificially coloured materials, like pastel papers, mounting card, plastic, dyed fabric etc.

Possibly the best surfaces of all are those you prepare yourself. Ready-made surfaces are rarely as versatile or satisfactory enough to suit all requirements. Those you prepare, moreover, have the advantages of better control of the work from its inception. The appropriate coloured surface will aid judgement of the tone of the colour – which a white or, for that matter, black, surface will rarely do. The reason for this is not difficult to find when considering tone. The addition of white or black to a

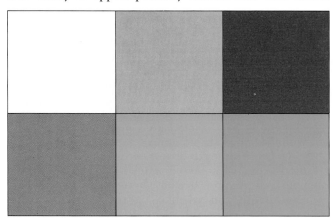

ABOVE *This chart shows the primary colours, yellow, blue and red with their contrasting complementaries, violet, orange and green, respectively.*

ABOVE RIGHT *A similar complementary contrast chart incorporating intermediate tones and tints.*

primary or secondary colour works within a tonal scale that has white at one end and black at the other. This is in accordance with one way the natural world is seen: as gradations of dark and light. This tonal scale moves in a series of progressions from one end of the scale to the other. To find the right balance within it is more difficult to judge, if we are forced to work from one end or the other. If instead we begin in the middle and work outwards, the result will be more successful, more visually effective and, more important, will be much more enjoyable to do.

Working in the middle of the tonal scale means darkening the white surface to a grey or neutral (middle tone) of colour. (As you rarely work on a black or very dark surface the problem won't arise with the same insistency.) For a white ground or surface the mid-tone can be varied in a number of ways:
1. It can be either flat or broken. A broken ground offers a number of additional possibilities over a flat ground, and was the kind often used by the old masters. Usually it was a wash or stain of diluted umber, but red ochre was also often employed, as well as neutral greys.
2. Greys can be mixed from complementaries and tinted with white, or from black; both make good backgrounds or underpaintings to work on.
3. Another practical neutral tint can be made with raw umber, rather than burnt umber which tends to be very warm. Raw umber, having a slightly greenish tinge, is cooler and just about right for making mid-tones that won't conflict with the colours painted over them.
4. A mid-grey tint can be further tinted with a primary to make a coloured grey, and a broken 'optical grey' can be made with patches of greys and coloured greys, to create a more lively surface to paint on – rather like an Impressionist painting in fact, but without the bright colours and the small brushstrokes.

Utilizing these kinds of grounds by painting the still lifes recommended in one of the exercises will be even more exciting because here you will be able to use with acrylic a number of accepted oil painting techniques with complete comfidence: impasto, palette knife, glazing and over-painting.

IMPASTOS

IMPASTOS ARE THICK, HEAVY strokes of paint made with brush or painting knife, and commonly associated with oil paint. With acrylic they can be achieved straight from the tube, like oil paint, and by the addition of either of two mediums, gel and texture or modelling paste, can be made as thickly as desired – something that can only be done with difficulty with oil paint, as oil paint dries slowly and cannot be thickened beyond a certain point without damage to its inherent and visual appeal.

Impastos have a direct, spontaneous visual impact, and are attractive to look at, and for many painters are easier to handle than thin paint, especially with a knife. But though attractive and pleasant to do, impastos can easily become an indulgence and so lose their initial charm unless

something is done about extending their capabilities by experiment and experience. Therefore they should be tried not only straight from the tube, but with gel and texture paste, and with a knife and brush separately and in combination. Impastos are intensified and conversely made more subtle when glazed.

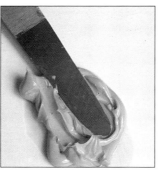

1 *The artist uses the knife to mix the paint on the palette. He then spreads it thickly in broad, textured ridges.*

2 *A heavy impasto may be sculpted to produce swirls and ridges.*

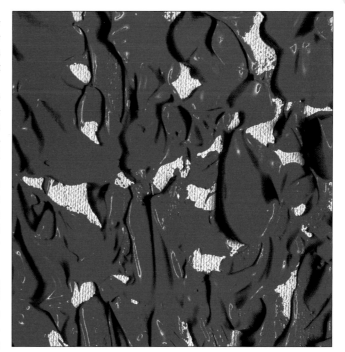

1 *Use undiluted acrylic paint from the tube, or mix tube colour with an equal proportion of gel medium.*
2 *Use a knife or a stiff bristle brush to spread the paint on the canvas.*

ABOVE *When applying impasto with a brush, mix the paint to a fairly stiff consistency. Dab the paint onto the support. Spread and shape it as required. The brushmarks will form part of the composition.*

KNIFE AND BRUSH

THE PAINTING KNIFE ON its own has an important role to play especially for those unused to a brush. But essentially what gives impastos their value is the directness with which they are done. Mess them about by too much overpainting and the vitality is severely reduced: you end with tinted mud.

The knife is probably less liable to mess, in spite of being clumsier than a brush. The flat blade of the knife constructed for mixing merely remixes the paint when applied to painting, whereas the brush being less able to mix, will only stir the paint up. Brushing paint should therefore be very deliberate, and if the sweeps and swirls fail to delight for whatever reason, scrape it off with a knife before it dries too hard, and start again.

The fact that some paint will be left will make a good underpainting for what is to follow, for some impastos work better, and look better, with an underpainting.

The main points to observe when mixing paint and medium for impastos are:
1. Make sufficient quantities of colour – you need more than you think.
2. Mix the medium well into the paint, take some time over the operation, or the impasto will lack the bulk the medium will give.
3. Impastos are also heavy, by comparison with thin opaque paint normally used, therefore only mix with a palette knife, never a brush. Application, on the other hand, can be done with either.
4. The visual impact of impastos are ridges of paint and lively brush or knife marks. These effects are best retained if the paint is not over-worked too much.

A glaze will bring out the unique features of impasto if applied carefully. But glazes can do a number of other things equally well. And because of the special qualities of acrylic mediums, they can do the job quicker and more effectively than oil paint, and may be used frequently without any bother, as the normal process of using acrylics.

ABOVE *An alternative method of applying impasto is to use a small palette knife. Scoop up some paint and lay it on the support. Spread and shape the impasto.*

TEXTURAL IDEAS

ABOVE A thick layer of acrylic mixed with modelling paste is applied with a painting knife and smoothed out.

ABOVE A kitchen fork is pressed into the wet paint to produce a pattern of grooves and ridges.

ABOVE An adhesive tool is used here. By twisting and turning it, many different patterns may be made.

GLAZES

IF IMPASTOS ARE THE thickest paint used with acrylic, then glazes are the thinnest – thinner even than the washes. Briefly, glazes are a mixture of medium and transparent pigment which is applied over dried underpaintings. The colour of the underpainting blends with that of the transparent glaze, and because it is not mixed with it, has an optical effect which is more vital than if it had been.

Glazes are, in effect, transparent coloured windows, and behave not unlike sunglasses – reducing the amount of light, and slightly changing the colour. Of course with coloured glazes, one tries to enhance, rather than reduce the colour, but to take the example of sunglasses further, glazes can and do have the power to unify the tones and tints of a work by reducing the colour, much as sunglasses do. Many a discordant work has been harmonized by placing a dark glaze over the whole of it.

Acrylic glazes are entirely free from being reduced to single colour glazing, because both they and the underpainting dry so quickly. As many glazes as required may be applied one after the other in a matter of minutes. The result is unique. Something that only stained glass could effect in the past – bright, rich, transparent colours, an effect that allows the light to pass through and so give an almost luminous glow to the colours. A good form of practice is to make glazes, on card (cardboard) or paper, using as a framework both the exercises given previously or the one that follows.

ABOVE To make this glaze, mix a small amount of colour with a lot of medium. Apply with a soft brush and allow to dry.

ABOVE A more transparent glaze can be made by adding extra matt medium to the pigment.

ABOVE A transparent scumble is made by mixing a lot of matt medium and water with the colour to produce delicate scumbles. Further scumbles can be built up in layers to give greater effect.

BELOW Use short, irregular strokes to produce an area of broken, scumbled colour.

EXERCISE IN GLAZING

FOR THE EXERCISE ONLY, a small piece of card (cardboard) or paper is necessary. But to get the most out of it, both plain and primed supports should be tried. Glazes should be as thin as possible, which makes them fragile, because the binders are weakened. Therefore the addition of a medium (in this instance the binder itself) is absolutely vital. Also the medium gives body to the glaze, which the pigment fails to give. As a beginning, to get used to the feel and visual impact of glazing, use the acrylic medium alone. If it feels too thick, add a few drops of water – the cardinal rule.

The exercise can be repeated with gel medium, both with brush and knife. Glazes can take on a different quality with a knife, and so should be tried.

The diagrams describe visually what takes place. On a grid of twelve squares, a layer of glaze is placed and allowed to dry. Another layer of glaze of a different colour is placed across it. Where the two glazes intersect, a third colour will be apparent. The rest of the grid can now be completed with further layers of glaze.

As you can see, the permutations of this principle are numerous:
1. Thin glazes over thin opaque paint,
2. Thin glazes over thin transparent paint,
3. Thin glazes over thick paint,
4. Thick glazes over thin paint,
5. Light glazes over light glazes,
and so on and so on. All these variations are fascinating to try out and will produce some very exciting effects.

SCUMBLING

THE BRUSH MARK THAT combines some of the transparent qualities of a glaze with the exuberant spontaneity of impasto is a scumble. Scumbling is a somewhat vague term for applying a thin coating of colour vigorously brushed over the entire work or parts of it to soften the effect, but the real point of a scumble is to

Yellow and green are scumbled together but not blended.

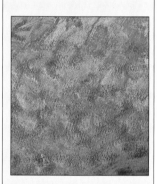

Scumbles must be applied thinly so that previous applied layers show through.

create a free or broken brush mark which will allow the underpainting to show through to animate the colour and the surface at the same time.

Unlike a glaze, a scumble may be applied without any additional medium, and be either semi-transparent or opaque. Provided the underpainting is perfectly dry, the scumble may be dragged, scrubbed, dabbed or brushed in any fashion suitable for covering the entire work, or parts of it, quickly and spontaneously.

Scumbling is cruder than glazing, which implies carefully controlled transparent layers over selected parts of the work. Scumbling by its very nature is more hit-and-miss, and will delight those who go for textural effects, the particular transitions of broken brushwork and changes of mind, and will give a great deal of pleasure, both doing it and looking at it afterwards.

Scumbling, as its name seems to imply, breaks all the accepted rules for the methodical application of paint. Dry paint, hitherto discouraged as being bad for brushes and palette, is looked upon with favour. 'Dry paint' – a term artists often use when referring to applying a scumble – is a stiff rather than thick paint, so that when it is dragged across a surface – underpainting or canvas – it will leave a pleasant broken effect. Consequently instead of throwing away old, worn out brushes you find that they are ideal for the job of creating textural effects, used with dry paint, and with the scrubbing and rubbing that characterizes scumbling. And when these old brushes finally collapse, use a wad of tissue paper and dab with that to get the kind of effect you want.

Scumbling is particularly effective for dragging light paint over a dark ground and vice versa, or dragging one complementary colour over another. It is the perfect foil to flat, carefully done painting, and should be resorted to from time to time, not only for the experience of creating broken colour effects, but as an exercise in improvisation. As an experiment, try scumbling over any discarded paintings, and observe how a once-rejected work takes on a new life when scumbled over.

WHITING-OUT

PERHAPS THE OPPOSITE OF the glaze and the scumble, despite its overlaying similarity, is the process I call 'whiting-out', or more accurately repriming, which is exactly what it is. The method I devised is ideally suited for acrylic, for it enables a painting to be continued indefinitely, or at least until you are satisfied with the result, without the repainted surface showing that it has been reworked in any way whatsoever.

Repriming is something that can be done without any difficulty with acrylic because of the quick drying and versatile textural qualities of rough or smooth, transparent or opaque. It cannot be done successfully with gouache or oil paint, because gouache picks up and oil paint is too thick and dries too slowly to make the operation worthwhile. It is worthwhile, if only for the following reason.

The recurring problem with paintings, illustrations and coloured drawings is that they frequently 'go wrong'.

SOME OTHER TECHNIQUES

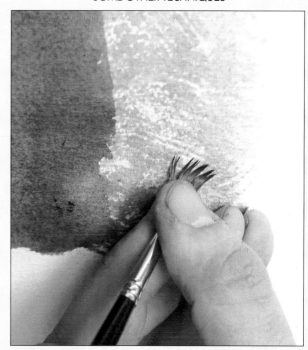

ABOVE *Using a dry brush, pick up colour on the brush and move it lightly across the support. The dry brush* technique *is used to blend or paint areas of finely broken colour.*

ABOVE *Scratching. Any sharp tool can be used to etch lines and texture into acrylic paint* while it is still wet. Here a *paint brush handle is being used.*

MIXED MEDIA

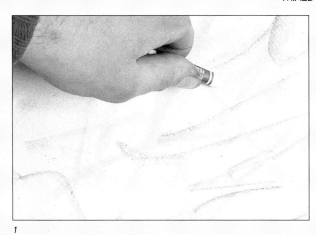

1

2

3

1 *TOP LEFT Wax resist. Wax crayon is applied to the support. Candles or any fatty, waxy material will do.*

2 *TOP RIGHT The next step is to paint acrylic over the crayon.*

3 *ABOVE The wax resists the paint, allowing a textured pattern to show through.*

They don't, in fact, go wrong, they go astray, or out-grow their original intention. Nevertheless, however natural this feature may be, it can cause frustration, helplessness and despair when you are faced with it. To circumvent or anaesthetize the pain it can cause, whiting-out or repriming will remove some of the sting. Moreover this can be repeated until the work adjusts itself and begins to flower again.

Only two conditions need be observed for this method to work properly.
1. The surface of the paint must be smooth. Any impastos or texturing will interfere with the successful application of the new paint.
2. The white paint (or tinted paint) must be semitrans-parent.

Whenever part of a painting needs correcting or chang-ing, or loses its freshness, or the whole of the painting needs altering, dilute some white priming or tube white with water to make a thin semitransparent wash, and white-out the part or parts to be repainted. The density of the paint must be gauged by eye, just so long as the underpainting isn't completely blotted out.

Whiting-out can be done over an entire work. Repaint-ing on still-discernible shapes can begin and whiting out can be done as often as necessary. With this method, the whiting-out is done with a painting knife. The white paint is gently spread over the work and allows the old work to show through better than if done with a brush, as it can be spread really thin with the blade of a knife.

Another way of using this method is to use it not only as a corrective device but as an actual technique of building up a work from the start. The design or drawing is painted on unprimed white card (cardboard), or paper, with monochrome washes, and then whited-out over the entire work, letting the drawing or design show through.

As a variation on the white tone, the paint can be tinted with a colour. Experiment will tell whether a particular colour is suitable for whiting-out in this way, but umbers and ochres are good colours to begin with, rather than the primaries (though I have used blue tints with a great deal of success). The best advice I can give is to try them all. The permutations are many, as with most things connected with acrylic. The advantage of white as a reprimer is that it is ideal for transparent rather than opaque application of colour. The sparkle of transparent washes will be more easily retained with repriming with white. A tinted white would not be of much help here, and, though some of the effects may be quite startling, white is probably the safest tone to use if you want to be certain of the results.

WASHES

WASHES USED IN WATERCOLOUR painting are perhaps the most difficult to control, and are probably one of the most difficult processes to master. Controlling them is a never-failing source of anxiety for some water-colourists, because if a wash goes wrong it cannot be put right, and so the work loses its point and purpose. Washes,

ABOVE *To lay a flat wash, prepare plenty of paint. Use a wide, flat brush and run the strokes in one direction only. Each stroke should slightly overlap the one before.*

even with acrylic, can be ruined, but because of the nature of the paint itself, you can use whiting-out and put it right again.

Although acrylic can be used like watercolour, it must be clearly understood that acrylic washes function differently from watercolour washes. The main difference is the paint composition itself, for though the pigments may be iden-tical, the binders are not. Watercolours can be diluted so thinly that they have hardly any body at all. The gum binders are capable of holding the pigments together despite overthinning. Acrylic, on the other hand, has a binder that imparts weight and substance to the paint which must be considered, especially when overthinning the paint, and it cannot be ignored without breaking down its inherent qualities. A useful measure to adopt is always to add a good few drops of the acrylic medium when diluting acrylic paint for washes, as a precaution. It will keep the wash from looking thin and lifeless, and will add a sparkle that ordinary watercolour sometimes lacks.

Acrylic washes can be varied in a number of ways not unlike watercolour, but happily because the particular characteristic of the medium is to impart bulk to a paint once thinned, it is easier to manage. A simple trial with watercolour will prove this quite conclusively. Watercolour occasionally behaves in a capricious way that some painters find almost impossible to control. By comparison, acrylic, by the very nature of its medium, is less temperamental, always provided that additional medium is reintroduced into the wash and can be manipulated by even the most inexperienced with relatively little skill.

There is perhaps only one rule to observe, that like pure watercolour, once a wash is applied, leave it alone.

Acrylic washes can be formed by:
1. flooding one wash into another
2. adding fresh colour to an already applied wash
3. adding colour to moistened paper
4. gradated tones from dark to light
5. flat
6. animated by brushstrokes
7. overlay
8. allowing the surface to play its part
9. allowing the wash to run freely, without any control whatsoever.

The following experiments should give a great deal of experience. They should be tried on paper, card (cardboard) and even canvas, with and without priming. Vary them by using both smooth and textured surfaces. The addition of the water tension breaker or wetting agent will ensure that washes will flow and absorb well on to the support. It is important to experiment in the following ways occasionally, so that you become familiar with the effect each method has.

Sables are traditionally more suitably for washes than hog's-hair brushes, and should be as large as possible (number 7 or 8). Hog's-hair may be tried but are less flexible for gradating and spreading a wash smoothly. As long as you recognize this, they can be tried as a means for creating variations of the basic wash technique.

EXPERIMENT 1 – FLAT WASH

☛ Squeeze out ½ in/1 cm of paint into a clean container.
☛ Add water to dilute, mix well to make sure that there are no lumps of undissolved paint as this will ruin a wash.
☛ Add some acrylic medium last – about a teaspoon will do.
☛ With a large brush spread the wash down the paper or card (cardboard), working from the top, to make a flat wash. Whatever happens, do not touch the wash once it has been applied. Let the colour find its own level.
☛ The application can be carried out upright or on the flat. If upright the wash will run down rather quickly.

EXPERIMENT 2 – GRADATED TONES

EXACTLY THE SAME AS Experiment 1, only in this experiment instead of painting the wash completely in one colour, halfway through continue with clean water only and let the colour blend into it. This is easy to do with pure acrylic colour, provided there is plenty of medium in the wash, and water tension breaker (wetting agent) in the water.

ABOVE *Experiment 2. To achieve a gradated effect, work quickly, adding water to the paint in increasing quantities with each successive band of colour.*

ABOVE *Experiment 4. To produce this wet-in-wet, the artist began with a graded wash of cobalt blue and added a graded wash of lemon yellow.*

ABOVE *Experiment 3. Single colour wet-in-wet wash, made by covering the support with a layer* *of water and allowing a wash of colour to flood into it.*

EXPERIMENT 3 – MOISTENED PAPER

FIRST COVER THE PAPER or card (cardboard) completely with water. Then, before it has properly dried, flood a wash into it as above.

EXPERIMENT 4 – ADDING COLOUR

THIS EXPERIMENT CAN COMBINE any or all of Experiments 2 and 3. Proceed as above, and before the colour has dried flood another colour into the wet surface. Usually known as wet-in-wet.

ABOVE Lay the palest colours first, so that the light reflects off the white paper.

ABOVE It is vital to allow one colour to dry completely before applying the next one.

ABOVE The artist applies a thin wash of Hooker's green over the first colour. Where the two washes cross, a third hue is produced.

EXPERIMENT 5 – OVERLAY

THIS IS EXACTLY LIKE glazing. Proceed as above, but let the colour dry out thoroughly. Then apply further washes over the dried paint. In pure watercolour, the paint may pick up, but with acrylic this can never happen.

EXPERIMENT 6 – ANIMATED BRUSHSTROKES

FOR THIS EXPERIMENT, USE an ample amount of acrylic medium with the paint and, when well mixed, the wash can be applied, letting the brush play its part by animating the wash with brushstrokes. Hog's-hairs can be used for this experiment with profit.

Washes are one kind of effect that looks well without under- or overpainting, hence their popularity for immediate statements, especially for figurative work like landscape painting where, being outdoors in all kinds of weather, speed and spontaneity are vital. Immediacy and fluency, however, are easily lost if these washes are overworked, which may be the reason why flooding and merging of one colour into another is not really possible with opaque or more solid paint which depend on their effects by overpainting in layers.

Washes can, of course be overpainted, which, as has been pointed out, is similar to glazing, but unlike glazing – which can be carried out on all kinds of surfaces, under-paintings and impastos – overpainting washes is always better on a white surface. This ensures the retention of the transparency and sparkle so typical of watercolour.

BELOW The use of animated strokes with a hog's-hair brush produces a very active texture.

ABOVE: Hatching using ink. By varying the density of the lines, a wide variety of tones is achieved. Freely drawn lines look more lively than perfectly straight, mechanical lines.

RIGHT An old, splayed brush was used to create this slightly rough, hatched texture in acrylic. The underlying colour glows through the overpainting to great effect.

HATCHING

HATCHING IS A VERY old and basic means for gradating tones on white paper with something as dense and impenetrable as pen and ink. Gradating tones with a pencil is much easier, as most of us will have experienced before now, and painted washes are perhaps one of the simplest and best means of achieving it in the most subtle and effective way. When painting expanded from simple washes to the more complex paints like gouache, tempera and fresco, the technique that was adopted was that of hatching, which reached its full development in the 14th and 15th centuries, before the introduction of oil paint rendered it obsolete. Oil paint could render gradated tones so much more realistically than hatching with tempera – but at a cost. The qualities of texture and colour that hatching brought were sorely missed, until renewed interest in water-based painting revived the method. Acrylic, being one of these, is ideally suited to hatching.

Hatching consists of the criss-crossing of hundreds of small lines over each other to produce a rich variegated tone. The more these fine lines are hatched the more dense the tone becomes. Many drawings by the old masters were done this way, and so inevitably became the basis of the way they painted. When one examines a 14th- or 15th-century tempera panel, it will be seen to be made up of hundreds of tiny strokes of colour, sometimes going around the forms, to accentuate the solidity, sometimes across the forms to show the play of light and dark.

In painting with a hatching technique, the open network

of lines means that not only are the tones gradated, but the underpainting can filter through as well, thus enhancing both tone and colour at the same time – another reason why, perhaps, tempera painting has a brilliance that oil painting seems to lack over the centuries.

Hatching with acrylic will involve small sable brushes (0, 00 or 1) as well as thin paint, which can be either transparent or opaque, or even a mixture of both. But it must not be too thick, or the hatching will lose its delicacy, and be more difficult to manipulate.

Hatching is a delicate and painstaking operation, but with patience can produce remarkable and effective results that are well worth the trouble they involve.

EXPERIMENT IN HATCHING

DRAW A SMALL GRID of 1-in/2.5-cm squares. About four will suffice. Try filling them with a variety of hatching as follows:
1. cross hatching with one colour,
2. cross hatching from dark to light,
3. cross hatching from the centre outwards,
4. cross hatching from the outside inwards.

Vary the hatching with both transparent and opaque lines, and short and long, thick and thin strokes, to create as much variety of texture as possible.

STIPPLING

STIPPLING IS SOMEWHAT LIKE hatching in that it is the building up of tone with hundreds of tiny marks. But with hatching, the marks are strokes of the brush – long, short, thin or thick – whereas with stippling, dabs are made with the point or end of the brush.

If sables are used for stippling, it is wiser to use the older, more worn out brushes, as stippling can be very hard on them unless used with a very gentle kind of stipple, which is not easy to do as the dabbing action is a forceful one. As with hatching, the process is a painstaking one. The overpainting of hundreds of tiny dots one on the other gives a pleasing effect, and the tonal gradations are even more delicate than with hatching. However it is unnecessary to cover the work completely with stippling. You can confine it to the parts with a more telling effect.

Georges Seurat, the pointillist painter, who took Impressionism one stage further, stippled his tones and tints of pure colour, without mixing them, throughout the painting. The intention was to let the eye do the mixing. Unfortunately his paintings were not carried out in acrylic, as they hadn't been invented at that time – but there is no reason why acrylics shouldn't be tried in this manner, provided the stippling has some kind of colour system as a foundation for the design, or that the stippling is consistent in its marks throughout the work.

Experiment with stippling in the same way as hatching. The paint can be thicker than with hatching, if desired, and stippling can also be carried out with materials other than brushes: sponges, wads of paper, toothbrushes, even fingertips will do as an alternative.

LEFT *Stippling with a brush is carried out by holding the brush at right angles to the painting surface, and repeatedly touching the tip to the surface.*

BELOW *The effect is an area of colours that appears lighter and brighter than the equivalent colour applied in a flat wash.*

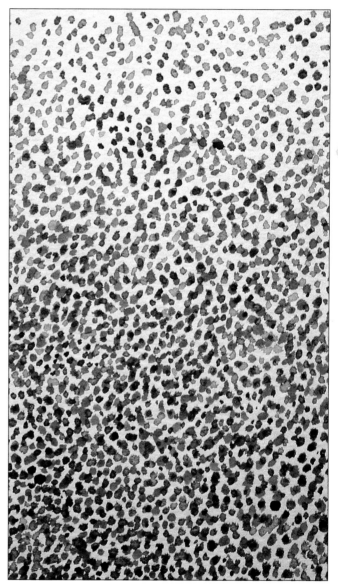

As with hatching, the aim should be to keep the dabs as separate as possible to achieve the maximum effect. The dabs should be as crisp as possible, though piled up over each other; they should not smear or smudge into each other. As with hatching, allow any underpainting to filter through if possible.

CHAPTER FOUR

THE
PROJECTS

PAINTING IS about looking and
seeing and translating what you see
in the three-dimensional world around
you, through selective and imaginative
processes, into pictures. Visual source
material for your paintings is everywhere around you, on a table, in your
room, through a window or even in
your mirror. Look at your everyday surroundings with new eyes for a subject
and you will find plenty of inspiration.

SWIMMERS IN HONG KONG

WATERSIDE PICTURES are popular subjects for artists, not only because they conjure up holidays, but also because they offer at least three quite separate elements to work on, the water, the landscape and the sky. This picture was painted essentially as a landscape and then brought alive by the addition of figures, buildings and other points of human interest.

The artist used the photographs as starting points only, identifying major features in them, particularly the vegetation, the mountains and the water, before creating his own imaginary landscape. The form of the trees will be treated with adjacent areas of light and shadow while the hazy distant mountains will be emphasized by the use of colours, mainly white and blue.

The almost impressionistic finish was achieved by the use of soft, carefully directed brushstrokes and reinforces the relaxed holiday atmosphere which is the central theme of the painting.

1 Two photographs of the city provide the artist with basic ideas for his picture. He will 'sandwich' these with other images in his own mind to compose the scene he wishes to paint.

2 The artist fills the water in primarily with phthalocyanine blue and titanium white which effectively reflect the colours of the sky and background landscape. The trees are strengthened with Hooker's green and the hills given more weight and bulk with medium magenta.

2

3

MATERIALS USED

SUPPORT
- prepared, acrylic-primed canvas board measuring 36 × 25in/92 × 64cm

BRUSHES
- Nos. 2 and 5 round bristle and synthetic
- Nos. 2, 4, 6 and 11 flat bristle and synthetic

COLOURS
- Hooker's green
- ivory black
- phthalocyanine green
- medium magenta
- titanium white
- cobalt blue
- phthalocyanine blue
- raw sienna

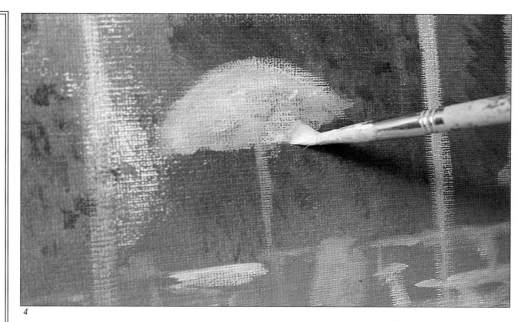

4

3 The sky is brought on further with cobalt blue which is also added to the water to deepen and brighten its colour.

4 Detail in the foreground is now developed, with the correct emphasis on form retained, in keeping with the overall picture.

5 Although the figures are very much in the foreground detail would have been impossible here, as the perspective of the composition, with mountains and tall skyscrapers in the background, requires that they be fairly small.

5

5

6 The trees are darkened with Hooker's green and highlighted with phthalocyanine green, again in broad brushstrokes.

6

7

8

7 *The skyscrapers are blocked in with strong simple brushstrokes and are set off against each other with varying mixtures of blues and white.*

8 *The figures have plenty of movement and definition as a result of the careful combination of different colours and tones.*

9 *The finished painting is very successful and owes much of its success to the way in which the brushstrokes were applied to the canvas. The texture of the canvas itself has also been used to advantage to give depth to the picture and to convey the steamy atmosphere characteristic of Hong Kong.*

Swimmers in Hong Kong

YOUNG MAN IN A STRIPED SHIRT

THIS IS EFFECTIVELY a rapidly-done sketch on a large scale. It could have been taken much further, but the bold and quick brushstrokes, and the scale, allow it to work as a vigorous and lively piece already. The spontaneous use of colour, to catch the most significant elements in the composition, was more important than filling in all the finer details.

Try painting quickly as it is a useful discipline that will teach you to structure and compose the whole picture and stop you from becoming too distracted by less important minor details.

2

3

MATERIALS USED

SUPPORT
■ prepared board, measuring 24 × 20in/ 60 × 50cm

BRUSHES
■ Nos 6 and 10 round bristle
■ No. 4 flat bristle

OTHER MATERIALS
Oil Pastel
Soft Pastel
Pencil

COLOURS
■ ivory black
■ titanium white
■ chrome oxide
■ naphthol red
■ yellow ochre
■ cerulean blue.

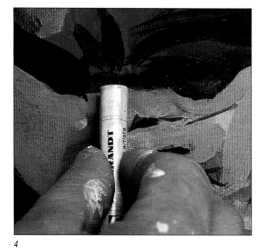

4

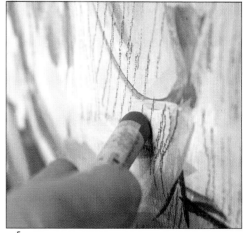

5

Young Man in a Striped Shirt

6

1 The artist will attempt to work as quickly as possible as the model is sitting up fairly straight, quite a tiring position to maintain for any length of time.

2 The artist paints directly onto the support without bothering to make any rough drawing or outline sketch. The shadow tones of the head and torso are blocked in first.

3 The main blocks of colour, the hair, the trousers, the arms and the face are built up quickly with relaxed brushstrokes, and then the shirt with a mixture of all the colours.

4 A soft pastel is used to give extra life and colour to the flesh tones; the texture of the pastel allows the artist to obtain firm edge on the arms and hands.

5 The combination of different mediums such as soft pastel, oil pastel, and pencil injects variety of texture into the picture.

6 The finished picture has a delightful informal sketch-like quality and shows just what can be achieved by working quickly and confidently without dwelling too much on relatively unimportant superficial details.

FOOD ON THE FARM

STILL LIFE is one of the simplest and most accessible of painting subjects. Unlike landscapes, for example, still lifes give you the opportunity to choose and arrange objects in any way you like. There is no need to stage an elaborate arrangement of objects, either, especially if time is pressing. In this painting the artist has chosen as his subject the remains of a simple rustic meal left on the table. An arrangement such as this can have great appeal, because somehow it captures a moment in time: it isn't merely a collection of lifeless objects.

In keeping with the earthy simplicity of the subject, the artist used a painting knife to give a rough-textured surface to the painting. Acrylic paint has a thick, buttery consistency, and can be 'sculpted' to create interesting surface effects that lend character to the painting. A knife can not only pile on thick paint successfully, it can also be used for scraping out unwanted passages. You must work quickly, though, due to the fast drying time of acrylic paint.

Another interesting point about this picture is that it was painted, not onto a white support, but over another painting beneath. This was an unfinished painting which the artist had rejected. Because the original work had not reached an advanced stage it was an easy matter to overpaint it, especially since acrylics have such good covering power. Rather than paint out the original image, however, the artist chose to work directly onto it, so that faint lines and shapes showed through the blocks of colour as the new work progressed. This method has one great advantage: it alleviates the problem of facing a glaring white canvas and being afraid of 'spoiling' it. Having shapes and colours already there on the canvas is much less inhibiting.

4

5

6

1

2

3

1 *Simple and uncontrived, this still life group nevertheless contains an interesting variety of shapes and textures.*

2 *Working over an old painting, the artist begins by blocking in the main colour areas with loose brushstrokes.*

3 *The forms of the still life are drawn in with a brush and diluted*

paint. Parts of the old painting still show through in places.

4 *Now the image is beginning to take shape.*

5 *This detail shows the various textures that can be achieved with a painting knife, from the smoothness of a knife blade to the rough, stippled texture of a crumbled brown loaf.*

6 *The paint is used thickly, often being mixed directly on the canvas instead of on the palette. Note the rough-hewn texture created by the knife.*

7 *This close-up of the earthenware jar shows how the artist has used the painting knife to partially mix the colours and build up a textured impasto.*

8 *The finished painting shows how bold and direct a knife painting can be. The artist has deliberately left the paint surface rough and unfinished, preserving a lively spontaneity that is entirely in keeping with the rustic simplicity of the subject.*

7

MATERIALS USED

SUPPORT
- prepared board primed with acrylic, measuring 24×20in/60×50cm

BRUSHES
- No. 7 flat hog's-hair
- Nos. 2, 4 and 6 round sable
- Nos. 3 and 5 synthetic fibre

COLOURS
- burnt umber
- yellow ochre
- cadmium red medium
- ultramarine
- ivory black
- titanium white

Food on the Farm

8

STILL LIFE WITH BOTTLE, FRUITS AND VEGETABLES

FOR THIS STILL LIFE PAINTING, the artist has used an intriguing combination of a modern medium – acrylic – and a traditional oil painting technique dating back to the days of the Old Masters: namely, that of developing a detailed underpainting over which transparent glazes of colour are applied, layer upon layer, to achieve a translucent and shimmering surface.

Hundreds of years later, the miraculous effects achieved by the Masters still fill us with admiration and awe. However, the technique which they used was a slow and laborious one, since each layer of paint had to be left for several days to dry out before the next one could be applied. If a layer of oil paint is applied over an underlayer that is not completely dry, cracking ensues and the painting can be ruined in a very short time.

With the advent of acrylic paints in the 1950s, this problem was at last solved. Like oil paint, acrylics can be used thickly or in thin washes; but, unlike oils, they dry very quickly and repeated layers of colour can be built up without any danger of cracking.

Acrylics, then, can achieve all that oil paint can, but much more quickly and with less risk.

Following the traditional method, the artist has here worked on a tinted ground, painting from dark to light with very thin layers of colour. Before starting to paint, the artist drew a detailed sketch of the still life. This, coupled with the quick-drying properties of the acrylic paints, allowed him to complete the painting rapidly once begun, as all preliminary planning and decision-making had been finished beforehand.

1

1 For this still life, the artist chose objects whose soft colours and shiny textures would lend themselves well to the glazing technique.

2 The first step is to tone the canvas with a thin wash of burnt umber, well diluted with water. This sets the tone for the whole painting, and softens the stark white of the canvas. The still life objects are then indicated with thin black paint and a No.2 brush.

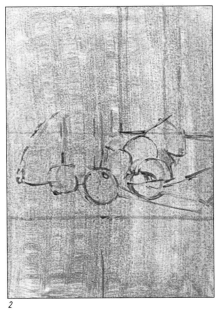

2

3

4

5

6

7

8

3 *Next the artist blocks in the lightest areas of the painting with thin white paint and a No.10 brush, blending them with a rag.*

4 *Working over the entire surface, the artist blocks in the strong highlight areas with a No.4 brush and pure white paint, used a little more thickly this time.*

5 *With a No.2 sable brush, the artist redraws the outlines of the subject in black thinned with water.*

6 *A dilute mixture of cadmium yellow and white is used for the onions. Then the shadow areas around the onions and the table are strengthened with thin washes of ivory black.*

7 *A cool tone of white and yellow ochre is now applied with a No.10 brush and worked well into the surface. Note how the warm underlayer still shines through.*

8 *With a fine brush and white paint, the artist develops the highlights and reflections in the bottle and the onions.*

9 *The completed painting has all the vigour of an* alla prima *painting, yet is also has a subtlety and delicacy. The dark underpainting ensures a unity in the painting as it permeates all subsequent layers of paint giving an overall warmth.*

Still Life With Bottle, Fruits and Vegetables

9

MATERIALS USED

SUPPORT
- prepared canvas board measuring 16×20in/ 40×50cm

BRUSHES
- Nos. 2, 4 and 10 sable round oil brushes

COLOURS
- ivory black
- burnt umber
- cadmium yellow light
- yellow ochre
- titanium white

Interior

7

INTERIOR

YOU DON'T NEED TO TRAVEL FAR and wide in order to find a suitable subject to paint; often the most interesting pictures are those which feature familiar objects and ordinary places. An interior scene, for example – perhaps the very room you are sitting in now – can provide an endless source of inspiration for the creative artist.

As with still lifes, you can arrange the objects in an interior, and also control the lighting, to express a particular mood or to make a personal statement. In this painting, for example, the artist has created a spare, almost abstract composition which captures the melancholy mood of a large, bare room on a cold winter's day. Through the window we catch a glimpse of the grey, wintry landscape beyond. The shadow of the window slants across the cold, empty wall. And in the corner stands a grand piano, half-hidden by a shroud-like dust sheet. Altogether, an atmospheric and thought-provoking composition.

To capture the mood of the scene, it was essential to work quickly before the light changed, and this is where the fast-drying properties of acrylics saved the day. The artist worked with a limited palette of neutral colours, and applied the paint directly onto the canvas with broad, flat washes.

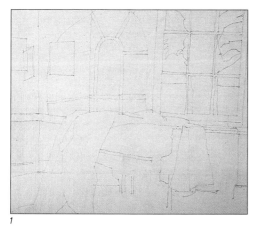

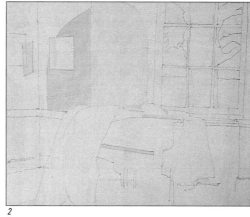

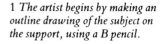

1 *The artist begins by making an outline drawing of the subject on the support, using a B pencil.*

2 *The pale tones of the wall are established first, using yellow ochre mixed with white, and lemon yellow in the lightest parts.*

3 *Using a No. 4 flat brush, the artist paints in the lines of the window frame, and its shadow cast on the wall, with raw sienna.*

4 *Now the dark tones of the foreground are blocked in with burnt umber darkened with black.*

5 *The artist paints 'negatively', working the dark tones around the white shape of the dust sheet covering the piano. The folds in the dust sheet are indicated with strokes of burnt umber.*

6 *The shadows on the background wall and on the dust sheet are now built up using Payne's grey, cobalt blue, yellow ochre and titanium white.*

7 *Finally, the scene outside the window is painted in, using Payne's grey, Mars black, burnt umber and titanium white. Subtle, neutral colours have been used throughout, and this contributes to the quiet, introspective mood of the painting.*

MATERIALS USED

SUPPORT
■ Gesso-primed hardboard measuring 10×12in/ 25×30cm

BRUSHES
■ Nos. 4 and 7 flat synthetic hair

COLOURS
■ raw sienna
■ yellow ochre
■ Payne's grey
■ Mars black
■ titanium white
■ burnt umber
■ cobalt blue

IRISES IN A GREEN VASE

A STILL LIFE SUBJECT such as a vase of flowers may seem like a simple one, but it is nevertheless very important to plan the composition carefully in order to create a pleasing image.

Because this vase of irises was such a symmetrical shape, it could have produced a stiff, boring picture. But the artist has avoided this problem by lighting the subject from one side to create interesting elongated shadows. He also arranged the subject on the canvas in an interesting way. Rather than place the vase of flowers in the centre of the canvas, which would have been the most obvious solution, he chose to place it off-centre, where it interacts with the rectangles created by the shelf and the side of an alcove.

Part of the appeal of this painting is in its crisp, clean edges. The artist used masking tape as a stencil in order to achieve the clear-cut characteristics of the highlights and shadows on the vase and the leaves.

In painting the subtle colours of the irises, the artist has used oil paint over an acrylic base. Because oil paint is slow-drying, it can be blended to create soft gradations of tone and colour – something which cannot be done with acrylics because they dry so fast. Do remember, however, that oil paint can be used over acrylic, but not vice versa. Acrylic paint will not adhere to an underlayer of oil paint, and starts to crack off in a very short time.

1

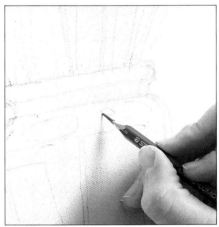

2

3

4

5

6

1 *The tall, elegant irises are placed against a cool, grey background which complements the cold blues and greens in the arrangement.*

2 *The artist places the subject off-centre, to create an interesting visual tension with the surrounding space.*

3 *Because the artist intends to build up the picture systematically, the drawing is detailed enough to act as an accurate guide to the placement of each area of tone and colour.*

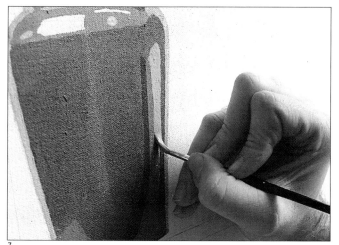

7

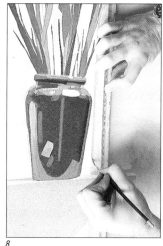

8

4 *The artist begins by painting the flowers. A purple-blue is mixed from ultramarine, white, black and a little crimson.*

5 *The irises are developed from light to dark, each tone being completed in flat patches of colour. More white is added to the lighter areas.*

6 *The leaves are painted in three tones of green mixed from chromium oxide, ultramarine and white. Touches of cadmium yellow pale are added to the centres of the irises.*

9

10

11

12

7 *The vase is painted with a mixture of emerald, chromium oxide and raw umber. For the shiny highlights, the artist uses the basic vase colour with added white and yellow ochre.*

8 *The straight edge of the background shadow on the left is achieved with the aid of a ruler. The shadow area is then painted with a mixture of Payne's grey and ultramarine.*

9 *The rest of the background is a very pale grey, made from white with touches of black and ultramarine. A slightly darker tone of grey is used for the shadows of the flowers, which are softened and blurred at the edges.*

10 *The shelf is painted next, using a mixture of raw sienna and white. The dark shadow is mixed from black, white, ultramarine and raw umber.*

11 *The final details of the flowers are completed in oil paint because the colour is slow-drying and easier to manipulate. The darks in the flowers are mixed from ultramarine, alizarin crimson and a touch of white.*

12 *When the paint is dry, the artist begins work on the crisp shapes of light and shadow on the leaves. He uses masking tape as a stencil, sticking it firmly to the canvas so that no paint can seep under the edges.*

13

14

13 *The delicate shapes to be painted are cut out with a sharp scalpel or blade, being careful not to cut the canvas. These shapes are then peeled away.*

14 *Thick oil paint is used to paint the shapes which have been cut out of the stencils.*

15 *When the paint is thoroughly dry, the masking tape is gently peeled off the canvas, revealing the sharp, clean lines of colour on the leaves.*

16 *Because the style of the picture is so graphic, the artist decides to add texture to the flat background colour using a soft pencil.*

17 *The finished painting has a pleasing sense of harmony and balance. The square canvas is divided into three geometric shapes, whose straight lines provide a contrasting setting for the organic flower forms and their soft shadows cast upon the wall behind. The loose pencil strokes are in complete contrast to the tight composition and precise shapes.*

15

16

MATERIALS USED

SUPPORT
■ stretched canvas treated with acrylic primer, measuring 30×30in/ 76×76cm

BRUSHES
■ No. 3 bristle
■ No. 4 sable

OTHER EQUIPMENT
■ masking tape
■ a sharp scalpel
■ a B pencil

ACRYLIC COLOURS
■ napthol crimson
■ ivory black
■ cadmium yellow pale
■ emerald green
■ chromium oxide
■ raw umber
■ yellow oxide
■ yellow ochre
■ ultramarine blue
■ cobalt blue
■ titanium white

OIL COLOURS
■ ultramarine blue
■ alizarin crimson
■ sap green
■ chrome green
■ ivory black
■ yellow ochre
■ cadmium yellow
■ raw umber
■ titanium white

Irises in a green vase

17

LANDSCAPE WITH SHED

ACRYLIC IS WITHOUT DOUBT one of the most versatile painting mediums to date. This landscape demonstrates how techniques and methods borrowed from other mediums can be effectively and harmoniously combined in one picture. For example, the artist has used a sheet of stretched heavy white paper, as one would with watercolour, but has begun the painting using the traditional oil technique of underpainting.

The artist continued to develop the picture using both watercolour and oil techniques. For example, thick paint has been scumbled and dragged in places, in the manner of oil paint. In other areas, the wash, a traditional watercolour technique, is used to exploit the underpainting and create a light, subtle tone which complements the heavier, opaque passages. All of which goes to show that there are few rules in acrylic painting, and that a wide range of expressive techniques can be used to get the most out of your subject.

MATERIALS USED

SUPPORT
- stretched heavy white drawing paper measuring 20×23in/50×58cm

BRUSHES
- Nos. 4 and 6 synthetic fibre

COLOURS
- alizarin crimson
- ivory black
- burnt sienna
- cadmium red medium
- cerulean blue
- chrome green
- yellow ochre
- titanium white

1

2

3

4

5

Landscape with shed

6

1 *Working on stretched and dampened paper, the artist begins by lightly sketching in the subject with a pencil. Then he starts to block in the shed with washes of alizarin crimson and burnt sienna.*

2 *The main shapes and outlines are further developed with very wet washes of burnt sienna. In places the tip of the brush is used to 'draw' the outlines.*

3 *The roof colour is put in next, using a mixture of burnt sienna and cadmium red. The* darker grass and shrub colours are flicked in with pure chrome green.

4 *Now the painting is taking shape. A thin wash of cerulean blue is used for the sky, with pale scumbles of alizarin crimson for the clouds. The light and dark tones of the foliage are developed with mixtures of chrome green and white.*

5 *A light green tone is used for the highlights in the foliage and grass. A wash of burnt sienna is brushed into the foreground area.*

6 *The artist now covers the foreground with a light green tone of dryish consistency, allowing the brown underpainting to show through. With a No.4 synthetic brush, the artist works over the painting putting in the final details, such as the tiles on the roof. Notice how the artist weaves warm reds and cool greens through the painting to create a vibrant colour harmony.*

BOATS ON THE BEACH

OFTEN THE MOST DIFFICULT STAGE in the painting process is that of actually getting started. A sheet of stark white canvas can be quite intimidating – one is nervous of applying the first brushstroke for fear of making a mistake.

The application of a toned ground can help by providing a more sympathetic colour upon which to begin work. Traditionally used in oil painting, a toned ground is a thin wash of colour which is brushed over the entire canvas prior to commencing the painting.

A toned ground serves two purposes: firstly, it provides a more neutral colour than that of the canvas itself and makes it easier to judge the relative intensity of the colour mixtures which are applied over it. Secondly, if the toned ground is allowed to show through the overpainting in places it acts as a harmonizing element, tying all the other colours in the painting together.

Traditionally, a toned ground is a neutral or earth colour, or it can give a generalized idea of the overall colour scheme of the subject. In this painting, for example, the artist uses a warm, earthy tone which harmonizes with the colours laid over it.

TONED GROUND

1 Generally, the colour for a toned ground is mixed on the palette and applied to the support with smooth, even strokes. Here, however, the artist begins by applying the colour in loose strokes which will be blended together on the canvas. Cadmium red, yellow, ochre and white, well diluted with water, are freely and loosely painted over the white surface.

2 When the canvas is well covered, and thoroughly dry, a thin wash of white paint is scumbled over it. The result is a medium-to-light toned surface in which the brushstrokes are only partially blended. The colours blend in the viewer's eye, however, and the effect is more vibrant than a flat wash of colour mixed on the palette.

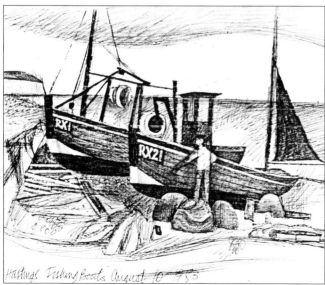

Hastings Fishing Boats August 10 1985

3

4

5

3 *Several charcoal pencil studies were made of individual elements and used as a basis for the final composition. This preparatory sketch concentrates on the beached boats.*

4 *A key drawing is made from the sketches, which will be traced onto the painting at a later stage.*

6

5 *With the toned ground now completely dry, the artist blocks in the sky area with a very pale wash of white and ultramarine, toned down with a touch of burnt umber. The foreground is brushed in with burnt umber, yellow ochre and white.*

6 *The artist now adjusts the tones in the scene, darkening the sea with ultramarine and lightening the foreground with pale washes of white, yellow ochre and ultramarine.*

7 *The line of surf is painted with pure white. The key line drawing is traced onto the painting and outlined in burnt umber with the tip of a No. 2 sable brush.*

7

MATERIALS USED

SUPPORT
- prepared board primed with acrylic, measuring 24×20in/60×50cm

BRUSHES
- No. 7 flat hog's hair
- Nos. 2, 4 and 6 round sable
- Nos. 3 and 5 synthetic fibre

COLOURS
- burnt umber
- yellow ochre
- cadmium red medium
- ultramarine
- ivory black
- titanium white

Boats on a beach

8

8 *The outlines of the figures and the boats are*
filled in with colour, using burnt umber, ivory
black, titanium white and ultramarine.
Stippled dots of yellow ochre mixed with white
are used to create the texture of shingle on the
foreshore. The charm of this picture lies in its
simple, 'naive' style. The fishing boats and the
figures are composed and arranged in such a
way as to lead the viewer's eye from
foreground to background.

A CORNFIELD IN SUMMER

ACRYLIC PAINT is extremely versatile, having many of the advantages of other mediums but few of the disadvantages. In this landscape composition the artist has combined a number of different painting techniques, from thin washes and glazes to thick impasto. Since acrylic paint dries in minutes, the artist was able to build up succeeding layers of paint very rapidly. In addition, the efficient covering power of acrylic means that light colours can be painted over dark ones without any danger of the underlying colour showing through. This gives the artist considerable freedom to experiment and make alterations to the composition and colours as the painting progresses.

Many landscape artists work out of doors on small pencil or watercolour sketches of the subject and return to the studio, using the drawings as reference material for larger paintings. This is far more convenient than carrying cumbersome equipment from place to place – especially if the weather is unreliable. It also allows the artist to observe the subject more closely and gather a great deal of information on form, colour changing light, textural details and so on.

Simple sketches are also an invaluable way of 'editing out' superfluous details and helping to capture the essence of the subject; painting in the field, it is all too easy to become overwhelmed by the complexity of the scene. Working from sketches, back at the studio, also allows the artist to use his or her imagination to play about with the subject and get closer to the original experience.

MATERIALS USED

SUPPORT
- prepared canvas board measuring 20×24in/ 50×60cm

BRUSHES
- Nos. 3, 6, 8, flat bristle brushes
- No. 4 sable

COLOURS
- ivory black
- burnt umber
- cadmium yellow
- chrome green
- cobalt blue
- gold ochre
- lemon yellow
- olive green
- raw umber
- ultramarine blue
- viridian
- vermilion
- titanium white

1

2

3

1 *A common practice with landscape artists is to make rough sketches, which often include written notes on colours, lighting and so on. The painting demonstration that follows is based upon this sketch.*

2 *The artist starts with a broad underpainting of thinly diluted paint. The basic forms of the*
landscape *are indicated with a mixture of gold ochre and raw umber, applied with a No. 8 bristle brush.*

3 *A thin glaze of warm orange is applied in the foreground, and olive green over the distant hills. A thicker layer of lemon yellow is applied across the centre.*

10

10 *The finished painting. The artist has
exploited both the opacity and the transparency
of acrylic to build up a variety of subtle
textures and forms. The measured use of
horizontal and vertical strokes enhances the
mood of calm and tranquility. Note, too, how
the warm yellow underpainting is allowed to
break through the subsequent layers of colour,
helping to harmonize the colour scheme.*

4

5

6

7

8

9

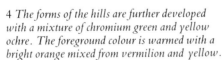

4 *The forms of the hills are further developed
with a mixture of chromium green and yellow
ochre. The foreground colour is warmed with a
bright orange mixed from vermilion and yellow.*

5 *The artist applies thinly diluted cobalt blue
over the sky area, spreading the colour with a
rag. The foreground is further developed with
a vivid green made of chrome green and lemon
yellow.*

6 *The artist develops foreground details with a
variety of greens and greys, working with thin
glazes of colour and thick dabs of opaque paint.*

7 *Background details are added with a No. 3
bristle brush and a thick mixture of chrome
green and black. The foreground is lightened
by adding small patches of light green and white.*

8 *The artist lightens the tone of the sky and
links it with a pale blue-green in the
foreground. A mixture of light orange and
white is used to intensify the colour of the
distant cornfield.*

9 *The tone of the central field is brightened
with a smooth layer of creamy yellow mixed
from gold ochre, white and a touch of green.*

LIGHTHOUSE

ALTHOUGH ACRYLIC PAINTS are a relatively new arrival in the painting world, their use has spread rapidly, since they are flexible enough to accommodate traditional styles of painting as well as modern styles. For example, their fast drying time and ability to be thinned to the consistency of watercolour make them ideal for the classical approach of building up layers of colour one upon the other: a technique known as glazing.

In the past, almost all paintings were done this way. Many of the Old Masters spent a great deal of time developing the underpainting, which was then finished off with thin glazes of colour through which much of the underpainting remained visible. What we see when we look at a Velasquez or a Rubens are simply the last steps the artists took to complete the picture, hiding much of the underpainting below the surface.

For this painting of a seascape at dusk, the artist chose to use a reddish underpainting which would give the whole picture a warm tone. He has also used the traditional method of working from dark to light, and building up slowly from general forms to more specific details.

MATERIALS USED

SUPPORT
- prepared canvas board measuring 24×26in/ 60×65cm

BRUSHES
- No. 3 synthetic fibre brush
- Nos. 2, 3 and 4 bristle brights
- Nos. 4 and 5 sable rounds

COLOURS
- alizarin crimson
- burnt sienna
- burnt umber
- cadmium green
- cadmium red light
- cadmium yellow
- cobalt blue
- phthalo blue
- ultramarine
- titanium white

1

2

3

4

5

Lighthouse

6

1 *The artist mixes burnt sienna with water to a thin consistency and applies it quickly and loosely with a broad brush, blocking in the main areas of the composition.*

2 *The sky tone is a thin wash of alizarin crimson, again brushed in loosely. The lighthouse is painted with a thin wash of burnt sienna, and the ground is covered with a darker, more opaque tone.*

3 *A thin wash of ultramarine is brushed into the sky area. Small patches of grass are indicated with chrome green and cadmium yellow medium. When this is dry, the foreground is lightened with vertical strokes of yellow ochre and white.*

4 *A very thin wash of phthalo blue is put in for the sea, and highlights are redefined with yellow ochre and white.*

5 *The artist mixes alizarin crimson and burnt sienna and carefully puts in the lighthouse stripes with a small sable brush.*

6 *In the finished painting, you can see how the reddish tone of the underpainting glows up through the succeeding layers of colour, imparting an overall warmth that enhances the peaceful mood of a seascape at dusk.*

VIEW ACROSS THE ROOFTOPS

THESE DAYS, many of us dwell in towns and cities, and are often far removed from the traditional subjects of the landscape painter: hills, valleys, rivers, coastlines and so on. The city does, however, offer exciting opportunities for those artists who are prepared to seek out more unusual subjects.

One of the most accessible subjects we have is the view from our own window. A high window, in particular, offers an excellent vantage point and can be just as exhilarating as looking at a view from a mountain top. The geometric shapes of buildings and rooftops, for example, can afford the opportunity to create bold, dynamic compositions in which shapes, colours and patterns are emphasized.

The particular view illustrated in this painting is a fine example of how an artist with a searching eye can find a certain beauty in even the most commonplace subject. Out of a cluttered jumble of buildings and rooftops, he has created a calm and ordered composition in which roughly half the canvas is given to empty sky and the other half to lively geometric patterns.

1

2

3

4

1 *The subject is complicated, and the artist starts by making a drawing in which he simplifies the tones and colours.*

2 *A fairly detailed outline drawing is made on the support. The artist begins by blocking in the darkest areas using a mixture of black and raw umber, well diluted.*

3 *The middle tones are blocked in next, using Payne's grey and a No. 3 sable brush.*

4 *The artist now begins to add colours over the original dark tones, using mixtures of white, yellow ochre, cadmium red and burnt sienna.*

5 *The painting is now developing into an interesting pattern of abstract shapes and colours.*

6 *This detail reveals the thinness of the paint, and how simply the blocks of colour are applied.*

5

6

View across the rooftops

8

7 *The artist adds details using rich reds and beiges mixed from Payne's grey, yellow ochre and white.*

8 *In the final painting the sky has been added with a flat wash of cerulean blue mixed with titanium white, toned down with a thin glaze of raw umber. The artist has resisted the temptation to fill the picture with too much detail; the large, empty space of the sky provides an exciting contrast with the clutter of roofs beneath.*

7

MATERIALS USED

SUPPORT
■ hardboard primed with emulsion measuring 22×26in/56×66cm

BRUSHES
■ No. 6 sable
■ No. 10 synthetic fibre

COLOURS
■ Payne's grey
■ ivory black
■ cadmium yellow
■ yellow ochre
■ cadmium red
■ burnt sienna
■ raw umber
■ titanium white

FRUIT TREES

THE CENTRAL THEME of this picture is the brightly coloured fruit trees sparkling in the sunshine, contrasted against the slanting shadows of the street below.

The painting is based on a small sketch, rapidly executed while the artist was on holiday in the Mediterranean. Over the years he has amassed a large collection of sketches like these, which he does not regard as 'finished drawings' but rather as records of interesting scenes or objects, which can be used later, either as foundations for complete paintings done later in the studio, or as fragments to be inserted into other compositions.

The habit of always carrying a sketchbook is an invaluable one, particularly when travelling abroad. You may be just 'passing through' a place, and yet a scene or objects presents itself as an ideal subject for a painting. A sketch can be done in minutes, and provides enough information about the subject to allow you to make a painting at a later date. A photograph may also help, but with a sketch you can make a more personal statement, isolating and emphasizing those elements which particularly appeal to you. A photograph is much less selective, and besides, there is no guarantee that it will turn out as you expected!

Because acrylic is adhesive, the paint can be mixed with other substances such as sand or grit and thus interesting textural effects can be obtained. In this painting the artist has mixed ordinary builder's sand with the paint in order to capture the rough sandy surface of the stone wall.

1

2

1 *This small sketch was made several months prior to the painting, yet it gives the artist enough to kindle his imagination and memory because it includes written colour notes and details about the play of light and shadow.*

2 *The artist begins by transferring the image onto a primed canvas in black paint applied with a sable brush.*

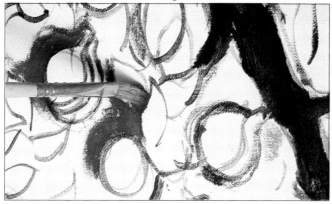

3

3 *Changing to a bristle brush, the artist blocks in the dark tones of the tree trunk and leaves.*

4 *The artist mixes ordinary builder's sand with the paint to capture the rough, sandy texture of the wall. Only a little sand is necessary, otherwise the effect can look too crude and there is a danger of overloading the paint.*

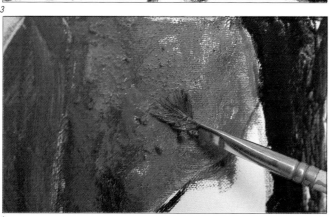

4

5

5 *Colour is laid on in small, thick dabs to create a lively surface texture. The artist moves across the whole canvas, building up the image bit by bit.*

MATERIALS USED

SUPPORT
- hardboard treated with acrylic primer, measuring 18×14in/ 46×36cm

BRUSHES
- Nos. 2, 5 and 10 flat bristle
- No. 2 round sable

COLOURS
- cadmium yellow
- cadmium red
- red oxide
- chrome green
- Hooker's green
- bright green
- burnt sienna
- raw sienna
- raw umber
- cobalt blue
- cerulean blue
- ultramarine
- ivory black
- titanium white

6

6 *Tones of warm brown are worked into the black tree trunks. Because acrylic dries to an opaque finish, light tones can be laid over darker ones without any danger of the darker colour showing through.*

7

7 *The painting is now almost complete. The paint is applied directly, in the alla prima technique, in keeping with the liveliness of the scene. The colours, too, are selected for their suitability to the bright, sunny nature of the subject.*

Fruit Trees

8

8 *The artist has created a highly personal interpretation of the scene, which is much more exciting than a mere photographic copy. Because the scene is viewed from the shade of a pavement café, there is a frame of shadow around the picture which helps to focus the eye upon the brilliantly sunlit street. Although the colours are bright, they are nevertheless harmonious; yellows, greens and earth colours have been skilfully woven throughout.*

THE THAMES AT RICHMOND

THIS LEAFY RIVER SCENE is one which is very familiar to the artist who painted it, since it lies directly beneath the window of his studio. It provides an endless source of inspiration to the artist, as the colours change with the passing of the seasons.

The success of this picture lies in its simplicity, which captures the tranquil calm of a summer's day. Acrylic paint can be diluted with water or medium to the consistency of watercolour, allowing delicate, translucent effects to be obtained. For this painting, the artist chose to work in the manner of a watercolour. Without any preparatory drawing or underpainting, he applied his colours directly onto a sheet of stretched paper. Working from light to dark, in the traditional watercolour manner, the artist applied the colours in thin, transparent glazes which allow light to reflect off the white of the paper and up through the colours, giving them a luminous quality.

Because the washes are so transparent, mistakes cannot be covered up, so it is important to get things right first time – especially since acrylic dries so quickly. The best way to work is boldly and decisively – as the artist did in this painting.

1 *A photograph of the view from the artist's window. Compare this to the finished painting, and notice how the artist has simplified much of the detail to arrive at the essence of the scene.*

2 *Without any preliminary underdrawing, the artist begins by blocking in the main areas of the composition with pale tints of Payne's grey and raw umber.*

3 *While the first tones are still damp, washes of Hooker's green mixed with a little raw umber in the shaded areas, are worked into the trees and the foreground.*

4 *The quiet ripples on the water's surface are indicated with pale lines of Payne's grey and raw umber.*

5 *The artist uses sable brushes throughout the painting process, to achieve the softness of form and delicacy of detail necessary.*

6 *The artist strengthens the tones in the painting by applying glazes of colour, one on top of the other. The glazes are very thin and transparent, allowing the underlayer to glow up through the overlayer and create the luminous effect of a watercolour painting.*

1

2

3

4

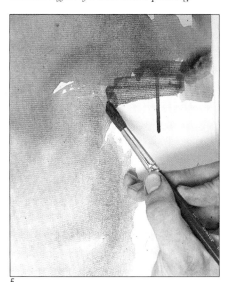

5

6

The Thames at Richmond

8

7 *Opaque white is used to redefine complicated edges such as the leaves on the trees. The paint is not used thickly but is still watery in texture.*

8 *The completed painting has all the freshness and sparkle of a watercolour. The artist has resisted the temptation to overwork the washes or to build up the paint in opaque layers. In addition, he has cut out much of the detail in the scene and presented us with his own personal interpretation of a much-loved subject.*

7

MATERIALS USED

SUPPORT
- stretched Bockingford watercolour paper measuring 16×12in/ 40×30cm

BRUSHES
- Nos. 4, 6 and 10 sable

COLOURS
- Payne's grey
- ivory black
- Hooker's green
- yellow ochre
- raw umber
- burnt sienna
- titanium white

1

1 *One of the drawings that became the basis of the horse in the painting – though in reverse.*

2 *The artist makes a detailed drawing of the subject with a 3H pencil. He then applies a very dilute wash of burnt sienna over all the parts of the horse which will be brown.*

3 *The background and foreground are washed in with very pale tints of blue and green.*

SUFFOLK PUNCH

ACRYLIC is a popular painting medium with animal artists. Its rapid drying time means that artists do not have to struggle home with a wet canvas after a day's work in the field. In addition, its versatility means that it can be used to render a wide range of textures, from the softness of fur to the clean, sharp lines of a bird's feathers.

The artist has been painting animals all his life and so has an extensive knowledge of their anatomy, appearance and characteristics. This painting was developed from two separate drawings of the horse and the dog, made at different times and then combined into a picture that derives as much from imagination as from fact. It is a good idea to keep a sketchbook with you at all times, so you can make drawings of things that interest you and which can later be incorporated into your paintings.

As is often the practice with acrylics, the artist has here used a combination of transparent and opaque techniques. This combination of thin washes and opaque colour creates a range of textures which reflect the quality of the surfaces they describe. The finished result resembles transparent watercolour and body colour, because very little thick paint has been used and only sable brushes have been employed.

MATERIALS USED

SUPPORT
- cartridge paper measuring 11×15in/ 28×38cm

BRUSHES
- No. 6 sable

COLOURS
- raw umber
- burnt sienna
- bright green
- cadmium yellow
- cadmium red
- cobalt blue
- ivory black
- titanium white

4 *To create an impression of mistiness in the foliage, the artist wets the paper in that area and allows the colours – raw umber and bright green – to blend so that they diffuse with soft edges.*

2

3

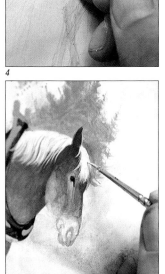

4

5

6

7

8

9

Suffolk Punch

10

5 The trees are treated in a similar way, but more opaque paint is added for the fir trees. When the background washes are dry the artist continues to work on the body of the horse, using a series of transparent washes of burnt sienna.

6 The artist works on one of the trees, stippling opaque colour over a pale underwash to build up texture and form in the foliage.

7 With the broader areas now established, the artist starts on the finer details. Here he is using a fine brush and thick white paint for the horse's mane.

8 For the grass the artist uses bright green and a No.6 sable brush, adding raw umber and white in the shadow areas.

9 This detail shows how the artist works around the shape of the dog.

10 The final painting. Only in the latter stages does the artist add the finer details. The dog's coat, and the characteristic plumes of hair on the horse's legs, are added using thin white paint, and then the harness and chains are added with black, red, yellow and white. The lesson we learn from this painting is that it is better to begin broadly and only finalize our work, and adding in the detail, in the latter stages. Working from large to small, and from light to dark, is the ideal way to control a painting.

1

1 *The painting evolved from these sketches made at the zoo.*

2 *The artist begins by making an accurate drawing of the subject on the canvas with a B pencil.*

CHIMPANZEE

APES RESEMBLE HUMANS in many ways, except that they have a good deal more charm. Chimpanzees are particularly endearing, with their bright, curious eyes and their impish behaviour – qualities which are captured in this delightful 'portrait'.

This painting was developed from sketches made at the zoo, supplemented by photographic reference in natural history books. The artist's approach, however, is not merely to make a slavish copy of the subject; rather, he aims to capture something of the character of the animal, to reach further than just surface appearance. A great deal of imagination is brought into play, and the artist allows the medium itself to play its part in translating the essential character of the subject.

Another important aspect of painting is choosing the format and viewpoint that best express what you want to say. In this painting, for example, the artist has chosen a landscape format, rather than a portrait shape which might seem more obvious, given the shape of the subject. The chimpanzee is placed low down in the picture, and this somehow communicates a clownish, comical air which is entirely in keeping with the subject of the painting.

3 *The main shapes of the body are blocked in with broad strokes of raw umber, burnt sienna, ivory black and Payne's grey.*

4 *The sky is blocked in with a mixture of cerulean blue and titanium white, applied with a No. 6 flat bristle brush.*

5 *The artist now begins work on the chimpanzee's face – the most important part of the composition. He starts by laying in the darkest tones using a mixture of yellow ochre, raw umber, ivory black and cadmium red. The colour is thinly diluted with turpentine and applied with a No. 7 Dalon brush, with a No. 2 sable brush for the finer lines.*

6 *The artist lightens the mixture used for the face by adding more white and yellow ochre and starts to lay in the middle tones.*

2

3

4

5

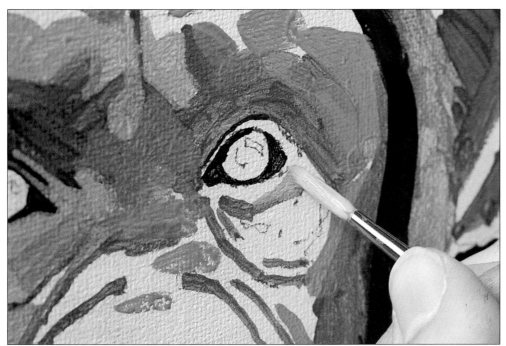

MATERIALS USED

SUPPORT
- prepared canvas panel measuring 20×24in/ 50×60cm

BRUSHES
- No. 2 sable
- No. 7 synthetic
- No. 6 bristle

COLOURS
- raw umber
- burnt sienna
- Payne's grey
- ivory black
- cerulean blue
- yellow ochre
- cadmium yellow
- sap green
- cadmium red
- titanium white

6

7

7 Because all the large areas have been dealt with the painting builds up very quickly. This is useful, because it gives the artist something against which to judge subsequent tones and colours.

8 The lightest tones in the face are now added, by adding cadmium yellow and more white to the original mixture. When the paint is thoroughly dry the artist scratches into it with a craft knife, making fine marks which indicate the whiskers on the chimp's chin.

8

Chimpanzee

10

9 *Using mixtures of sap green and ivory black, the artist indicates the trees in the background. When the first paint layer is dry the artist puts in the lighter foliage, created by adding white and yellow ochre to the original green mixture.*

9

10 *Using masking tape to protect the surrounding areas, the artist blocks in the grey background with Payne's grey, yellow ochre and titanium white. The finished painting has a charm and directness which is perfectly matched to the character of the subject. The way the subject is placed within the edges of the support creates a series of simple shapes which are an important feature of the composition.*

1

1 One of the many charcoal sketches which the artist made, using photographs as reference. The end of a thin stick of willow charcoal is used to achieve crisp lines, while tone and modelling are achieved by smudging and smearing the charcoal.

2 Before starting to paint, the artist makes a simple charcoal drawing on the canvas to fix the position of the subject and outline the main features.

TIGER

PAINTING AN ANIMAL involves much the same sort of challenge as painting a human portrait: we must aim not only to capture a likeness of our subject but also to convey something of their character and personality. In this painting of a tiger the artist has used his skill to portray the animal's strength, intelligence and awesome beauty.

The power and directness of this painting belies the fact that the artist worked entirely from photographic reference. He did not merely copy the photographs, however; instead, he used them as a starting point for the study. His own imagination, and his feeling for the subject, provided the spark of inspiration that turns what could have been an ordinary painting into something more meaningful.

Another point to bear in mind is that the artist did not begin painting straight away. Instead, he made many pencil studies of his subject, in which he investigated the facial markings, the structure of the head, the proportions of the body, and so on. This process can be compared to a dancer learning steps, or a musician practising scales: all the sweat and labour of the preliminary work is what, in the end, will lead to success.

3 The loose particles of charcoal dust are flicked off the canvas with a duster to prevent them from contaminating subsequent paint layers. The artist deliberately chose a long, narrow canvas which emphasizes the lean power of the tiger's body.

4 The artist starts to lay in broad strokes of colour immediately, without any underpainting. The paint, raw sienna and cadmium yellow deep, is applied with a 1-inch decorator's brush to encourage a free, spontaneous approach.

5 The artist now blocks in the background with vigorous brushstrokes, using the same decorator's brush and sap green diluted with water. Notice how the brushstrokes remain visible, adding drama and movement to the image of the tiger.

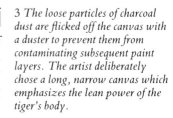

2

3

4

5

6

7

8

6 *With the main areas established, the artist begins to work on the details of the tiger's features. Here a No. 12 ox-hair brush is being used to paint the striped markings on the face.*

7 *The artist continues to apply colour all over the painting, often stepping back from the picture to assess its progress. The broad strokes of yellow, white and black are now beginning to come into focus*

8 *In this detail we see just how exciting the paint surface is. The broad, loose marks create a dynamic force which animates the picture and makes us feel as though the tiger is about to pounce.*

9 *The finished painting demonstrates how a fast, vigorous, alla prima technique creates an exciting impression of a subject such as a wild animal. Acrylic paint dries quickly, allowing the artist to work fast and keep the paint surface fresh and lively. The image of the tiger emerges convincingly from the vigorous brushwork, the separate areas of bright colour merging in the viewer's eyes. Note also how the artist deliberately confines the subject within the narrow limits of the picture's boundaries, giving the impression that the tiger is about to burst from the painting.*

MATERIALS USED

SUPPORT
- ready-primed flax canvas measuring 30×20in/ 76×50cm

BRUSHES
- 1-inch decorator's brush
- No. 12 round ox-hair
- No. 8 sable round
- No. 4 bristle round

COLOURS
- raw sienna
- cadmium red
- cadmium yellow
- cadmium yellow deep
- sap green
- ivory black
- titanium white

Tiger

1 *The subject of this painting was the artist's own falcon, sitting on an Arab-style perch.*

LANNER FALCON

THE SUBJECT OF THIS PAINTING is a Lanner falcon, a native of the Mediterranean and North Africa. This particular bird, posing regally on its Arab-style perch, belongs to the artist. Falcons are his special love, and he knows the subject so well that he is able to paint the details and wing patterns of these birds virtually with his eyes closed!

What we can learn from the artist is that the better you know your subject, the more likely that you will be able to do justice to it. If you really want to succeed, it isn't enough to paint a subject just once and then forget it. The more you practise the more skillful you become; there is, unfortunately, no other way to fulfill your hopes and ambitions when trying to master acrylic. Fortunately, the practice of painting with acrylics always offers some kind of pleasure. And if you see every attempt that you make not as a final attempt, but just another form of practice, the fear of failure will be lessened. In turn, your more relaxed attitude will show in your paintings, which will show a bolder, more confident use of form and colour.

MATERIALS USED

SUPPORT
■ gesso-primed hardboard measuring 20×16in/ 50×40cm

BRUSHES
■ Nos. 4 and 7 synthetic and a 1-in bristle brush

COLOURS
■ burnt sienna
■ cobalt blue
■ Turner's yellow
■ yellow ochre
■ brilliant orange
■ cadmium red medium
■ ultramarine
■ Payne's grey
■ titanium white

2

3

4

2 *The artist begins by making a drawing on paper. He transfers this to the canvas by covering the back of the drawing with charcoal powder and tracing over the lines of the drawing with a 4B pencil.*

3 *The artist starts the painting with the head because the eye and the beak are important in capturing the personality of the subject. If he gets these right, the painting will succeed.*

4 *Now the artist blocks in the body of the bird with a mixture of Payne's grey and raw umber. He then draws the scalelike shapes of the feathers with a small brush and light grey paint.*

5

6

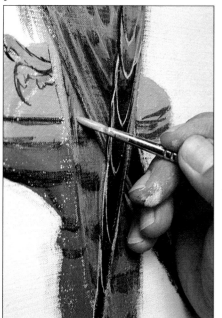

7

5 *He then develops the shading on the feathers with tiny hatched brushstrokes of raw umber and black, applied with a No. 2 brush.*

6 *The artist develops the details on the neck of the bird with white paint, smudging it with his finger to give a soft texture. He then continues working over the plummage, and lightly blocks in the background with loose strokes of white and yellow ochre.*

7 *The artist highlights the tips of the wings with light grey, then gently smudges the paint with his finger to create a soft, feathery edge.*

8 *The background is darkened with a mixture of burnt sienna and yellow ochre, applied loosely with a No. 5 bristle brush. The artist is not happy with this, however, as he feels it detracts from the main subject.*

8

Lanner Falcon

9

9 *In the finished painting, we can see how the artist has overlaid the dark background with a pale, neutral one which gives much greater force and power to the image of the falcon. The removal of the dark background was easily accomplished thanks to the efficient covering power of acrylic paint; even the darkest colour will not show through a light one laid over it. Also, acrylic paint dries to a hard, impermeable finish which means that a fresh layer of paint cannot 'pick up' the colour underneath and cause muddiness, as sometimes happens with other, less versatile painting media.*

SELF-PORTRAIT

IF YOU ARE LOOKING FOR a convenient model for a portrait painting – someone who is inexpensive, reliable and available at times that suit you – then there is no better subject than yourself. Painting a self-portrait also has the added advantage that you don't have to worry about flattering your sitter!

Acrylic paints are an especially suitable medium for self-portraits. Their consistency can be varied to suit a whole range of styles, from loose and impressionistic to tight and realistic, depending on the mood you wish to convey.

Strangely, it is usually difficult to 'see' ourselves properly. You may think you know your own face extremely well, but when it comes to painting a portrait it is essential to study your features as if for the very first time. If necessary, make a series of sketches before you begin the actual painting.

When posing for a photograph, many of us tend to look awkward and self-conscious. The same thing can happen with a self-portrait, so try to relax in front of the mirror and select a comfortable pose. It is a good idea to mark the position of the easel, the mirror and your feet so that when you come back to the painting you will be able to take up the position again.

For this self-portrait the artist chose an unusual but effective composition in which his own image is cropped off at the corner. His shadow cast on the wall behind helps to stabilize the composition and adds three-dimensional depth to the image.

1
1 *The artist begins by making an outline drawing of himself on the canvas, using a B pencil. He then blocks in the main light and shadow areas on the face with broad strokes of burnt sienna, diluted with water for the light areas.*

3 *This close-up reveals how the artist is building up the broad masses and planes of the face with thin washes of colour which indicate the light, medium and dark tones.*

2
2 *Now the dark tones of the hair, beard and moustache are put in with burnt sienna darkened with cobalt blue.*

4 *The artist continues to model the face using various tones of earth colours such as burnt sienna, burnt umber, Turner's yellow, brilliant orange and raw sienna. The eyes are painted with Payne's grey and black, and the mouth with red ochre.*

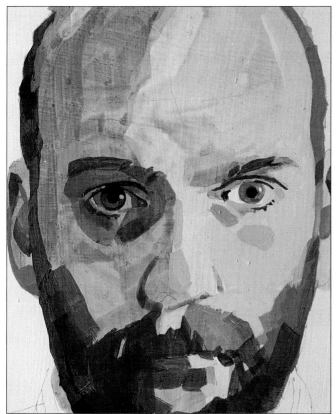

3

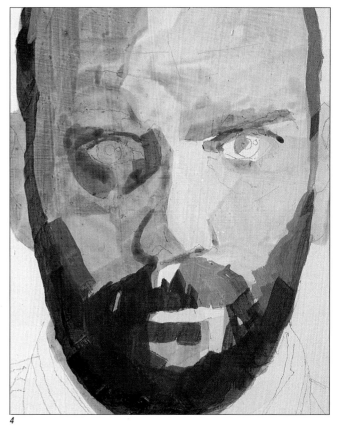

4

5

6

7

5 *Now the cast shadow on the wall is brushed in with a 1-in bristle brush and a weak solution of Payne's grey, white and yellow ochre.*

6 *The details of the shirt and tie are painted with a No. 3 sable brush and cadmium red medium and brilliant orange.*

7 *Washes of ultramarine blue complete the colouring of the shirt. These bright, vibrant colours are deliberately chosen to bring a touch of vitality to the otherwise sombre composition.*

8 *The artist now completes the modelling of the head and the facial features. The highlights in the skin tones are added with thin washes of Turner's yellow and white, and white highlights indicate the reflections on the mouth and eyes.*

8

MATERIALS USED

SUPPORT
- gesso–primed hardboard measuring 20×16in/ 50×40cm

BRUSHES
- Nos. 4 and 7 synthetic and a lin bristle brush

COLOURS
- burnt sienna
- cobalt blue
- Turner's yellow
- yellow ochre
- brilliant orange
- cadmium red medium
- ultramarine
- Payne's grey
- titanium white

9 *The finished portrait. Notice how the unique placement of the figure and the use of clean, white space around it force the viewer's eye into the face of the subject. The strong colours of the shirt and tie contrast boldly with the white of the paper and create a dynamic visual tension.*

Self Portrait

1 *Before starting to paint, the artist made sure that the model was sitting comfortably and in a relaxed position.*

2 *Working with black, white, vermilion and burnt sienna, the artist blocks in an overall impression of the figure. The colours are loosely applied with thin paint to allow for correction as the painting develops.*

WOMAN IN A SPOTTED DRESS

PAINTING A PORTRAIT makes more demands on an artist than any other subject. In creating a likeness, every feature of the head and face must be carefully analyzed in terms of colour, shape and tone. Because the character of the image is dependent upon this detailed analysis, small adjustments at any stage of the painting can make all the difference between success and failure.

The sympathetic nature of acrylic paints can help to overcome some of the problems of portrait painting. Unlike watercolours, which are difficult to control, and oils, which are slow-drying, acrylics allow you to work at a comfortable pace, building up the colours layer upon layer. In addition, the opacity of acrylics allows you to make adjustments or cover up mistakes without any danger of the colours turning muddy.

For this portrait, the artist worked 'from the general to the particular'. That is, he established the basic forms quickly with thin layers of paint, gradually working up to the finer details so essential to the individuality of the human face.

This is a standard three-quarter portrait, in which the head is facing at an angle halfway between a profile and a full frontal view. This pose is favoured by many artists, as it has a pleasing naturalness and also creates an interesting shape on the canvas.

MATERIALS USED

SUPPORT
- stretched and primed cotton duck canvas measuring 20×18in/ 50×45cm

BRUSHES
- No. 6 flat bristle
- No. 4 round sable

COLOURS
- burnt sienna
- burnt umber
- cadmium yellow
- cobalt blue
- vermilion
- yellow ochre
- ivory black
- titanium white

3 *The light flesh tones of the face are applied. Cobalt blue is added to the basic flesh tone mixture for the cool shadow areas. When these are dry, rich reds and browns are used to define the mouth. Deep shadows on the underside of the chin and nose are painted as precise shapes of cool, grey purple.*

4 *The background colour is applied with a mixture of cobalt blue, yellow ochre, black and white. A thin glaze of black is then applied over the model's dress.*

Woman in a spotted dress

8

5 *The artist adopts an unusual technique to paint the small coloured spots on the model's dress. Using a piece of perforated scrap metal as a stencil, he stipples the opaque paint into the holes with a bristle brush.*

6 *The stencilled dots are now strengthened with a small sable brush, using white, cadmium yellow and vermilion.*

7 *The artist continues to build up the pattern on the dress. Larger spots are painted freehand.*

8 *The finished painting. By starting with broad strokes and thin paint, the artist was able to establish the pose and the correct proportions of the model in the early stages, without building up a thick, dense layer of paint. Working from this firm* *foundation, he was able to work quickly and confidently when applying the finer details. The completed portrait retains some of the lively, spontaneous strokes made in the early stages of the painting.*

CHAPTER FIVE

DESIGNING WITH ACRYLICS

A HANDBOOK of this kind can only touch briefly on design. Such a subject would need a book of its own to do it justice. So I have confined myself to highlighting some of the more obvious things that acrylic is capable of doing.

SOME USES OF ACRYLIC

- Collage
- Simple surface modelling and textural effects
- Staining
- Spraying
- Taping
- Wall decoration and murals
- Drawing and illustration

I try to define design and design methods as exactly as possible.

However, the result will inevitably take on a personal note. As someone who has worked as a painter and designer for many years, I have naturally come to a number of conclusions, some of which are very personal. One conclusion is that all the disciplines – painting, drawing, design and sculpture – have a great deal in common, and relate closely to each other.

I prefer to think of drawing not as a separate activity, but as the base connecting painting and design, for drawing serves them both equally. Therefore if you draw, you are directly concerned with painting and designing, even though the ends to which they are put may differ appreciably.

Without going too deeply into the philosophy of the visual arts, I have taken the view that design has, basically, a decorative function, which confines itself to environment, objects and communication media, and does this principally by the use of colour, shape and form, pattern and texture, and imagery.

Painting, however, though using the same elements of colour and form, is more concerned with expressing an individual point of view. Moreover it may incorporate research of an aesthetic or philosophical nature quite outside the province of design, though design itself may be indirectly related to these researches in no small way. Drawing spans both activities and can be research and communication, decorative and creative, all at the same time.

That painting has influenced design over the centuries is obvious. A great many innovations in posters, furniture, textiles and interiors can be more or less traced to the experiments of painters during this century. Many of these painters were also sculptors and became, in turn, designers themselves, of no mean achievement. Picasso and Braque spring readily to mind as two important artists who left their imprint on design as much as on painting. In many instances the public will reject an artist's researches out of hand, but accept them eagerly when transformed into design. Those who intend to design should bear this in mind and recognize that research is important to all areas of art, and that drawing is perhaps the best form of it.

It is also interesting to note that in French and Italian the word for drawing is the same for design.

Acrylic is also an ideal medium for research and experiment because, like drawing, it is immediate, and research depends on spontaneity and the quick grasp of ideas. Acrylic can offer extended opportunities for going over the same ground until something exciting emerges. In addition it is able to do things that other mediums cannot attempt.

COLLAGE

(1) *ABOVE Acrylic medium can be used for collaging. Cut the canvas shape and paint one side with medium.*

(2) *ABOVE Press the shape onto stretched canvas. Rub it down with a clean, dry brush.*

(3) *ABOVE Collage can also be done using the adhesive qualities of acrylic paint.*

COLLAGE

THE WORD COLLAGE COMES from the French *coller* to stick – an apt description for a picture or design that is made up from pieces of paper, cloth or other material and stuck to a firm support.

This method of creating images was extensively used by the Cubists, the two main innovators being Picasso and Braque, both painters. In his later years Matisse used pieces of coloured paper as a substitute for painting.

Collage can literally transform discarded bits of cloth and wood and other materials into interesting schemes of colour, tone, form and texture.

Another sort of collage can be made from waste pieces of wood sawn off frame mouldings. When stuck together in varying combinations, interesting ideas for three-dimensional designs emerged, not apparent in the original material. When the discarded bits were reassembled, completely new forms were created.

You can see even from a few examples the potential of collage, and in particular its pronounced three-dimensional qualities. None has paint added to them in these instances, though it can be tried with equal success.

In what way exactly does collage involve acrylic, if no paint is used? Quite simply the strong adhesive qualities that the base medium possesses. With it you can stick almost anything to a support.

MODELLING AND SURFACE TEXTURES

ADHESION IS ONLY ONE of the many attributes of acrylic modelling or texture paste. Another is its modelling ability and the way it may be used to make exciting surface textures, with or without the addition of paint. With the simplest of modelling techniques, surfaces can be transformed simply by using this paste.

Sawdust can be added to the acrylic paste to give it more bulk and texture, also a little white primer to give it more body. It can then be thoroughly mixed and spread on to a piece of card (cardboard). Pattern effects can be made by impressing various shapes or edges into the drying surface. Alternatively the paste could be mixed with a little sand, white primer and umber to darken it. Lines can be scratched into it very freely with the back of a brush to create a relief effect. It may then be further stained with colour, and the surplus wiped off.

As another variation, some cellulose filler can be added and some blue to give it a little colour. Lines could be incised on the surface with a comb. When dry this surface could be stained with umber and wiped off before nearly dry. The mixing of the paste with sawdust, sand and cellulose filler, as well as white primer and a little tube colour, gives the paste that is formed an entirely different texture each time. The addition of the white primer to the other aggregates changes the qualities of the paste, for without it the paste dries somewhat transparent.

These few variations give unlimited scope for experiment and if pursued further, would aid an interior designer or stage designer in discovering interesting surfaces by trying out the paste on models or on pieces of card (cardboard), and then lighting them from various angles.

Another method for creating surface textures of a completely different kind is to embed small regular or irregular fragments of objects into a smooth paste. Make up a smooth texture paste of cellulose filler with a touch of

TEXTURES WITH GEL

ABOVE *Equal proportions of gel and paint are mixed. The thickened colour should be used immediately, as it dries quickly.*

ABOVE *A painting knife is used to mix the gel and paint.*

ABOVE *The result is a paint with a stiff, buttery consistency which retains the shape of the knife marks.*

ABOVE *Alternatively, a brush may be used to mix the gel and paint in equal quantities.*

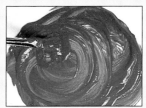

ABOVE *Used with a stiff brush, gel lends itself to rugged brushwork which retains the impression of the bristles.*

ABOVE *The mixture is then applied to the support with direct, spontaneous strokes.*

TEXTURE WITH FOIL

(1) *Modelling paste is spread evenly over the support.*

(2) *A piece of crumpled foil is pressed into the paste while it is still wet.*

(3) *The modelling paste takes on the texture of the foil.*

When the paste is dry, it is ready to be overpainted.

The rougher texture creates broken colour where the paint is applied. The finer texture on the right produces mottled patches of colour.

TEXTURE PASTE

ABOVE *Texture paint is applied directly to the support with a knife.*

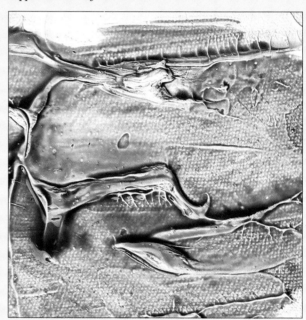

ABOVE *The textured surface is painted over to create a delicate glaze.*

white primer, and experiment with all kinds of materials – buttons, hairpins, tacks, or staples for regular shaped objects, and peas, lentils, seeds or macaroni for irregular ones.

Three other ways of using acrylic which are ideal for designing purposes are staining, spraying and taping.

STAINING

BECAUSE ACRYLIC IS QUICK drying and water-resistant, and can be used thick or thin with equal ease it can be painted on unprimed cloth, and not only is it perfectly safe, but if it is thin enough, it soaks into the fibres of the material without any loss of brilliance, with remarkable affinities to dyeing and screen printing.

STAINING

ABOVE To stain a support, mix the tube colour with a medium to produce a thin, fluid consistency.

ABOVE Work the colour into the weave of the support using a decorator's brush or a sponge.

This opens up a wealth of possibilities for painting and fabric designing.

Thin colours can be sprayed, dribbled or splashed on to various kinds of cloths to produce a diversity of effects quickly without the bother of any kind of printing process to intervene.

When you try the staining technique, add some water tension breaker (wetting agent) to the water diluting the paint, as this will increase the surface wetting and penetration properties of the colours. The addition of a few drops of matt medium will ensure that the thinned colour will flow well, dry matt and retain the binding properties of the medium.

SPRAYING

THIN ACRYLIC PAINT CAN also be sprayed from an airbrush or spray-gun. The mixture can be as transparent or opaque as you like. The dilution can be as great as 50/50 water to acrylic or as little as 25% water to 75% paint. The addition of either gloss or matt medium is recommended to ensure maximum adhesion of the paint. Spraying can be carried out on any kind of surface as recommended in Chapter 1. Spray-guns are delicate instruments and the makers' directions regarding the application of the paint and cleaning should be followed scrupulously.

The results of spraying can vary from gently gradated tones to more brilliant effects. Spraying is a flexible way of creating realistic and decorative effects, and to carry it out numerous masks and stencils are needed. One way to protect parts of the work from undue spraying is to apply masking tape to them.

TAPING

THE USE OF MASKING tape to protect parts of the work not to be damaged or painted accidentally has given rise to a number of techniques which can be used for certain kinds of painting.

For example, if the work is to be very flat, and very precise in its form, masking tape placed at the edges of the area to be painted, will protect that edge, and ensure that a good flat paint can be produced without the fear of going over the edges. The masking tape will give a good hard edge to the areas of paint.

The paint can be brushed over the masking tape with complete confidence. When the paint is thoroughly dry, the masking tape can be removed leaving behind a crisp, flatly painted area with hard edges.

However, it is advisable to make sure that the masking tape is carefully stuck down, and that there are no bubbles in it. Also the density of the paint should not be too thin. For the best results, the paint should be really opaque, if necessary applied in a thick layer. The addition of a matt or gloss medium or water tension breaker (wetting agent) will ensure that the paint flows well.

SPRAYING

ABOVE Use the spray-gun with masking fluid to create a pattern.

ABOVE When the masking fluid has dried, spray a layer of paint over it.

MASKING

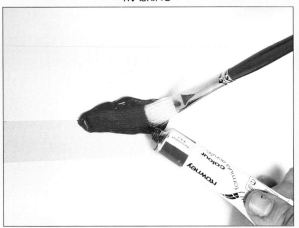

ABOVE *Masking tape is placed across the support in the appropriate place. The artist* works with colour from the tube, spreading it across the tape with a small brush.

ABOVE *The artist continues to spread the paint, working* away from the masked area.

ABOVE *When the paint is dry, the tape is removed. The underlying support has been* protected and a hard line of paint produced.

MURAL PAINTING

IN ALL MY EXPERIENCE as a mural designer, I have found acrylic to be the best all-round paint for painting on walls. Wall painting is at best an arduous task which can be made unnecessarily difficult if the paint used is unsympathetic to work with.

Problems with murals arise because you never know how the walls will be deployed from site to site. Sometimes they can be ideal – the right height, good light, easy access, plenty of room to work in. In such circumstances the problems of the paint are not so imperative.

But very often the walls will be high, the light poor or changeable, and so work has to be carried out on steps or scaffolding, which means that the mixing table might be elsewhere, and the paint carried to the wall for application. If the mix is wrong, the whole operation has to be repeated: mixing in one place, and painting in another, which can be very tedious to say the least. I find acrylic easy to mix, store and transport up and down ladders, and it is easily brushed on to the wall, and you know that the paint film is tough enough to withstand the wear and tear a wall painting has to endure.

When I used acrylic for the first time on a mural, I devised a completely new method to deal with it. First the walls were primed with acrylic primer, which was a delightful surface to draw on, and when completed the drawing was covered over with a semi-transparent wash of pale ochre, umber and white.

The intention was to create a neutral tone over the whole work so that the lighter and the darker tones would relate properly with each other.

When the underpainting was dry the major areas of the mural were filled in carefully, including some of the detail. Because of the neutral tone covering the whole work, this could be done with confidence, whereas if it had been attempted on a white ground all kinds of problems would have ensued.

The method adopted here was to become the foundation of the whited-out method discussed earlier. Though it wasn't used in this instance, it was used in later works of this kind.

As will be seen in the colour reproduction, the colours are rich and bright, the detail sharp and clear. This could not have been achieved so successfully with other paints, as they do not possess the quick-drying properties and translucency of acrylic, therefore the overpainting method cannot work as well.

As will be observed in the almost completed wall, large areas of the underpainting have been left untouched, and remain as they were originally painted with the free brushwork contrasting with the clear-cut shapes of the design.

Acrylic is ideally suited to murals and wall decoration, not only as paint, but as a means of creating textures, and surface variation so that the light can play its part as well. For those unused to painting on a wall, who would like to try some of the methods suggested in this section, if the work cannot be carried out directly on the wall, it can be done on sheets of card (cardboard) or hardboard first, and

placed into position afterwards. This means that if the work is not immediatcly successful, it can be removed easily, and a new section put in its place.

Of course, the real satisfaction of mural painting is to paint or work *in situ*, but working on removable panels is a good introduction to seeing if the design is effective without harm to the wall.

DRAWING AND ILLUSTRATION

THOUGH DRAWINGS AND ILLUSTRATIONS can be adequately carried out in most other mediums, acrylic offers tremendous scope for the further exploration of tones, shapes, textures and colour, which would be of inestimable value in both areas.

Black and white drawings can be enhanced by the addition of washes of transparent or semi-opaque acrylic colour, provided a few conditions are observed. Charcoal, charcoal pencils, conté crayon, carbon pencils, chalks and pastels will tend either to run or be picked up by any washes or overpainting, and unless this particular quality is especially needed, it is advisable to fix the drawing first. The ordinary type of fixative is not recommended as it might impair the adhesive qualities of the acrylic, therefore some acrylic gloss or acrylic matt medium can be sprayed with safety over the drawing with a spray diffuser and will hold the drawing in place.

Alternatively the drawing can begin with washes and then be drawn over with pen, charcoal pencil, crayon and so on. Ordinary pencils smudge less and pick up less than carbon pencils and can be painted over quite easily.

Pure charcoal, however, is prone to smudging and picking up as it does not contain any binder whatsoever. And though most other drawing mediums contain a little binder, it is safer to fix them as a precaution.

Melissa

EPILOGUE

CRYLIC — as I hope I have amply demonstrated — is a wonderful paint, in fact, a magic paint that can do everything other paints can do, and in many instances far better — more transparent than watercolour, more opaque than gouache, and thicker than oil paint. It dries quicker, is more resilient to damage, and more versatile than any known paint today.

TO MAKE ACRYLIC PRODUCE WONDERS is not the province of the manufacturers, but of the user. The magic, alas, won't happen by itself.

Technique will enable acrylic to go some of the way to fulfil its potential, but the magic needs imagination. Whereas oil paint demands years of discipline to allow any magic to come through, acrylic can accommodate lots of imagination to let it happen sooner. You can experiment with acrylic in a way that would seem presumptuous with other mediums. There are no rules you break at your peril, only a few simple conditions that should be observed, to get the magic working. They can be summarized thus: Use plenty of clean water. Keep brushes clean by washing immediately after use. Mix the paint well. Don't be cautious about adding extra acrylic medium to mixtures; additional medium always makes paint flow better. To produce the maximum visual qualities of acrylic in a subtle and arresting way, let the painting show on its surface the effect of the layers beneath. Vary the layers and allow each one to show through. Starting with lean paint, and finishing with thick is better than starting with thick paint, because once acrylic is dry it is almost impossible to remove. Allow washes to show the white surface through the transparent layers. Unlike glazes which can cover any surface or underpainting, both thick and thin, washes depend on the white surface to give the sparkle needed When in doubt white it out. Enjoy the process.

Whoever said, 'Paints were invented solely for enjoyment. . .' made a good point. They undoubtedly are, and acrylic paints even more so. But to enjoy them fully a number of conditions have to be considered. Some are familiar; others might be somewhat strange. But they are all relevant, as much to the amateur, as to the professional.

Briefly they are: Liking what we do, rather than doing what we like. Accepting that means are more important than ends. Letting the ends take care of themselves. It is the process that matters. An attitude of optimism. Aim to be natural, and not to strive too hard. Cultivate patience. Allow progress to develop at its own pace. Decide and act. Practice constantly.

Liking what we do means accepting our own efforts as valid – even if they don't come up to our own expectations – because they are our own and not somebody elses's. Of course it is natural to admire the achievements of others, and wish to do likewise, but this kind of ambition will only lead to disappointment. Equally we may like to impress others with what we do, and because it fails to excite the admiration we would like, we will tend to

PAGE 112 *This portrait of a young girl was painted on primed hardboard using as reference a colour photograph blown up to life size.*

RIGHT *David Hockney,* Mr and Mrs Clark and Percy. *The artist achieved the fine translucent finish of the vase and flowers and general even tone by using paint in a carefully controlled manner.*

Lanyon Quoit

Wintry Landscape

Bottle, Fruits and Vegetables

become discouraged. And when this happens, enjoyment flies quickly out of the window. The ends we choose will have a direct bearing on the way we enjoy our work – hence means being more important than ends. If we enjoy the means the ends will take care of themselves.

This is not to say that ends are not without value and that aims, ambitions or intentions are unnecessary. Far from it. In their proper context, they can be the motive or spur for what is to be done; moreover they can provide the excitement that goes towards the creating of significant work. But for the successful realization of these goals, each stage of the process must be given due attention and not be rushed or skimped (hence the need for patience), or despaired over (hence the need for optimism).

Whatever the personal target, working towards it should be enjoyable. For if we enjoy what we do, the enjoyment becomes part of the work and will be seen and enjoyed by others in turn. What we should realize is that our work is like an open book, available for all to dip into and read. What we put into it, someone else can take out.

Painting and designing are processes that need constant practice. This is the secret: only practice will encourage skills to grow, understanding to ripen, and allow work to develop and, above all, for enjoyment to increase.

Practice *is* everything. It is the centre of an artist's working life and, consequently, looked forward to, if only for an hour a day.

Of course 'mistakes' will be made, but they should be seen as part of the process. Making errors of judgement is the only way to develop, make us more critically aware, and so build up confidence in what we are doing.

If making mistakes is a persistent worry remember that 'those who never make mistakes, never make anything . . .' and take heart.

The methods that I have described in this book take all this into consideration. The suggested painting exercises and experiences will do a great deal to forestall many of the major difficulties that may occur when using acrylic for the first time. This is because the exercises bring into play natural abilities. There is no need to learn any special way of doing things as one would when learning a performing art. These exercises can and should be adapted to suit the individual personality of the user. They can be played by the book or turned upside down if need be, without harm. The information is there to be used, and how it is done is a personal matter, whether you are an amateur dabbler or an aspiring professional.

Expertise should be acquired slowly on your own terms. The principle to follow is to do things gradually and deliberately at your own pace, in your own way.

If I were asked to sum up this book in one word, it would be action. Painting is an immediate activity that takes place only in the present. In short, it happens now. To enable this to happen, the best procedure to adopt is to decide and act. The secret is to make up your mind as clearly and firmly as possible and then, without any hesitation, act. For whatever is decided – and this is the point – will be correct. The success of the outcome depends not on what is decided, but on the act of decision itself.

PAGE 116 *An understated composition, subdued colours and restricted tonal contrast are masterfully combined in this painting to create this sombre and overcast scene.*

PAGE 117 *An advantage with acrylic is that light colours can be laid on top of dark. Here, the warm, dark undertones provide a contrasting base to the cold, light tones of the snow and sky.*

LEFT *Acrylics were chosen for this still life because of the bold colour scheme of the subject. The aim of the artist was to create a composition using the classical triangle, with the bottle as the focal point.*

ABSTRACT Relying on colour, pattern and form rather than the realistic or naturalistic portrayal of subject matter.

ABSTRACTION The creation of an abstract image by the simplification of natural appearances.

ACTION PAINTING Splashing and dribbling paint on canvas. The technique is supposed to be derived from Leonardo's suggestion of using stains on walls as a starting point for a design.

ADVANCING COLOURS Colours which appear to be near the viewer. Warm, strong colours seem to advance whereas cool colours recede.

AERIAL PERSPECTIVE The use of colour and tone to indicate space and recession. Warm colours, clearly defined forms and sharp contrasts of tone tend to advance towards the picture plane whereas cool colours, less clearly defined forms and tonal contrasts appear further away.

ALLA PRIMA Completing the painting in one session with neither underdrawing nor underpainting.

AQUEOUS A term which refers to a pigment or medium soluble, or capable of being suspended in water.

BINDER The adhesive which holds the powdered pigment together in a form suitable for painting. See **Medium**.

BLENDING Merging adjacent colour areas so that the transition between the colours is imperceptible.

BLOCKING IN The process of putting down roughly the main areas of tone and colour in a composition before the work begins.

BODY COLOUR Paint, such as gouache, which has opacity and therefore covering power. Body colour may be used to add highlights or colour.

BROKEN COLOUR A term used in colour theory to describe a colour mixed from two secondary colours. These colours tend towards grey. It is also a method of painting in which colours are applied as areas of pure paint rather than being blended or mixed. These colours combine in the eye of the viewer to create new colours. The paint may be applied in small discrete patches, as in the Pointillist technique, or it may be applied in such a way that initial paint layers show through subsequent layers to create new colours.

BRUSHWORK The personal handwriting of a painter. May be thick or thin, gentle or vigorous depending on the form of expression of the artist. It may be aesthetically pleasing in itself.

CALLIGRAPHIC A term referring to a linear style of painting or drawing characterized by flowing, rhythmic marks.

CHARCOAL A drawing material made by reducing wood, through burning, to charred black sticks. All charcoal tends to powder but sticks are available in different thicknesses so the qualities in a charcoal drawing can be varied.

CHIAROSCURO This term literally means 'light-dark' and originally was used in reference to oil painting with dramatic tonal contrasts. It is now more generally applied to work in which there is a skilfully managed interplay of highlight and shadow.

COLLAGE From the French word *coller*, meaning 'to stick'. A picture or design built up from pieces of coloured paper. Devised by the Cubists. Any materials may be used likewise.

COMPLEMENTARY COLOURS There are three basic pairs of complementary colours each consisting of one primary and one secondary colour. These are opposite colours in that the primary is not used in mixing the secondary, thus blue and orange (red mixed with yellow) are complementary colours. On an extended colour wheel, a warm red-orange is opposite green-blue.

COMPOSITION The arrangement of various elements in painting or drawing, for example, mass, colour, tone, contour etc.

COVERING POWER This term refers to the opacity or transparency of a paint. Some paints are transparent and are therefore more suitable for glazing whereas opaque paints are used for areas of dense colour or where it is important to obliterate underlying colour.

CROSS HATCHING A technique of laying on areas of tone by building up a mass of criss-cross strokes rather than with a method of solid shading.

DESIGN Roughly has the same meaning as composition, but applies also to artefacts and decorative objects, and functional equipment. Also has the same meaning as the Italian word *disegno* to mean drawing.

DILUENT A liquid such as turpentine which is used to dilute paint. It evaporates completely and has no binding effect on the pigment.

DISEGNO An Italian word capable of many meanings, the simplest of which is drawing and the next simplest design.

DISTEMPER Powdered colour mixed with glue size. Because of its relative simplicity and cheapness was often used as a household paint for decoration, but since superseded by acrylic paints. Not to be confused with tempera.

DRAWING The simplest way to plot out an image; to organize shapes and tones preparatory to painting or designing. To put down what is seen in an ordered way so that it is immediately understood. The way artists and designers think about their work. The artists' way of making notes and observations for future reference.

DRY BRUSH In this technique a brush holding relatively dry paint is dragged across the surface giving a broken or feather effect.

EARTH COLOURS A range of pigments derived from inert oxides, for example, ochres, siennas and umbers.

FERRULE The metal section of a paintbrush which holds the hairs.

FIGURATIVE This term is used in referring to paintings and drawings in which there is a representational approach to a particular subject, as distinct from abstract art.

FIXATIVE A kind of thin varnish sprayed on to drawings and pastels to prevent their being rubbed (or picked up if overpainted).

FORESHORTENING The effect of perspective in a single object or figure, in which a form appears considerably altered from its normal proportions as it recedes from the artist's viewpoint.

FRESCO Wall painting with a medium like watercolour (but without any binder) painted on to wet plaster which when

dry acts as the binder by 'locking-in' the paint. Absolutely permanent when favoured by a dry and warm climate.

FUGITIVE This term describes pigments which fade on exposure to light.

GESSO Name of the ground used for tempera painting, and sometimes oil. Not recommended for acrylic.

GLAZING The process of applying a transparent layer of paint over a solid one so that the colour of the first is blended or modified by the second.

GOUACHE A water based paint made opaque by mixing white with the pigments. Known variously as poster or designer's colour.

GRAIN The texture of a support for painting or drawing. Paper may have a fine or coarse grain depending upon the methods used in its manufacture.

GRAPHITE A form of carbon which is compressed with fine clay to form the substance commonly known as 'lead' in pencils. The proportions of clay and graphite in the mixture determine the quality of the pencil, whether it is hard or soft and the density of line produced. Thick sticks of graphite are available without a wooden pencil casing.

GROUND The surface preparation of a support on which a painting or drawing is executed. A

tinted ground may be laid on white paper to tone down its brilliance.

GUM ARABIC A water soluble gum made from the sap of acacia trees. It is used as the binder for watercolour, gouache and soft pastels.

HALF TONES A range of tones or colours which an artist can indentify between extremes of light and dark.

HANDLING The name given to the most personal part of the work -- the actual execution.

HATCHING A technique of creating areas of tone with fine, parallel strokes following one direction.

HOT COLOUR Colour which tends to be reddish in hue. The red end of the spectrum. Similarly, cool colours would tend to be blue, or at the blue end of the spectrum.

HUE This term is used for pure colour found on a scale ranging through the spectrum, that is red, orange, yellow, green, blue, indigo and violet.

IMPASTO Paint applied thickly so that it retains the mark of the brush or the knife.

KEY Colour is said to be high or low in key according to whether nearest to white (high key) or black (low key).

LEAN A term used to describe oil paint which has little or no added oil. The expression 'fat over lean' refers to the use of

lean paint (thinned with turpentine or white spirit) under paint layers into which more oil is progressively introduced. This method of working prevents the paint surface from cracking as it dries.

LINEAR PERSPECTIVE A method of creating an illusion of depth and three dimensions on a flat surface through the use of converging lines and vanishing points.

LOCAL COLOUR The actual colour of the surface of an object unmodified by light, shade or distance.

MAHL STICK A cane used for steadying the painting arm when putting in fine detail. One end is covered with a soft pad to prevent the point from damaging the support.

MAROUFLAGE Process of affixing canvas to a wall by means of cement. Can also mean glueing canvas to a support.

MASKING The technique of covering areas of the support (with either masking fluid or tape) in order to create a hard edge to the area being painted. The artist is free to use loose brushstrokes, while at the same time protecting the covered area.

MEDIUM 1 The liquid constituent of a paint in which the pigment is suspended. **2** Liquid with which the paint may be diluted without decreasing its adhesive, binding or film-forming properties. **3** The mode of expression employed by an artist, e.g. painting, sculpture or etching. 4 The actual instrument used by an artist: acrylic or oil paint, chisel, needle etc.

MIXED METHOD Originally oil glazes over a tempera underpainting, but can also mean mixing compatible mediums like collage and paint; painting over drawing with inks, acrylic, and vice versa; adding three dimensional objects to a flat surface.

MODELLING In painting and drawing modelling is the employment of tone or colour to achieve an impression of three-dimensional form, by depicting areas of light and shade on an object or figure.

MONOCHROME A painting executed in black and white, or black, white and one other colour.

MURAL or wall painting is a term to describe any kind of wall decoration. Not interchangeable with fresco.

NEGATIVE SPACE The spaces between and around the main elements of the subject -- the background in a figure painting, for example.

NOT A finish in high quality watercolour papers which falls between the smooth surface of hot-pressed, and the heavy texture of rough paper.

OCHRES Earth colours derived from oxide of iron in a range from yellow to orange-red.

OPACITY The quality of paint which covers or obscures a support or previous layers of applied colour.

OPTICAL COLOUR MIXING Creating new colours by mixing pigments optically on the canvas rather than on the palette. The Pointillists placed small dots of unmixed colour on the canvas so that viewed from a distance the dots are no longer visible and, for example, dabs of yellow and red would combine in the eye of the viewer to create orange.

PAINT QUALITY One of the desirable visual attributes of a finished painting. The term does not refer to good or bad ingredients. Paint quality is intrinsic for material beauty or successful surface effect. Something that comes with skilful handling, but often helped by the paint concerned.

PAINTING KNIFE A knife with a thin flexible blade used for applying paint to a support. These knives generally have a cranked handle and are available in a range of shapes and sizes.

PALETTE The tray or dish on which an artist lays out paint for thinning or mixing. This may be of wood, metal, china, plastic or paper. By extension the term also refers to the range of colours used in making a particular image or a colour scheme characteristic of work by one artist.

PALETTE KNIFE A knife with a straight steel blade used for mixing paint on the palette, cleaning the palette and for scraping paint from the support if necessary.

PASTEL A drawing medium made by binding powder pigment with a little gum and rolling the mixture into stick form. Pastels make marks of powdery, opaque colour. Colour mixtures are achieved by overlaying layers of pastel strokes or by gently blending colours with a brush or the fingers. Oil pastels have a waxy quality and a less tendency to crumble, but the effects are not so subtle.

PERSPECTIVE Systems of representation in drawing and painting which create an impression of depth, solidity and spatial recession on a flat surface. Linear perspective is based on a principle that receding parallel lines appear to converge at a point on the horizon line. Aerial perspective represents the grading of tones and colours to suggest distance which may be observed as natural modifications caused by atmospheric effects.

PICKING-UP What happens when a colour is laid over another incorrectly, so that the two colours combine and become muddy.

PICTURE PLANE The vertical surface area of a painting or drawing on which the artist plots the composition and arranges pictorial elements which may suggest an illusion of three-dimensional reality and a recession in space.

PIGMENT A substance which provides colour and which may be mixed with a binder to produce paint or a drawing material. Pigments are generally described as organic (earth colours) or inorganic (mineral and chemical pigments).

PLANES The flat surfaces of an object. These are revealed by light and can be seen in terms of light and dark. Even a curved surface can be regarded as an infinite number of small planes.

PLEIN AIR A French term meaning 'open air' used to describe pictures painted out of doors.

PRIMARY COLOURS In painting the primary colours and red, blue and yellow. They cannot be formed by mixtures of any other colours, but in theory can be used in varying proportions to create all other hues. This is not necessarily true in practice, as paint pigments used commercially are unlikely to be sufficiently pure.

PRIMING Also known as ground, this is the layer or layers of materials applied to a support to make it less absorbent or more pleasant to paint on. A suitable priming for canvas could consist of a layer of size, followed by an oil grounding.

RENAISSANCE The cultural revival of classic ideals

which took place in Europe from the 14th to the 16th centuries.

RESIST This is a method of combining drawing and watercolour painting. A wash of water-based paint laid over marks drawn with wax crayon or oil pastel cannot settle in the drawing and the marks remain visible in their original colour, while areas of bare paper accept the wash.

RETARDER An additive to lay the drying process of acrylic paint.

SABLE Small rodent-like animal, the fur of which goes to make fine, high-quality (and often expensive) brushes.

SATURATED COLOUR Pure colour, free of black and white and therefore intense.

SCUMBLING A painting technique in which opaque paint is dragged or lightly scrubbed across a surface to form an area of broken colour which modifies the tones underneath.

SECONDARY COLOURS These are the three colours formed by mixing pairs of primary colours; orange (red and yellow), green (yellow and blue) and purple (red and blue).

SIZE Used both as a noun and a verb. Size is the solution that is used to coat a support in order to render it less absorbent. To size is to carry out this process.

SPATTERING A method of spreading paint with a loose, mottled texture by drawing the thumb across the bristles of a stiff brush loaded with wet paint so the colour is flicked onto the surface of the painting.

STAINING POWER The colour strength of a pigment and its ability to impart that colour to white, or to a mixture. If a pigment has good staining power you will need only a little of it to impart colour to a mixture.

STIPPLING The technique of applying colour or tone as a mass of small dots made with the point of a drawing instrument or fine brush.

STUDY A drawing or painting, often made as preparation for a larger work, which is intended to record particular aspects of a subject.

SUPPORT The term applied to the material which provides the surface on which a painting or drawing is executed, for example, canvas, board, or paper.

TEMPERA Any kind of binder that will serve to temper powdered pigment and make it workable. In practice the term is usually confined to egg tempera only, yolk of egg being the binder. A unique but very slow medium to master.

TONE In painting or drawing, tone is the measure of light and dark as on a scale of gradations between black and white.

Every colour has an inherent tone; for example, yellow is light while Prussian blue is dark, but a coloured object or surface is also modified by the light fallng upon it and an assessment of the variation in tonal values may be crucial to the artist's ability to indicate the three-dimensional form of an object.

TOOTH A degree of texture or coarseness in a surface which allows a painting or drawing material to adhere to the support.

TRANSPARENCY A quality of paint which means that it stains or modifies the colour of the surface on which it is laid, rather than obliterating it.

UNDERDRAWING The preliminary drawing for a painting, often done in pencil, charcoal or paint.

UNDERPAINTING The preliminary blocking-in of the main forms, colours and tonal areas.

VALUE The character of a colour as assessed on a tonal scale from dark to light.

VEHICLE A liquid used as the carrier of pigments in a paint. The term is interchangeable with medium, but is perhaps more properly applied to the liquid used as an ingredient in manufacture than to a liquid added during painting procedure.

WASH An application of considerably diluted paint to make the colour

spread quickly and thinly.

WATERMARK The symbol or name of the manufacturer incorporated in sheets of high quality paper. The watermark is visible when the paper is held up to the light.

WET INTO DRY (wet in dry) The application of paint to a completely dry surface.

WET INTO WET (wet in wet) The application of wet paint to an already wet surface. Used in *alla prima* technique. Wet into wet allows the artist to blend colours and tones.

WHITING-OUT or repriming is the process of covering a painting or part of a painting that has 'gone wrong' with a semi-transparent layer of white or tinted paint.